Building a Community of Self-Motivated Learners

Award-winning teacher, blogger, and author Larry Ferlazzo is back with more insightful research and strategies for helping students want to care more about school and learning. In his previous books on motivation—*Helping Students Motivate Themselves* and *Self-Driven Learning*—he tackled ways to help students build intrinsic motivation through how you use class time, manage your class, encourage students to feel positive about learning, help them not feel burned out by testing, and more. In this book, he looks at how teachers can create classroom conditions that are needed for motivation to grow in the first place. Ferlazzo provides research-based suggestions on what you can do *today* to help students want to develop qualities like physical health, grit, flow, and a desire to transfer what they're learning to life outside of school.

At the end of each chapter, you'll find high-interest lesson plans, correlated to the Common Core ELA/Literacy Standards, that set the stage for long-term positive impacts. Students will read about sports stars, how maintaining a healthy lifestyle can help them achieve their goals, and other engaging topics. They will integrate information from various texts and make connections to their own lives, hopes, and dreams—a more powerful way to learn to care than being told they should. The readings for these lessons and other tools are available as free eResources on our website so you can easily print them for your students.

Larry Ferlazzo (@Larryferlazzo) is an award-winning teacher at Luther Burbank High School in Sacramento, California. He writes a popular education blog and a teacher advice column for *Education Week Teacher*.

Building a Community of Self-Motivated Learners

Strategies to Help Students Thrive in School and Beyond

Larry Ferlazzo

Routledge
Taylor & Francis Group

NEW YORK AND LONDON

First published 2015
by Routledge
711 Third Avenue, New York, NY 10017

and by Routledge
2 Park Square, Milton Park, Abingdon, Oxon, OX14 4RN

Routledge is an imprint of the Taylor & Francis Group, an informa business

Library of Congress Cataloging-in-Publication Data

Ferlazzo, Larry.
  Building a community of self-motivated learners : strategies to help students thrive in school and beyond / Larry Ferlazzo.
    pages cm
  Includes bibliographical references.
  1. Motivation in education.   2. Effective teaching.   3. Classroom management.   I. Title.
  LB1065.F46   2015
  370.15'4—dc23   2014035549

ISBN: 978-0-415-74665-6 (hbk)
ISBN: 978-0-415-74666-3 (pbk)
ISBN: 978-1-315-79747-2 (ebk)

Typeset in Palatino LT Std
by Apex CoVantage, LLC

Printed and bound in the United States of America by Publishers Graphics, LLC on sustainably sourced paper.

Contents

eResources

The figures in this book can be downloaded and printed for classroom use. You can access these downloads by visiting the book product page on our website: http://www.routledge.com/books/details/9780415746663. Then click on the tab that says "eResources," and select the files. They will begin downloading to your computer.

Figures

Bonus: With the eResources, you'll also find a document with all the URLs from the book hyperlinked, so that readers of the paperback version can easily click on the ones they want to use.

Meet the Author

Larry Ferlazzo teaches English and social studies to English language learners and mainstream students at Luther Burbank High School in Sacramento, California. He has written six previous books: *Helping Students Motivate Themselves: Practical Answers to Classroom Challenges; Self-Driven Learning: Teaching Strategies For Student Motivation; The ESL/ELL Teacher's Survival Guide* (with co-author Katie Hull Sypnieski); *English Language Learners: Teaching Strategies That Work; Building Parent Engagement in Schools* (with co-author Lorie Hammond); and *Classroom Management Q & As: Expert Strategies For Teaching.*

He has won numerous awards, including the Leadership for a Changing World Award from the Ford Foundation, and was the grand prize winner of the International Reading Association Award for Technology and Reading.

He writes a popular education blog at http://larryferlazzo.edublogs.org and writes a weekly teacher advice column for *Education Week Teacher* and a regular column about teaching English language learners for *The New York Times.* His articles on education policy regularly appear in the *Washington Post* and the *Huffington Post.* In addition, his work has appeared in publications such as *ASCD Educational Leadership, Social Policy,* and *Language Magazine.*

Ferlazzo was a community organizer for nineteen years prior to becoming a public school teacher. He is married and has three children and two grandchildren.

Acknowledgments

I'd like to thank my family—Stacia, Rich, Shea, Ava, Nik, Karli, and especially, my wife, Jan—for their support. In addition, I need to express appreciation to my longtime teaching colleagues, especially Katie Hull Sypnieski, Dana Dusbiber, Lara Hoekstra and Pam Propeck Buric. I would also like to thank Kelly Young at Pebble Creek Labs and my many other colleagues at Luther Burbank High School, including Principal Ted Appel, Jim Peterson and Mai Xi Lee, for their assistance over the years. And, most importantly, I'd like to thank the many students who have made me a better teacher—and a better person. In addition, thanks to David Powell for his continued assistance in making my manuscripts presentable. Finally, I must offer a big thank you to Lauren Davis at Routledge for her patience and guidance in preparing this book.

Introduction

Did you really need to write a third book in five years on student motivation?

I don't think any teacher—myself included—can know too many strategies to help students develop intrinsic motivation to learn what we're teaching in our schools. Research might be able to identify the most effective ways for students to learn, and Standards might prioritize what skills and content they should learn. However, none of that matters if students are uninterested in implementing those learning strategies and/or don't want to acquire those skills and content.

Fortunately, there is growing recognition of the value in helping students develop their own motivation and other related Social Emotional Learning (SEL) skills like perseverance, self-control, and personal responsibility. Public surveys also clearly show that parents support schools reinforcing these "character" traits in the classroom (Brenneman, 2013).

Unfortunately, at the same time, there is an increasing danger to SEL of being "co-opted" by well-financed and well-known groups and individuals, ranging from some "school reformers" (Educators 4 Excellence, n.d.) to columnists like *The New York Times'* David Brooks (2014), and converted into a "Let Them Eat Character" strategy. I fear those "Blame the Victim" efforts may be used to distract from the importance of supplying much needed financial resources to schools, providing increased support to families by dealing with growing income and wealth inequality, and developing a comprehensive anti-poverty strategy.

Recent research (Ferlazzo, 2013) reveals the toll that poverty takes on one's ability to execute SEL skills. People aren't poor because they don't have self-control or grit—poverty itself helps create a lack of those qualities. The cognitive "bandwidth" required to deal with financial problems, stress and constant "trade-offs" (healthy food for the family tonight or new school clothes; doing the homework or taking care of younger siblings so that parents can work) makes it more difficult to maintain the mental reserve needed for those SEL skills.

None of these concerns, however, mean that we shouldn't help our students develop these SEL skills in ways that are healthy for them, for their families, for us and for our schools. The strategies and lessons in this book, and in the two previous volumes in this series—*Helping Students Motivate Themselves* (Ferlazzo, 2011) and *Self-Driven Learning* (Ferlazzo, 2013)—are efforts to do just that. The first volume, *Helping Students Motivate Themselves*, discusses motivation with particular attention to class time and structure, such as getting the year off to a good start, using leftover class time, managing the class, incorporating games and technology, and keeping kids focused at the end of the year. The second volume, *Self-Driven Learning*, looks at intrinsic motivation with respect to what students are learning and being asked to do—how teachers can encourage them to feel positive about learning, to enjoy reading and writing, to want to think critically, and to not be burned out by tests.

Now, this third volume looks at the classroom conditions that are needed for motivation to grow in the first place. Each chapter provides specific research-based suggestions on what teachers can do *today* to help students want to develop qualities such as physical health, grit, flow, and a desire to transfer what they're learning to life outside of school. At the end of each chapter are lesson plans (correlated with Common Core Standards that include literacy development) that can "set the stage" for long-term positive impacts. Time and time again research shows that simple actions and lessons like these that teachers can easily integrate into their regular classroom routines are more effective than extensive and complicated "character" programs (Kamenetz, 2014; Sparks, 2012). Easy ways to supplement these lessons with technology "extension" activities are included, and all figures are available as eResources for free download (see page ix for details).

A note of caution, however, should be applied to anything in this book—and, in fact, to anything in education—that says it is "research-based." As a major study found, only 0.13 percent—less than half of 1 percent—of studies published in the top 100 education journals had been replicated (Strauss, 2014). This shocking and depressing statistic raises questions about how much credence should be placed on education policy or classroom strategies that purport to be based on research. I recommend that educators follow a guide of being "data-informed" instead of being "data-driven" (Ferlazzo, 2011, January 28) in all things, and take research as just one of many pieces of evidence to consider as they take action. Fortunately, in addition to being research-based, all the strategies and lesson plans in this book and in the previous volumes in this series have been used successfully in countless classrooms, including my own. That's no guarantee that everything suggested here will be effective for everybody all the time, but I do believe that real-world experience tends to provide the most reliable evidence that a classroom practice will be successful.

As I mentioned earlier, concerns about research and how SEL is being promoted in some circles as the cure-all for challenges facing many of our students (particularly ones in low-income communities) should not dissuade us from effectively teaching SEL in schools. Nevertheless, we should remain vigilant about who is doing what and why they are doing it in the name of Social Emotional Learning. A recently published chart (Ferlazzo, 2014) showed the results of using Google's Ngram Viewer to search all indexed books and identify how often the phrase "teaching character" was used since 1840. The two peak years that phrase was used most often were in the depths of the Great Depression and our more recent Great Recession. It goes without saying that "teaching character" is a less monetarily expensive strategy to responding (or, to pretend to be responding) to economic crises than other potential solutions.

We need to remember that Social Emotional Learning has an important place in teaching and in learning. It is also critical to remember that it has to be kept in its appropriate place, and is not a substitute for appropriate public policy responses to the challenges our students may face in the 80 percent (Ferlazzo, 2010) of their lives (economic, geographic, family, etc.) that we teachers cannot affect in the classroom. Even with that major caveat, though, I am unable to think of another *teaching* strategy that can have a more dramatically positive impact on our classes than one that helps students to motivate themselves.

George Eliot wrote, "What makes life dreary is the want of motive" (*Daniel Deronda*, Book VIII, Chapter LXV). All of our students have motivations inside of them. The strategies in this book are one way to help create a setting where those motivations can come out, and where they can also find new ones to inspire them to even greater dreams.

References

Brenneman, R. (2013, August 21). More social-emotional learning in schools, please, poll says. *Education Week*. Retrieved from: http://blogs.edweek.org/edweek/rulesforengagement/2013/08/poll_more_social-emotional_learning_in_schools.html?cmp=ENL-EU-NEWS2

Brooks, D. (2014, July 31). The character factory. *The New York Times*. Retrieved from: http://www.nytimes.com/2014/08/01/opinion/david-brooks-the-character-factory.html?_r=0

Educators 4 Excellence (n.d.). *True grit: The game-changing factors and people lifting school performance in LAUSD.* Los Angeles: Educators 4 Excellence. Retrieved from: http://educators4excellence.s3.amazonaws.com/8/4f/c/2001/TrueGrit Publication_Final.pdf

Ferlazzo, L. (2010, December 28). The best places to learn what impact a teacher & outside factors have on student achievement. *Larry Ferlazzo's websites of the day.* Retrieved from: http://larryferlazzo.edublogs.org/2010/12/28/the-best-places-to-learn-what-impact-a-teacher-outside-factors-have-on-student-achievement

Ferlazzo, L. (2011). *Helping students motivate themselves.* Larchmont, NY: Eye on Education.

Ferlazzo, L. (2011, January 28). The best resources showing why we need to be "data informed" & not "data driven." *Larry Ferlazzo's websites of the day.* Retrieved from: http://larryferlazzo.edublogs.org/2011/01/28/the-best-resources-showing-why-we-need-to-be-data-informed-not-data-driven/

Ferlazzo, L. (2013). *Self-driven learning: Teaching strategies for student motivation.* New York: Routledge.

Ferlazzo, L. (2013, August 30). The best articles about the study showing social emotional learning isn't enough. *Larry Ferlazzo's websites of the day.* Retrieved from: http://larryferlazzo.edublogs.org/2013/08/30/the-best-articles-about-the-study-showing-social-emotional-learning-isnt-enough

Ferlazzo, L. (2014, February 1). Response: 'Character is Not Compliance Out of Fear.' *Education Week.* Retrieved from: http://blogs.edweek.org/teachers/classroom_qa_with_larry_ferlazzo/2014/02/response_character_is_not_compliance_out_of_fear.html

Kamenetz, A. (2014, July 14). Teaching 4-year-olds to feel better. *NPR.* Retrieved from: http://www.npr.org/blogs/ed/2014/07/14/330761945/teaching-four-year-olds-to-feel-better?ft=1&f=1013

Sparks, S.D. (2012, March 24). Study finds social-skills teaching boosts academics. *Education Week.* Retrieved from: http://www.edweek.org/ew/articles/2011/02/04/20sel.h30.html?tkn=WQNFELArcqZMg0R5kEANZ%2By%2BUZUtqEboYqjH&cmp=clp-edweek

Strauss, V. (2014, August 21). A shocking statistic about the quality of education research. *The Washington Post.* Retrieved from: http://www.washingtonpost.com/blogs/answer-sheet/wp/2014/08/21/a-shocking-statistic-about-the-quality-of-education-research

I Still Want To Know

How Do You Motivate Students?

Motivation ideas from your first two books have been very helpful. I can always use more, though, and I suspect many other educators out there are thinking the same thing. Do you have any more suggestions?

Intrinsic Motivation: Why It's Better and How It's Nurtured

> There are three things to remember about education. The first is motivation. The second one is motivation. The third one is motivation.
> (Former U.S. Secretary of Education Terrel Bell;
> in Hacker, Dunlosky, & Graesser, 2009)

When students feel more motivated to learn, they perform better academically, show improved classroom behavior, and gain a higher sense of self-esteem (Hattie, 2011, p. 252; Usher et al., 2012, p. 1). Unfortunately, data—and the direct experience of many educators reading this book—shows that lack of motivation affects many of our students, and appears to increase each year from middle school through high school (Busteed, 2013; Committee on Increasing High School Students' Engagement and Motivation to Learn, 2003). Students can demonstrate this lack of engagement by withholding effort and by "voting with their feet" through rising chronic absenteeism as they get older (Balfanz & Byrnes, 2012, p. 18), and chronic absenteeism is among the highest predictors of dropping-out of school (Balfanz & Byrnes, 2012, p. 25). To use terms first used by Albert O. Hirschman (Gladwell, 2012), it appears that the lack of student motivation is a major contributing cause to many choosing this option of "exit" (withdrawal from active engagement) over "voice" (active participation) in academic life.

How can we respond effectively to this "motivation crisis"?

One way to is to "double-down" on the common belief in the power of extrinsic motivation—bonuses, points, stars, etc.—and its equivalents in the punishment arena. This chapter and book, as well as the previous books in this series, *Helping Students Motivate Themselves* (Ferlazzo, 2011a) and *Self-Driven Learning* (Ferlazzo, 2013), provide a different perspective, one best characterized by Sir Ken Robinson, author and speaker on education issues, who has said:

> Farmers and gardeners know you cannot make a plant grow . . . the plant grows itself. What you can do is provide the conditions for growth. (Ferlazzo, 2012, June 4)

One of the key ways to "provide the conditions for growth" or, as the National Research Council put it, "create a set of circumstances" (National Research Council and the Institute of Medicine, 2004, p. 14; National Research Council and the Institute of Medicine, 2004; as cited in Committee on Increasing High School Students' Engagement and Motivation to Learn, 2003) is by emphasizing intrinsic motivation (choosing to do an activity in order to gain pleasure from it or in order to help achieve an internalized goal) instead of extrinsic motivation (doing a specific behavior in order to gain an outside reward).

Before reviewing what those "conditions for growth" might be, let's quickly review some of the overwhelming research on "reward undermining" (Klass, 2012) that demonstrates why a reliance on extrinsic motivation should *not* be on that list:

♦ Extrinsic motivation can be effective over the short term in encouraging mechanical tasks and compliance, but tends to be destructive in advancing creative and higher-order thinking (Pink, 2009, p. 46).

♦ Extrinsic motivators, though possibly effective in the short term to gain compliance to do a task, tend to diminish intrinsic motivation for that same activity over the long term (Deci et al., 1999, p. 659).

♦ A recent study of 200,000 employees found that that those who were more intrinsically motivated were three times more engaged in their work than those who focused more on external rewards (Chamorro-Premuzic, 2013).

These critiques, however, do not mean that extrinsic motivation has no role in the home, classroom, or workplace. Even Dr. Edward Deci (perhaps the world's foremost researcher on intrinsic motivation) recognizes that there are going to be times when carrots or sticks need to be used to encourage or stop a behavior because of the immediacy of a challenging situation. As he told *The New York Times*:

> If you're under a lot of stress or in a bad place, then having a conversation at that moment is not going to work.
>
> But, he emphasized, don't let the situation end there. "You need to sit down the next afternoon when everyone's calm, talk it through from both sides, then discuss ways so the behavior doesn't happen again," he said. "Always use the blow up as a learning moment the next day." (Feiler, 2013, January 11)

In addition, author Daniel Pink discusses the need for "baseline rewards" (Pink, 2009, p. 35)—the basic and fair "compensation" that we must all receive in order to have any motivation at all. In school, that might mean a caring teacher, a clean classroom, and engaging lessons. In other words, extrinsic motivators have their place, but they must also be kept in their place.

So, if extrinsic motivation is not one of those "conditions for growth," what *is* on the list?

Self-Determination Theory, one of the most respected theories on human motivation, was originally developed by Professors Edward Deci and Richard Ryan (Ryan & Deci, 2000), and suggests that three elements combine to nurture intrinsic motivation—autonomy (having a degree of control over what needs to happen and how it can be done), competence (feeling that one has the ability to be successful in doing it), and relatedness (doing the activity helps them feel more connected to others, and that they feel cared about by people who they respect).

Many other reports and research related to education, including from the National Research Council, generally concur that these three elements are critical for the kind of environment that should be created for our students (Farrington et al., 2012, p. 32). In addition, most also explicitly add a fourth criteria—that the work must be seen by students as being interesting and valuable to them (Usher et al., 2012, p. 4). In other words, they should see it as relevant to their present lives and/or hopes and dreams for the future (Self-Determination theorists often include this quality of relevance within their "developing autonomy" category, Assor et al., 2002, p. 264).

The ideas and lessons in this chapter, as well as those found in the entire book (and the first two books in this series), are designed to help our students motivate themselves through cultivating these four qualities and to counter what the National Research Council suggests—that these four elements become less and less visible as students move into secondary schools (Committee on Increasing High School Students' Engagement and Motivation to Learn, 2003).

Years ago, I lived in an elevated house that was at the bottom of a small hill. It had a storm drain on the street in front of it. During the summer, I would pour wood chips in the small dirt area between the sidewalk and the curb, and during heavy winter rainstorms the drain would get clogged up with debris floating downhill. Water would go over the curb, and all the wood chips would float away leaving a muddy area. Each year my wife would strongly suggest I plant grass or bushes in that area so that it could withstand the water, and each year I instead chose the short-term solution of wood chips—it appeared easier to me and seemed to work most of the time—until the bad weather hit. I chose this solution even though planting grass and bushes would have saved me time and money over the long term, made the neighborhood look better and, in fact, would have probably attacked the cause of the problem by reducing the amount of debris that was clogging the drain. I had other things on my "to do" list that I felt were more important and I was more comfortable with a problem I was familiar with than with a solution that was new to me—having a "green thumb" was not on my resume.

Let's see how we can get rid of the wood chips of extrinsic motivation. Instead, let's plant some nice grass and bushes, and create the conditions in which they can grow well . . .

Ed Tech

Research on motivation continues to be done regularly around the world. Stay updated on the latest studies, and how to apply them in the classroom, at "The Best Posts & Articles On 'Motivating Students'" (http://larryferlazzo.edublogs.org/2010/05/17/my-best-posts-on-motivating-students/).

Immediate Actions

Here are some strategies to support the four qualities critical to intrinsic motivation—autonomy, competence, relatedness, and relevance—that teachers can keep in mind during day-to-day work in the classroom. Though they are categorized into those four qualities for organizational clarity, many of the suggested strategies cover more than one area—for example, building a trusting relationship with students is listed under "relatedness," though it's also critical for differentiated instruction under "competence." Obviously, the idea is not necessarily to apply every quality all the time—we're not Supermen or Superwomen, after all. However, they provide a variety of tools to keep in mind in lesson planning and implementation.

Promoting Autonomy

Choice

Providing students with freedom of choice is one strategy for promoting learner autonomy. Educators commonly view this idea of choice through the "lens" of "organizational" and "procedural" choice. Organizational choice, for example, might mean students having a voice in seating assignments or membership of their small learning groups. Procedural choice could include a choice from a list of homework assignments and what form a final project might take—a book, poster, or skit.

Some researchers, however, believe that a third option, called "cognitive" choice, is a more effective way to promote longer-lasting student autonomy (Stefanou et al., 2004, p. 101). This kind of cognitive autonomy support, which is also related to the idea of ensuring relevance, could include:

♦ problem-based learning, where small groups need to determine their own solutions to teacher-suggested and/or student-solicited issues—ways to organize school lunchtime effectively, what it would take to have a human colony on Mars, strategies to get more healthy food choices available in the neighborhood, etc.

♦ students developing their own ideas for homework assignments related to what is being studied in class

♦ students publicly sharing their different thinking processes behind solving a similar or the same problem

♦ teachers using "thinking routines" like the one developed by Project Zero at Harvard which consists of a simple formula—the teacher regularly asking, "What is going on here?" and, after a student response, continuing with "What do you see that makes you say so?" (Perkins, 2003, para. 7).

This is not to suggest that asking students where they might want to sit or how they want to display their class project is bad or does not support autonomy. It does suggest, however, that we might not want to stop there.

Supporting Competence

Here are a few ways teachers can help students feel that they can be successful in learning activities:

Feedback

Feedback, done well, is ranked by education researcher John Hattie as number 10 out of 150 influences on student achievement (Hattie, 2011, p. 251). The root of "feed" comes from the old English word "fedan," which means "nourish, sustain, foster" (Feed, n.d.) and the origins of "back" suggest "to support" (Back, n.d.). Let's look at some ways to ensure we respect the word's origins.

Praising effort and the specific work of students instead of their intelligence will help them lose their fear of making mistakes and recognize the truth in Woody Allen's statement that "eighty percent of success is showing up" (Barcelona, 2008, para. 12). Praising for intelligence makes people less willing to risk "their newly-minted genius status" (Dweck, as cited in Rock, 2011, para. 10), while praising effort encourages the idea that we primarily learn through our hard work: "Ben, it's impressive that you wrote two drafts of that essay instead of one, and had your friend review it, too. How do you feel it turned out, and what made you want to put the extra work into it?" Or tell them, "Boy, those two hours you spent working on the essay last night really paid-off—you described the characters in the novel so well" instead of, "Wow, you are a natural-born writer." Teachers can emphasize the *process* and not just the *product*. This kind of feedback supports students in believing that during times when they are not as successful as they would like to be, it's a matter of "not yet" rather than "never"—it's a question of needing to work harder or differently, not a question of a lack of intelligence or ability. Carol Dweck calls it the difference between a "growth mindset" and a "fixed mindset" (as cited in Rock, 2011).

But how do you handle providing critical feedback to students when it's necessary?

First, it's important to recognize that people who are beginning to learn any kind of skill tend to be more discouraged by critical feedback than those who are more "expert"—they want to hear more what they did wrong and how they can do better (Tugend, 2013). Novice or expert, however, much research shows that a ratio of positive to negative feedback of between three-to-one and five-to-one is necessary for healthy learning to occur (Pozen, 2013; Schwartz, 2013; Tugend, 2013).

Keeping those points in mind, teachers might consider a strategy called "plussing" that is used by Pixar animation studios with great success. *The New York Times* interviewed author Peter Sims about the concept:

The point, he said, is to "build and improve on ideas without using judgmental language."

   … An animator working on "Toy Story 3" shares her rough sketches and ideas with the director. "Instead of criticizing the sketch or saying 'no,' the director will build on the starting point by saying something like, 'I like Woody's eyes, and what if his eyes rolled left?'"

   Using words like "and" or "what if," rather than "but" is a way to offer suggestions and allow creative juices to flow without fear, Mr. Sims said. (Tugend, 2013)

"Ands" and "what ifs" could easily become often-used words in an educator's vocabulary!

Differentiation

Our students come to us with varying strengths and challenges, and few educators believe that "one size" of instruction will "fit all." In fact, John Hattie (2011) writes that a "truism in most schools" is that the spread of abilities in a class will be equal to the grade of that class. In other words, a third-grade class will have a three-year "spread" among them, while a ninth-grade class is likely to have a nine-year "spread" (Hattie, 2011, p. 97).

   There are many books written on the topic of differentiation, with ones by Carol Ann Tomlinson (for a list of her books on differentiation see http:// www.caroltomlinson.com/books.html) and Rick Wormeli (for a list of his books see http://www.amazon.com/Rick-Wormeli/e/B001JS321Q) being stand-outs among them, so this short section is certainly not designed as the "be-all, end-all" on the topic. Instead, it is designed to provide an introduction (also note that Chapter 3 discusses a specific differentiation strategy for writing). It is, after all, a critical tool in helping develop self-motivated learners.

   It's important to keep in mind that, as Diane Heacox says, "authentic differentiation is not tricks or tips" (Heacox, 2012). Instead, it's more of a "mindset" (Ferlazzo, 2012, June 4). Nevertheless, there are some specific research-based strategies that have been shown to be effective in mixed-ability classes (Huebner, 2010). We can keep them in mind when working with our diverse students to help them all develop needed skills and feelings of competence and confidence.

"Planning for the Unpredictable"

Carol Ann Tomlinson (2011) talks about differentiated instruction as "planning for the unpredictable." With each additional year of teaching our classes, we begin to know where the challenging spots tend to be—which words or concepts in what thematic unit a number of students might find particularly challenging, what assignments tend to require several examples of teacher modeling for some, what essay assignments may have a handful of students requiring more detailed graphic organizers for planning, etc. We may just not necessarily know *which* students might require that assistance, though as the year goes on we may be able to anticipate that better. Tomlinson suggests that putting time and effort into this kind of "proactive instruction" will be a far more effective differentiation strategy than the "improvising" many well-intentioned teachers do by teaching the same lesson the same way to everyone and then "reacting" to the different difficulties some might face (2011). We can't anticipate each challenge that every student will have, but we can prepare for many of them. Here are some of those preparation "tools" we can have in our toolbox ready for use:

♦ **Use formative assessments regularly.** In fact, Carol Tomlinson recommends becoming an "assessment junkie" (2003). Formative assessment is done during the instructional process, as opposed to a summative assessment, which is done at its end. It's ongoing, and is used by both teachers and students to evaluate evidence so that teachers can make adjustments to their teaching and students to their learning. It's a critical way for teachers to check students' understanding and then use the information to guide instruction.

♦ **Formative assessment can be almost anything**—teacher observations; review of student work; a quick ungraded quiz; checking for understanding by asking students to give a thumbs-up, thumbs-down, or thumb sidewise (always with a teacher statement saying that it's fine for students to not put their thumbs up); asking students to quickly answer one to three key questions as an ungraded "exit slip" to give you on their way out the door (those questions include: "On a scale of one to five, with one being no confidence at all and five being you get everything we covered today, how would you rate your level of understanding?"; "What questions do you have about what we covered today?"; "Can you please summarize in one to three sentences the major point of the lesson today?").

♦ **Use flexible groupings**—working individually, in partners, in larger groups, mixed-ability, similar-ability, student choice, etc. Tomlinson calls this opportunities to "audition" so the teacher can see what might work best for students in particular situations and also so that students can see what they can contribute in different contexts (Rebora, 2008). Limiting students to same-ability groups can contribute towards students developing a fixed mindset, which is the opposite of what they need for the development of intrinsic motivation. The jigsaw method is a small group activity that's particularly suited for differentiated instruction (Hattie, 2011, p. 99). One way to use this strategy is to start with similar-ability small groups that are assigned an appropriate text or assignment connected to a broader theme. Students in the groups then develop a plan and materials for teaching or applying their information. Next, one person from each group comes together into mixed-ability groups to then teach or contribute their work.

♦ **Use visual aids** such as sentence starters and paragraph frames, pre-teach key vocabulary words with visual support, have students complete graphic organizers, and provide written as well as verbal directions. Sentence starters and/or paragraph frames are simple sheets or posters with "fill-in-the-blanks" that students can use as scaffolding for writing or speaking. Many examples can be found online and teachers can easily write them to target a specific learning activity. Perhaps the most common are "question starters" aligned with Bloom's Taxonomy levels. They are a research-supported differentiation tool (Donnelly & Roe, 2010), and build on the Zeigarnik Effect (Konnikova, 2012, April 30), which finds that people are more motivated to finish something once they have begun—even if it means just copying the first few words of a sentence starter.

Pre-teaching a limited number of vocabulary words with visual support is another research-based differentiation strategy. Teachers could develop one list for the entire class, and/or different versions based on your expectation of various students' prior knowledge—recognizing, however, that it is not effective to pre-teach a large number of words at one time (some researchers recommend not more than six for a text [Cranmer, n.d.], while I go up to 20 for an extended unit). Criteria for choosing which words to pre-teach could include: that they are key to the upcoming lesson, they are unlikely to be known by many of students, and that they are likely to be used in other situations and texts (Sedita, 2005, p. 5). Recent research also suggests that students might be more likely to remember word definitions if they are first asked to guess what they mean (Willingham, 2013, July 8).

Education researcher Robert Marzano recommends a multiple-step procedure for vocabulary instruction, beginning with the teacher providing a definition or example, followed by students writing it in their own words and then drawing a representation of it. A few days later, he recommends that teachers begin to have students talk about the words with partners and play class vocabulary games, as well as regularly take notes about when they see the words used and make other comments that help them gain understanding (Marzano, 2009).

Research has consistently found that graphic organizers are an effective aid to learning in the classroom (Hall & Strangman, 2002; Lubin & Sewak, 2007). Examples of graphic organizers are ubiquitous online, and can easily be modified for just about any learning activity. Better yet, it's easy to increase or decrease the amount of scaffolded support present in them, so it's possible to have more than one type available for one lesson.

In addition to providing verbal instructions prior to a learning activity taking place, provide them in writing—either on the board/overhead and/or as a student hand-out. Consider if a simplified version would be better for some students.

Ed Tech

For additional resources on differentiation, visit "Not 'The Best,' But 'A List' Of Mind-mapping, Flow Chart Tools, & Graphic Organizers" (http://larryferlazzo.edublogs.org/2009/02/09/not-the-best-but-a-list-of-mindmapping-flow-chart-tools-graphic-org anizers/); "The Best Resources For Helping Teachers Use Bloom's Taxonomy In The Classroom" (http://larryferlazzo.edublogs.org/2009/05/25/the-best-resources-for-help ing-teachers-use-blooms-taxonomy-in-the-classroom/), which has links to many "sentence-starters"; and "The Best Resources On Differentiating Instruction" (http://larryferlazzo. edublogs.org/2012/01/09/the-best-resources-on-differentiating-instruction/).

♦ **Use modeling—mainly by the teacher but also by other students—of the desired learning activity.** This research-based differentiation strategy (Hogan & Pressley, 1997, p. 20) can take many forms—a "think aloud" where the teacher is sharing what she is thinking as she does a learning task; showing actual examples of the "product" from previous years—an essay, a poster, etc.; preparing a few students ahead of time to model a procedure and/or a small group discussion. Teachers might just use one example with the entire class and be prepared to offer multiple ones with particular students. Some researchers suggest that modeling prompts observers' brains to activate "mirror neurons" that make "practicing in the head" possible (Washburn, 2013).

♦ **Activate students' prior knowledge.** Numerous studies have found that students learn new information and concepts better when they can see relationships with their existing knowledge (Willis, 2006, p. 15). Teachers can help make this happen by developing relationships with students to learn about their interests and prior experiences; engaging in conversations with parents; and having students do activities like completing a K-W-L chart listing what they "Know" about a topic, what they "Want" to know about it; and then, as the lesson continues, what they have "Learned."

♦ **Use technology such as desktop computers, laptops, cellphones, and tablets.** Some technology can make the same classroom materials more accessible to students with special needs through providing audio support for text and the ability to click on words for immediate definitions in English or their native language. Other students might just *like* doing the same work on a computer more than if pen and paper materials are being assigned, while technology offers others who find the classroom materials or overall assignment too challenging tools to engage in the topic and still gain an understanding of the key points. For example, if the lesson is on figurative language, there are multiple leveled free and accessible online interactive lessons, games, and videos that a student can use for scaffolding tools towards understanding.

 Ed Tech

For a list of sites where students can work on computer assignments and their progress can be monitored by teachers, visit "The Best Sites That Students Can Use Independently And Let Teachers Check On Progress" (http://larryferlazzo.edublogs.org/2008/05/21/the-best-sites-that-students-can-use-independently-and-let-teachers-check-on-progress/). In addition, CAST, the Center for Applied Special Technology (http://www.cast.org/learningtools/index.html), has a long list of online tools appropriate for differentiation and examples on how to use them.

♦ **Use "Wait Time."** The average time between a teacher posing a question and a student giving the answer in a typical classroom is about one second. Multiple studies have shown that the quality and quantity of student responses increases when the wait time is increased to between three and seven seconds (Wait Time, n.d.). There may very well be times when that time should be extended further for individual students. For example, a teacher could pose a question to a student and say that he will return in a minute and expect an answer.

♦ **Make sure that all students have "respectful tasks."** Tomlinson writes that this is a "core principle" of differentiated instruction (Rebora, 2008). Though some students might have graphic organizers that look different or are given adjustable time limits, or are even being evaluated under different growth criteria, all must be assisted towards the primary learning tasks through engaging and pedagogically appropriate activities—no mindless word searches, drawing games busywork, or "drill and kill" worksheets for students who face exceptional challenges. These are just a few of many possible strategies that fall into a framework suggested by Tomlinson that encourage teachers to differentiate in "content, process, products and learning environment" (Tomlinson, n.d.).

Seeing Progress

Harvard professor Teresa Amabile is well-known for her identification of the "Progress Principle." Her research has found that it is critical for people to feel that they are making progress—even "incremental" progress—towards "meaningful" goals (Peer-to-Peer Support, n.d.). The section on goal-setting under "Setting the Stage" later in this chapter provides details about how to apply this strategy in the classroom.

Encouraging Relatedness

Teacher–Student

Students having a high-quality relationship with a teacher whom they respect is a key element of helping develop intrinsic motivation. Research also shows there is a direct connection between those positive relationships and higher academic achievement—students will work harder and longer if they like their teacher (Montalvo et al., 2007, p. 144). John Hattie (2011) ranks student-teacher relationships as number 12 out of 150 influences on student learning (p. 251). These facts also contrast with the fact that teacher-student relationships tend to begin to deteriorate during junior high school and get even worse in high school (Freeman et al., 2007).

What are some actions teachers can take to strengthen these relationships? Here are four simple suggestions adapted from Robert Marzano's ideas (Marzano, 2011a; Marzano & Marzano, 2003), followed by three additional ones:

- **Take a genuine interest in your students**. Learn about their interests, hopes, and dreams. Ask them about what is happening in their lives. In other words, lead with your "ears" and not your "mouth." Don't, however, just make it a "one-way street"—share some of your own stories, too.

- **Act friendly in other ways**—smile, joke, occasionally make a light supportive touch on a student's shoulder.

- **Be flexible, and keep eyes on the learning goal "prize."** One of my students had never written an essay in his school career. He was intent on maintaining that record during an assignment of writing a persuasive essay about what students thought was the worst natural disaster. Because I knew two of his passions were football and video games, I told him that as long as he used the writing techniques we'd studied, he could write an essay on why his favorite football team was better than its rival or on why he particularly liked one video game. He ended up writing an essay on both topics.

- **Don't give up on students.** Be positive (as much as humanly possible) and encourage a "growth mindset."

- Another suggestion would be to **be courteous**. Not only does saying "please," "thank you," and "I'm sorry" contribute to a positive relationship and classroom atmosphere, but there are additional benefits, too. People are more likely to comply with a task (and do so more quickly) if someone asks them instead of tells them (Yong, 2010). I've found that "Can you please sit down?" is more effective than "Sit down!" Saying thank you provides immediate positive reinforcement to students. Research (Sutton, 2010) shows that people who are thanked by authority figures are more likely to cooperate, feel valued, and exhibit self-confidence.

- **Have an *authoritative*, not *authoritarian*, classroom management system.** Being authoritarian means wielding power unilaterally to control someone, demanding obedience without giving any explanation for why one's orders are important. Being authoritative, on the other hand, means demonstrating control, but doing so relationally through listening and explaining. Marzano recommends a similar system, though he uses the terms of achieving a balance between teacher *dominance* and *cooperation* (Marzano & Marzano, 2003). Look for recommendations on how to implement this in Chapter 2 on classroom managment.

♦ One final idea to keep in mind would be **"attunement,"** which is the word Dan Pink uses to describe the act of being able to take the perspective of the other person—to understand the self-interests of that person and to imagine what they are *thinking* (Ferlazzo, 2013, February 17). That, combined with feeling empathy—trying to understand what the student is *feeling*—can go a long way to building a positive teacher-student relationship.

Student–Student

Here, too, there is substantial research behind the belief that facilitating positive peer-to-peer relationships in school can help develop students' intrinsic motivation (McGrath & Noble, 2007). Well-structured cooperative learning projects utilizing changing small groups during the school year is an obvious way to help students achieve that goal (McGrath & Noble, 2007, p. 4). Being part of a group with a shared purpose and committed to progress increases positive feelings and motivation (Markman, 2012, March 8).

Having students regularly share with classmates about positive events in their lives has also been shown to develop a more trusting and supportive environment (Seppala, 2012; What's an easy way?, 2010). On many Fridays, I have students list three positive things that happened to them during the week and then share with a partner. Psychologist Martin Seligman (2011) recommends that people doing this "three good things" exercise also answer one of the following three questions about each listed event: "Why did this good thing happen?"; "What does this mean to you?"; "How can you have more of this good thing in the future?" (p. 84).

Ensuring Relevance

Substantial evidence points to students' intrinsic motivation being built if they see what is happening in the classroom as relevant to their interests, hopes, and dreams (Kirk, n.d.; Usher et al., 2012, p. 6). Here are a few research-based suggestions that educators can apply in the classroom:

♦ **Have students write about how what they are learning is relevant to their lives.** Researchers had students write one paragraph after a lesson sharing how they thought what they had learned would be useful to their lives. Writing one to eight of these paragraphs during a semester led to positive learning gains, especially for those students who had previously been "low performers" (Hulleman & Harack-iewicz, 2009, p. 1411). It is not uncommon for *teachers* to explicitly make those kinds of real-life connections. However, research has also found that this kind of teacher-centered approach can actually be de-motivating to some students with low skills. A student who is having a very difficult time understanding math or does just not find it interesting, for example, can feel threatened by hearing regu-larly from a teacher about how important math is to his/her future. Instead of becoming more engaged in class, he/she may experience more negative feelings (Hulleman et al., 2010, p. 881). These same researchers write:

> a more effective approach would be to encourage students to generate their own connections and discover for themselves the relevance of course material to their lives. This method gives students the opportunity to make connections to topics and areas of greatest interest to their lives. (p. 881)

This experiment has been repeated with the same results (Hulleman et al., 2010). I have also used this process in my own classes—with some slight variations. I will often, though not always, tell students near the beginning of lessons (instead of waiting until the end) that they will be writing about how they can apply what we are going to learn in their own lives. I also might have them write just one or two sentences instead of a paragraph, and have them use them as an "exit slip" from class.

This is not to suggest that teachers should *always* leave making the "relevance" connections to students—sometimes our students won't be aware of them and sometimes we face classroom time constraints. In fact, other studies that have *only* looked at teachers pointing them out have found it more beneficial for most students than not discussing them at all (Sparks, 2013). However, since sub-stantial research demonstrates that "assisted discovery learning" (like the student-generated paragraphs described here) is generally more effective than direct instruction (Marzano, 2011b), the more we remember to incorporate it, the better.

♦ **Connect to student stories.** There has been extensive research done on how teaching through telling stories can result in greater academic achievement (Willingham, 2013, June 3). Neuroscience research-ers Renate and Geoffrey Caine have reflected on the importance of stories in their study of two types of memory systems: taxon and locale (Caine & Caine, 1994, p. 42; Construction of Individual Meaning, n.d.).

Taxon learning consists of lists, basic skills, and habits. Locale, on the other hand, involves creating stories out of a person's life experiences. Taxon tells us how to turn a key in our house door and locale tells us what to do when we lose the key. Taxon memories must be rehearsed regularly to move into long-term memory. Locale memories, however, *go automatically into long-term memory*. Taxon learning responds more to extrinsic motivation and is resistant to change once a fact or habit has been learned. Locale learning is more responsive to intrinsic motivation and is always evolving.

Professor Melanie Greene calls it "narrative transportation." Another researcher likens the effect of stories to a Trojan Horse—they make people let their guard down (Nussbaum, 2013). But just teaching information through storytelling is only part of the story. If we want to maximize the effectiveness of stories in the classroom, then not only should we tell stories, but we can also help students use their own personal stories to construct new knowledge. Here's one example: I used my Hmong and Latino immigrant students' locale memories to strengthen their reading skills during a unit on feudalism. The textbook's authors listed several key facts about feudalism: people spent most of their time working in the fields, they didn't own the land they farmed, and their homes had one or two rooms. The book flatly declared that feudalism had ended with the Renaissance. Instead of having students memorize these facts (taxon memory), I asked students to think about them, write about whether they'd experienced any of these conditions in their home culture, and ask their parents and grandparents the same question (locale memory). Every student commented that they were either experiencing some of those "feudal" conditions currently or had done so very recently, either before their families emigrated or while they lived in refugee camps. The class concluded that the textbook was mistaken in saying feudalism had ended.

Examining parallels between their lives and the lives of people in the Middle Ages strongly engaged students. Many clamored to read more challenging texts about the Middle Ages. This unit provided countless opportunities for my students to learn reading strategies, academic vocabulary, and grammar. They embraced those opportunities because the lessons took place within the framework of their own stories and those of their families (Ferlazzo, 2010, p. 31).

During my 19-year community organizing career (prior to becoming a teacher), our primary strategy was to learn people's stories, have them share those stories with others, and then help them develop a new interpretation of those stories. This new interpretation then was the engine that would propel themselves to action. It's similar to a challenge we face in the classroom—we need to help students connect our lesson content to their background knowledge and then attach new understandings and learnings to it—whether it's connecting their working in the fields to feudalism or connecting:

- their lives to the study of Mount Everest by reflecting on what its first blind summitter meant when he said, "There are summits everywhere . . . you just have to know where to look"

- stories of important women in their lives to learning about important women in history

- their experiences of using the scientific method to successfully learn anything (cooking, playing basketball) to its use in the scientific process.

By building on students' stories, we can also capitalize on what most of us know, and what researchers have recently confirmed—people enjoy talking about themselves. In fact, brain scans have found that talking about ourselves triggers the same reward sensations as food and sex (Hotz, 2012; Ward, 2013).

There is an additional benefit of sometimes incorporating family stories in these kinds of activities. Research has found that the more young people know about their family histories, the happier and more resilient they are, along with developing a sense that they are in more control of their lives—all elements that also contribute towards intrinsic motivation. Knowing these stories makes them feel that they are part of something bigger than themselves (Feiler, 2013, March 15).

We need to emphasize the use of stories in the classroom. But let's make sure they aren't just ones we originate. Let's make sure our students are tellers of their own tales, too.

♦ **Use the knowledge gained through relationships with students to "tweak" lessons so they seem more relevant to student interests and/or goals.** For example, many students in our school have been enamored with playing with a Japanese wooden toy called Kendama. I had seen other students doing paper-folding. When we began studying Asia in our Geography class, it was easy to integrate activities studying the history of wooden toys and origami there, and further explore how cultural influences spread across borders—not limited to toys. We were also able to study the significance of paper cranes to the atomic bombings of Japan, and how they were also used in the aftermath of the more recent earthquake and tsunami. It's safe to say the level of student enthusiasm was quite high, as was the level of reading and thinking—higher, I believe, than it would have been if we had followed the "typical" course of study.

♦ **Regularly take time to have students review, reflect, and discuss various goals they have made for themselves.** The section on goal-setting provides context for how to introduce this idea to students. Once goals have been set, however, this type of reflection can just take a few minutes of class time.

These next activities may require more planning and preparation but, nevertheless, are effective ways to do standards-based lessons with a high-degree of student relevance:

♦ **Use cooperative activities, such as project-based or problem-based learning, that provide substantial latitude to students about the topics they focus on.** Project-based learning is typically defined as students working on a task that results in a concrete project (report, online slideshow, PowerPoint, poster, etc.) and/or public presentation. Problem-based learning can also result in a similar product, but the topic is generally a real-world problem that students must solve. Either strategy can take anywhere from a few days to a few weeks to complete (Prince & Felder, 2007). This kind of activity can also promote the "cognitive autonomy" mentioned earlier. Both *Helping Students Motivate Themselves* (2011) and *Self-Driven Learning* (2013) have detailed examples of standards-based cooperative learning lessons that encompass multiple qualities that develop students' intrinsic motivation.

Ed Tech

"The Best Sites For Cooperative Learning Ideas" (http://larryferlazzo.edublogs.org/2010/04/02/the-best-sites-for-cooperative-learning-ideas/) contains an extensive list of resources on many kinds of cooperative learning activities and research that supports their use.

♦ **Try implementing 20 percent time in your classroom.** This classroom learning activity has been inspired by a number of business initiatives, particularly Google's history of giving its employees 20 percent of their time to work on a project of their choosing. A growing number of educators are applying this to the classroom—whether as a literal 20 percent time project one day each week or as an occasional lesson.

Ed Tech

"The Best Resources for Applying 'Fed Ex Days' To Schools" (http://larryferlazzo.edublogs. org/2012/05/28/the-best-resources-for-applying-fed-ex-days-to-schools/) shares many resources and examples on how to implement 20 percent time in the classroom.

Obviously, we should not base our lessons only on what students are interested in **now**—we have a responsibility to also help them expand their visions. But if we do not want to feel like we're "pushing a rope" most of the time, starting with where our students are at might be the best way to ensure that it's their energy that will be propelling them forward—not ours.

Setting the Stage

The next portion of this chapter will share specific lessons that support the qualities needed to help students develop intrinsic motivation. They typically require more planning than most of the ideas listed in the "Immediate Actions" section. This section first has short explanations and rationales for each lesson. Then, all the lesson plans can be found in the last part of the chapter.

Goals, Grit, and Deliberate Practice

Goals

Goal-setting, as has already been mentioned, can play a critical role in developing intrinsic motivation. Here's what the Center on Education Policy said in their research paper on student goals and motivation:

> Each of the four main dimensions of motivation—competence, control/autonomy, value/interest, and relatedness—can play a crucial role in goal-setting. To feel competent, students need to see

their goals as realistic and achievable, which may require altering the goals or altering students' perceptions of their own abilities. To feel in control, students must be able to see a clear path to achieving the goal, through means they can control rather than through luck or chance. Control is also maximized when students set goals themselves, or at least agree with and internalize goals set for them by someone else. Student support for the goal will also foster interest and value. Lastly, relatedness can be affected by what students perceive is expected of them by society, how they will be judged by people of social importance, or what goals other members of their own social group or another desirable social group are pursuing. (Usher et al., 2012, p. 2)

In other words, research shows that goals which are primarily student-chosen (limited teacher assistance can be helpful), challenging enough to drive performance but realistic enough to still be attainable, measurable and specific can help drive student intrinsic motivation. In addition, regular feedback—whether through student self-reflection, discussion with student "goal-buddies" (partners that meet regularly to review their progress) or teacher conversation—is critical for ongoing support and for potential goal modification. A goal or goal-setting process that does not meet all these criteria can result in the exact opposite occurring—students can feel *less* motivated (Goal Setting Theory Overview, n.d.).

When discussing goals, a critical distinction to make is between learning goals (also called mastery goals) and performance goals. Learning goals demonstrate increased understanding and the ability to apply it. Performance goals involved reaching a certain "score" or outperforming others. One simple example (others can be found in the goal-setting lesson plan) is that a learning goal would be to be able to speak Spanish, while a performance goal would be to get an "A" in Spanish class. People who focus on learning goals develop more of the kind of "growth mindset" discussed earlier in the chapter—they are less frustrated by challenges and see success as gained more by effort—there is always something more to strive for (Usher et al., 2012, p. 2). In fact, those who emphasize learning goals during a course have been found to have higher performance levels than those who focused on performance goals (Locke & Latham, 2006, p. 266).

Does this mean we should completely discourage students from considering performance goals? Of course not. There's no problem with students choosing to have some, especially since most school systems are structured to value and recognize them. As with extrinsic and intrinsic motivation, it's not a question of never having one, but more of which we try to support more in our instruction.

Setting goals and developing a plan to achieve them, and then beginning to execute that plan, has also been found to enhance people's sense of "hope." In fact, psychologists have used "hope surveys" to determine the hope levels of students, and suggest that 12 percent of academic achievement is directly related to how hopeful students feel about their future (Kluger, 2013).

The goal-setting lesson plan incorporates all the aspects that have been mentioned so far, and more. It's titled "Goal Setting Lesson Plan II" because there is a lesson plan in *Helping Students Motivate Themselves* that covers the same topic (Ferlazzo, 2011b, p. 19). That lesson plan, however, is substantially different. I give one lesson at the beginning of the year and the other during the second semester as a "refresher." Either can be give first, and they each work well as "stand-alone" lessons.

Grit

"Grit" is the word coined by Professor Angela Duckworth to describe perseverance—the ability and willingness to successfully overcome challenges in the pursuit of goals. More and more research is being done demonstrating its key role in academic and professional success (Schechtman et al., 2013).

As with goal-setting, there is also a lesson plan on grit in *Helping Students Motivate Themselves* (Ferlazzo, 2011b, p. 71). That lesson plan, however, is substantially different. As I do with the two goal-setting lessons, I give one lesson at the beginning of the year and the other during the second semester as a "refresher." Either can be given first, and they each work well as "stand-alone" lessons. However, the grit lessons should be given some time *after* a goal-setting lesson—one day, one week, or one month (or even longer) after the goal lesson

Deliberate Practice

Deliberate practice is a form of practice connected to grit/perseverance which—more than any other known quality—has been found to be the key to someone mastering a skill (Szalavitz, 2013). Persevering in the face of challenges is critical, but deliberate practice can be an effective strategy to use in order to overcome obstacles. It is not just mindless repetition of a task. Instead, it involves regularly doing increasingly challenging tasks and reflecting on the progress made and the problems encountered (Ericsson et al., 1993, p. 367).

This chapter contains a "mini-lesson" on deliberate practice and is connected to the previous goal-setting and grit lessons. There is an extensive lesson on deliberate practice in *Self-Driven Learning* (Ferlazzo, 2013, p. 155)

related to reading and writing, but this mini-lesson is entirely different. It can be taught on its own, and should follow the goal and grit lessons in this chapter.

Student Engagement

This activity is called a mini-lesson, but is basically an outline of a simple teacher research plan to determine how successful he/she has been in helping students develop intrinsic motivation.

Goal-Setting Lesson Plan II

Instructional Objectives for Students

- Further develop their ability to practice reading strategies to help comprehend a text.

- Understand the importance of setting goals and designing an effective action plan to achieve them.

- Identify long-term and short-term goals and an effective plan to achieve them.

Duration

Two 55-minute class periods and various short follow-up activities during the rest of the year.

Materials

- Access to the Internet, the web pages "The Best Video Clips On Goal-Setting" (http://larryferlazzo.edublogs.org/2013/07/11/the-best-video-clips-on-goal-setting-help-me-find-more/) and "The Best Resources For Doing A One-Sentence Project" (http://larryferlazzo.edublogs.org/2013/03/13/the-best-resources-for-doing-a-one-sentence-project/) and a computer projector.

- Student copies of Figures 1.1 through 1.7.

- Construction paper and color markers.

- For follow-up lessons in future days, weeks, and months, copies of Figures 1.8 through 1.13 and the article "Nine Things Successful People Do Differently" (http://blogs.hbr.org/cs/2011/02/nine_things_successful_people.html).

Common Core English Language Arts Standards

Reading:

- Determine central ideas or themes of a text and analyze their development; summarize the key supporting details and ideas.

- Read and comprehend complex literary and informational texts independently and proficiently.

Writing:

- Write arguments to support claims in an analysis of substantive topics or texts, using valid reasoning and relevant and sufficient evidence.

Speaking and Listening:

- Prepare for and participate effectively in a range of conversations and collaborations with diverse partners, building on others' ideas and expressing their own clearly and persuasively.

Language:

- Demonstrate command of the conventions of standard English grammar and usage when writing or speaking.

- Demonstrate command of the conventions of standard English capitalization, punctuation, and spelling when writing.

Procedure

First Day

1. Without any introduction, show the well-known three-minute basketball scene in the movie *The Pursuit of Happyness* that can be found on "The Best . . ." list. You also have the option of showing any one of the other clips on that list, instead.

2. Ask students to take five to ten minutes to write a short response to the prompt below, which is distributed to students (if you have chosen a different clip, adjust the prompt accordingly).

   In the video clip, what is Will Smith saying about goals? To what extent do you agree with what Smith is saying? To support your opinion, be sure to include specific examples drawn from your own experience, your observations of others, any of your reading, or from the movie clip.

   The prompt is presented in the style of the University of California Analytical Placement Exam. (More information on these types of prompts can be found at this post on writing prompts: http://larryferlazzo.edublogs.org/2013/04/03/writing-prompts-feel-free-to-contribute-your-own/)

   Explain to students that in the future, they may have to write a complete essay in response to a prompt like this one. Today, though, they just have to write a paragraph or two. Depending on student experience with prompts, you might want to number each of the three elements of the prompt to emphasize how students have to respond to all three.

3. At the end of five to ten minutes, explain that you are going to divide students into pairs and have each partner read what they wrote to the other one. Further explain that they should help each other ensure that each has covered all three elements of the prompt. Give them five minutes to share. While students are talking with each other, circulate to identify which students have written responses that would serve as good examples.

4. Ask for the class' attention, and ask one or two students to come up to the front, show their responses on the document camera (if available), and read them to the class.

5. Thank the class for taking the assignment seriously, collect the written responses, and explain that they are going to learning about goal-setting and set some goals for themselves over the next two days. First, they are going to start on a big goal. Write on the board: "What do you want people to say about you twenty or thirty years from now?" and pass out Figure 1.1, One-Sentence Project (this project was inspired by Dan Pink's book, *Drive*, 2011, p. 154).

6. Then show two short videos by Dan Pink introducing the project and the student videos modeling their sentences. All videos are short and can be found at "The Best Resources for Doing A One-Sentence Project."

7. Give students construction paper and markers to write and illustrate their sentences. Remind students to include sharing "why" they want to be talked about in that way. Researchers have found that identifying a "self-transcendent" goal (also called "Purpose For Learning")—in other words, one that will benefit others as well as themselves—tends to help students sustain a greater amount of "grit" and self-control (http://www. stanford.edu/~gwalton/home/Publications_files/Yeager_etal_inpress.pdf, p. 18). Though you do not need to share this information with students, ensuring that they include the reasons for their goal might tend to naturally get them thinking about how their goal can benefit the world, especially after seeing the examples in the videos. You can circulate to monitor to check that goals are classroom appropriate. If they are not completed by the end of the period the students must finish them as homework and bring them back the next day. Students can share their posters in small groups if they all are finished prior to the end of the class period.

Second Day

1. Begin by reminding students that the class had begun discussing goals yesterday, and that they were each to have completed their "One-Sentences" as homework if they had not completed them in class yesterday. Ask students to take them out and have students turn their desks so they are facing each other in rows. Depending on the number of students in class and the size of the classroom, there might be ten students sitting next to each other in one row, facing another ten in another row. Behind them, there could be another ten facing another row. Explain that this is a form of "speed dating." Each person will show their poster and say what they wrote to the student they are facing. At the end of one minute, yell "switch" for

one side of the rows to move down one (you can jokingly explain that since all your favorite students are in "this" row, then "that" row can be the one that has to move). This can go on for ten minutes—it's not necessary for every student to see what everyone wrote.

2. Bring the class together and collect the posters to put them up on the wall later to serve as reminders. Then explain that those are long-term goals, and a lot has to be done to get from here to there. Explain that now we have identified the long-term goals, let's start figuring out short-term goals they can achieve in class this year to help them accomplish their one-sentences. (Note: Some students might choose one-sentence goals—professional athlete, skateboarder, etc.—that they believe cannot be helped by what is being studied in class. The "Our World Of Text" lesson plan in *Self-Driven Learning* (Ferlazzo 2013) provides ideas on how to deal with this issue, and can be taught at any time prior to or after this goal-setting lesson is complete. Other responses could be pointing out that to get to college before the pros requires being able to do academic work, and the better skilled they are, the more time they can spend on athletics; also, you have to negotiate contracts, and there are many stories of agents and advisors who have taken advantage of athletes and left them bankrupt. In addition, I have worked with coaches at our school to develop a weekly evaluation form highlighting several qualities we believe are important in both the classroom and in athletics—see Figure 1.2, Weekly Evaluation For Athletes. If you anticipate this issue coming up in your class, you might want to consider having a similar conversation with your school's coaches to determine your own list of qualities and use them to help student athletes develop their short-term goals.)

3. Explain that before going on any further to set goals for this year, you will review what one of the most well-known researchers on goal-setting says about why and how we should do it. Show Figure 1.3, The Motivational Benefits of Goal-Setting, on the overhead or document camera and distribute copies to students. Then read it aloud.

4. Next, explain that now they've reviewed *why* we make goals, students will shortly begin to write down goals that they have for this year in this class that will help them move towards their "one-sentence" goals. Make one more point, though—the difference between "Learning Goals" and "Performance Goals." Pass out Figure 1.4, The Difference between Learning and Performance Goals, and explain that students will be divided into pairs and work for five minutes. One student is to read the first half and the other student is to read the examples out loud (with the other reading along silently). Then they should come up with the answer to this question, which you can write on the board and also distribute on the hand-out: "Why

Building a Community of Self-Motivated Learners

do you think students who focus on learning goals get better grades and scores than those who emphasize performance goals?" Explain that this question may not make sense to them now, but will after they read the hand-out. Every student should write their response on the paper—it may only be a sentence or two—and it can be the same response as their partner's. Then pair up the students and circulate to identify examples of good responses.

5. After five minutes, bring the class together again and call on students you have previously identified to share their responses to the question. Be prepared to add some responses of your own, including the points that were made earlier in the goal-setting section of this chapter—that students tend to be less concerned about grades and scores and focus more on truly understanding and applying what they are learning. Teachers might want to share this excerpt from *The New York Times* about the danger of focusing on performance goals:

> "If the goal is to earn a certain score on a math test, then that goal takes over," Professor Schweitzer said. "A love of learning or understanding of the elegance of math gets beaten out."
>
> And goals can have unintended consequences. A 1999 article on the use of incentives that appeared in *The Journal of Economic Literature* tells an anecdote about Ken O'Brien, the former New York Jets quarterback who had a tendency to throw interceptions early in his career. As a result, he received a contract that penalized him every time he threw the ball to the opposing team. It worked—he threw fewer interceptions. But that was because he threw fewer balls overall, even when he should have. (Tugend, 2012)

6. Next, distribute Figure 1.5, "Goal-Planning Sheet." Explain that you would like students to identify at least two and as many as three goals they would like to achieve this semester. They could be a mix of both learning goals and performance goals, but they should not be all performance goals. They should be challenging, but not too difficult. Students should write down why they chose that goal (how might it fit in with their one-sentence goal), and one or two specific things they can do over the next week to achieve each one of the goals. Show a model you have created for two or three goals on the overhead. Showing models of specific actions to take to achieve the goals will be particularly important. Explain that the students will be periodically reviewing the progress they are making towards their goals. In addition, point out that research has found that thinking about goals as "promotion"—in other words, in a positive way ("I want to focus more in class")—helps people become more likely to achieve their goal and actually helps them feel happier than thinking about goals as "prevention"—which

tends to be more negative ("I don't want to talk as much in class") (http://journal.frontiersin.org/Journal/10.3389/fpsyg.2014.00722/pdf, p. 5).

Note: Writer Samuel Thomas Davies (2014) has reviewed research that suggests that the chances of people being successful in achieving their goals has much to do with their self-perception (http://www.samuelthomasdavies.com/how-to-commit-to-your-goals-in-the-long-term/). In other words, instead of saying "My goal is to read higher-level books" it is better to say, "I am a reader; therefore I will read higher-level books"; or instead of saying "I want to focus more in class" it might be better to say, "I am a scholar; therefore I will focus more in class." You might want to share this research with students and suggest they apply it in their goal-planning.

7. Students can begin working on their goal-planning sheet. Once they are completed, they can hand them in to you to photocopy and then return to the students, asking that they put it in a separate section of a binder, or in a special folder, labeled "Goals."

Future Days

- A few days after teaching this lesson, perhaps on a Friday and announcing that it will be a regular Friday occurrence, ask students to take out their Goal-Planning Sheet. Distribute Figure 1.6, "Four-Week Goal-Tracking Sheet," and ask students to copy their goals and action plans into the first two columns of the new sheet. Then ask students to complete their assessment for the first week; you can show your own sheet as a model. Point out that it's okay for goals and action plans to change. Students can pair up to share what they wrote. Circulate throughout the room to identify students who might need some help. Students should keep these sheets in their binder or folder. At the end of each month, they can turn them into you for review. At that time, students can also review if they want to change any of their goals.

In order to ensure that this short weekly activity does not feel dreary, routine, and obligatory to students, consider varying what takes place. Here are some ways to easily "mix it up" a bit:

- In addition to having students complete their goal-tracking sheets, show one of the short videos on "The Best Video Clips On Goal-Setting" list some Fridays and ask students quick reflective questions about it.

- Ask students one day to share why they think they are tracking the progress they are making towards their goals. Follow up the discussion by sharing Figure 1.7, "Pursuing Goals Effectively," which is an excerpt from a paper by a prominent researcher on goals and goal-setting, as a read-aloud.

- Some days have students share their progress in pairs, other days in larger groups, and sometimes use the "speed dating" process from earlier in the lesson plan.

- At least once each semester, plan a curriculum-related project that students can do in small groups relatively independently so you can call each student one at a time to your desk for a two-minute conference about their goals.

- Periodically change the goal-setting sheet and process. In addition to teaching the goal-setting lesson found in *Helping Students Motivate Themselves* (Ferlazzo, 2011b), here are other ways students can set goals:

  — Researchers have found that it's particularly effective for people to actually see that they are making progress through some sort of visualization, such as drawing some kind of graph (Virginia Tech, 2011). This is not to suggest that teachers create big public achievement charts with gold stars. Instead, students can keep one for themselves that they could complete along with their regular goal-tracking sheet. Figure 1.8, "Bar Graph Goal-Tracking Sheet," can be used for students to "color in" a bar graph each week based on how much progress they feel they have made towards each goal during that time. I've found it particularly useful for the last several weeks of a semester or school year.

  — Figure 1.9, "Goal Report," is another option for a goal-tracking sheet.

  — Figure 1.10, "Goal Reflection," is a goal-setting sheet that can include school-related and non-school-related goals. This one can also be helpful leading up to a stressful time of the year.

  — An earlier section in this chapter discussed research that showed having students write a few sentences after a lesson about how they might apply what they had just learned to their lives enhanced academic achievement and engagement. Here's an exercise to combine that concept with goal-setting that I have done successfully later in the school year:

    First, give each student a sheet asking them to list *what* units and life skills (that's the term I use to describe lessons in this book and the previous ones in this series) the class has studied so far during the year, and *how* the class studied them (Figure 1.11). Then, after they have completed this, give them a sheet asking them to list their personal, academic, and professional goals (Figure 1.12). They can copy goals they have identified on previous goal-setting sheets. After that sheet is done, ask students to clear their desks, put the first sheet on their left and the second sheet on their right with space in the middle for the third sheet that is then given to them (Figure 1.13). That sheet says,

"List ways how what we have studied and how we have studied them this year can help you achieve your goals." In other words, how what we have done (on their left) can help them achieve their goals (on their right). The figures refer to what I cover in my classroom, so they should be changed to reflect the terminology used in your class.

— On a day when students can go to the computer lab or access individual laptops/tablets, tell students they are first going to read a short article on what successful people do to achieve goals, and then take a short online quiz (their final score can remain private) on how many of those actions they are taking to achieve their goals. First, give students copies of "Nine Things Successful People Do Differently" (http://blogs.hbr.org/cs/2011/02/nine_things_successful_people.html) and ask students to read it aloud in pairs, taking turns with each paragraph. If time permits, students could be asked to write a short phrase summarizing each of the nine "things." Next, students can take the online quiz "9 Things Diagnostic" (http://9thingsdiagnostic.com/index.php). It should only take a few minutes to complete it. Before taking it, explain to students that after they are done, the site will give them a "grade" (they don't have to tell anyone what it is), along with a recommendation of which of the "nine things" they might want to improve. If they agree, and it's fine if they do not, they can then look again at their goal sheets and action plans and make changes. Teachers should have taken the quiz earlier, and can model what they learned and the changes they will make. After they are done, students can share in partners or small groups what changes, if any, they made.

— The one-sentence goals and the shorter-term goals provide an exceptional classroom management tool to teachers. When students are not behaving appropriately, you can ask them, "Is what you're doing now going to help you achieve your goals?" (Obviously, it would be more effective if you can remember student goals so instead of saying "your goals" you can say the specific goals the students have chosen.)

— Sometimes, students can fall into the "doldrums" near the end of a semester or school year. A strategy to combat that challenge is to have students write and illustrate one goal they want to focus on during the last few weeks, share it in class, and put a little different twist on previous goal exercises by displaying their posters in the hallway or on a classroom window facing outward. Making it a widely public display can often generate more enthusiasm towards achieving it.

— January is a timely month for students to make "New Year's Resolutions," so a simple goal-setting review or mini-lesson might be particularly engaging. One potential exercise could be for you to choose one article or video (or, better yet, have each student choose their own preference) from "The Best Ways To Help Make Your New Year's Resolutions Succeed" (http://larryferlazzo.edublogs.org/2012/12/31/the-best-ways-to-help-make-your-new-years-resolutions-succeed/) and have students write a short essay in response to this prompt:

Describe two or three strategies from the list the author suggests to improve the chances of success for a New Year's resolution. Do you agree that they would help? To support your opinion you may use examples from your own experiences, your observations of others, and anything that you have read, including this essay (or video).

- When Goals Are Not Met:

There may be times when students are having difficulties meeting their goals. If and when that occurs, researchers recommend that accountability is still important and it should not be dismissed with a shrug (http://blogs.hbr.org/2011/02/making-sure-your-employees-suc/). Find out from the student why they think they are having difficulties, elicit from them ideas on what they can do differently and perhaps provide some of your own suggestions (remember the advice from Pixar mentioned earlier in this chapter to use "ands" and "what ifs"):

> If the problem was within his control, ask him to apply the possible solutions you've discussed, take another stab at reaching the goal, and check in with you more frequently. If it was something that was outside of his power or the goal was too ambitious, acknowledge the disappointment but don't dwell on it. "Do the diagnosis, get the learning, and move on," says [Harvard Professor Linda] Hill. (Gallo, 2011)

Dr. Robert Brooks suggests that this kind of feedback be prefaced with a "we" statement like, "This strategy you're using doesn't seem to be working. Let's figure out why and how we can change the strategy so that you are successful" (Brooks, as cited in Washburn, 2009, para. 11).

Assessment

1. The response to the first day's writing prompts can be reviewed to see if students responded to the three elements of the prompt.

2. Collect each goal sheet to make copies before returning the original to each student the following day. Assess if students followed instructions for both goals and action plans and, if not, provide students with additional instructional support.

3. If you feel a more involved assessment is necessary, you can develop a simple rubric appropriate for your classroom situation. Free online resources to

both find pre-made rubrics and to create new ones can be found at http://larryferlazzo.edublogs.org/2010/09/18/the-best-rubric-sites-and-a-begin ning-discussion-about-their-use/

Possible Extensions/Modifications

- Ask students to expand the paragraph they wrote on the first day of the lesson in response to the Will Smith video into a full-fledged essay.

- Students could make an online video of their one-sentence projects. See the Ed Tech box below for details.

Ed Tech

Students can make online videos either saying their one sentences and showing their posters, or combining that with actually acting them out. Videotaping them with a smartphone is easy, and many free and easy online video-editing tools are available at "Not The 'Best,' But A List . . . of Online Video Editors" (http://larryferlazzo.edublogs. org/2010/03/30/not-the-best-but-a-list-of-online-video-editors/). Be sure to obtain parent permission prior to posting student work online. Information, including model permission slips, can be found at "The Best Teacher Resources for Online Student Safety and Legal Issues" (http://larryferlazzo.edublogs.org/2009/08/10/the-best-teacher-resource s-for-online-student-safety-legal-issues/).

Figure 1.1 One-Sentence Project

Today and tomorrow we will be working on a "One-Sentence Project."
After watching some introductory videos, you will need to write one relatively short sentence explaining how you want your life to be remembered.

In this one short sentence, you will need to answer these questions:

How do you want to be remembered?

Why do you want to be remembered that way?

You will then create a poster sharing your sentence and illustrating it with a drawing.

For example, my sentence is:

He helped a lot of people to help themselves because it was important to him to leave the world a better place than it was when he entered it.

Figure 1.2 Weekly Evaluation for Athletes

Student Name _____

Date _____

Subject _____

1. Leadership (Has he/she been a role model for other students?)

_____

2. Cooperation (Has he/she worked well with teacher and students?)

_____

3. Respect (Has he/she been respectful to teacher and students?)

_____

4. Perseverance (Has he/she kept on trying, even if a task was difficult?)

_____

5. Preparation (Has he/she come to class ready to learn and completed homework?)

_____

Other Teacher Comments:

_____

Teacher's Signature:

_____

Building a Community of Self-Motivated Learners

Figure 1.3   The Motivational Benefits of Goal-Setting

Why is goal-setting effective?

The answer to this question is fourfold.

First, in committing to a goal, a person chooses to divert attention toward goal-relevant activities and away from goal-irrelevant activities.

Second, goals energize people. Challenging goals lead to higher effort than easy goals. This is true regardless of whether goal attainment requires physical or cognitive effort.

Third, goals affect persistence. High goals prolong effort; tight deadlines lead to a more rapid work pace than loose deadlines.

Fourth, goals motivate people to use the knowledge they have that will help them to attain the goal, or to discover the knowledge needed to do so.

Sources: From "The motivational benefits of goal-setting," *Academy of Management Executive* (2004), *18*(4), by Professor Gary Latham.

Figure 1.4 The Difference between Learning
Goals and Performance Goals

Learning goals demonstrate increased understanding and the ability to apply it. Performance goals involve reaching a certain "score" or outperforming others. People who focus more on learning goals tend to get higher "performance" evaluations (like grades) than those who emphasize performance goals.

That doesn't make performance goals "bad." Just make sure that, if you decide on performance goals, you have some learning goals, too.

Examples:

Learning Goals	Performance Goals
I want to be able to write a good essay here and in other classes.	I want to get an A in class.
I want to be able to read higher level books than I read now.	I want to read more books than anyone else in this class.
I want to be able to give a good class presentation.	I want to pass the class.
I want to be more of a leader in class.	I want to get a lot of extra credit points.
I want to be able to control myself in class and respect other students and the teacher.	I don't want to get any referrals to the office for misbehavior.

Question:

Why do you think students who focus on learning goals get better grades and scores than those who emphasize performance goals?

Figure 1.5 Goal-Planning Sheet

Name _____

Semester Goal	Reason for Goal	Is it a Learning or Performance Goal?	Specific Actions I Will Take Over the Next Week to Help Achieve Goal
I want to . . .			
I want to . . .			
I want to . . .			

Figure 1.6 Four-Week Goal-Tracking Sheet

Name _____

Goal	What I will specifically do to accomplish it	First Week	Second Week	Third Week	Fourth Week
		1. Did I make progress towards my goal? *2. What did I do?* *3. What will I do next week?* *4. Do I need to make adjustments to my goal?*			
		1. 2. 3. 4.	1. 2. 3. 4.	1. 2. 3. 4.	1. 2. 3. 4.
		1. 2. 3. 4.	1. 2. 3. 4.	1. 2. 3. 4.	1. 2. 3. 4.
		1. 2. 3. 4.	1. 2. 3. 4.	1. 2. 3. 4.	1. 2. 3. 4.

Figure 1.7 Pursuing Goals Effectively

For people to pursue goals effectively, they need some means of checking or tracking their progress toward their goal. Sometimes this is self-evident to perception, as when a person walks down a road towards a distant but visible town or cuts the grass on a large lawn. In such cases, deviations from the path to the goal are easily seen and corrected. Contrast this, however, with a sales goal whose attainment requires scores of sales over a period of many months [or an academic goal]. Here some formal means of keeping score is needed so that people can get a clear indication if they are moving fast enough and in the right direction.

Source: From "Motivation through conscious goal setting" (p. 120), *Applied & Preventive Psychology* (1996), 5: 117–124, by Edwin A. Locke

Figure 1.8 Bar Graph Goal-Tracking Sheet

Name _____

GOAL _____

Great										
Good										
Okay										
Little										
	1st Wk	**2nd Wk**	**3rd Wk**	**4th Wk**	**5th Wk**	**6th Wk**	**7th Wk**	**8th Wk**	**9th Wk**	**10th Wk**

GOAL _____

Great										
Good										
Okay										
Little										
	1st Wk	**2nd Wk**	**3rd Wk**	**4th Wk**	**5th Wk**	**6th Wk**	**7th Wk**	**8th Wk**	**9th Wk**	**10th Wk**

Figure 1.9 Goal Report

Name _____

Date _____

Learning Goal
I had said my learning goal this semester would be _____
and that I would _____
to achieve it.

Circle One of the Responses:
I made progress towards my goal this week.

I did not make progress towards my goal this week.

Next Step
I will _____
this week to make more progress.

Performance Goal
I had said my learning goal this semester would be _____
and that I would _____
to achieve it.

Circle One of the Responses:
I made progress towards my goal this week.

I did not make progress towards my goal this week.

Next Step
I will _____
this week to make more progress.

Learning Goal
Over the next two weeks, I want to _____ .
I will _____
to help achieve it.

Performance Goal
Over the next two weeks, I want to _____ .
I will _____
to help achieve it.

Figure 1.10 Goal Reflection

Name _____

1. What do you like about yourself? Name as many things as you like, but please list at least three:

2. What things about yourself would you like to change/improve? Name as many as you would like, but please list at least three. Please also say why you would like to improve them:

3. What can you do between now and the end of the school year to make those changes/improvements happen? Please be as specific as possible, and list at least three actions you can take:

4. What can your teachers do to help you make those changes? Please be as specific as possible, and list at least three actions they can take:

5. If you make those changes, can you think of some ways you can reward yourself for those accomplishments? List them:

Figure 1.11   What Have We Studied This School Year?

Units (Jamaica, etc):

Life Skills (self-control, etc.—review your notebook):

How have we studied them (writing ABC paragraphs, reading, data sets, etc.):

Figure 1.12   What Are Your Goals?

School (high school, college):

Professional (career):

Personal (family, etc.):

Figure 1.13 How What We Have Studied and How We Have
Studied Can Help You Achieve Your Goals

List Ways How What We Have Studied and How We Have Studied This Year Can
Help You Achieve Your Goals

Grit Lesson Plan II

Instructional Objectives for Students

- Further develop their ability to practice reading strategies to help comprehend a text.

- Understand the importance of grit/perseverance in achieving their goals.

- Further develop their ability to write academic text.

Duration

One fifty-five minute class period if the student computer activity is not included. If it is included, twenty minutes will have to be added to the next day.

Materials

- Access to the Internet, the web pages "The Best Video Clips Demonstrating Grit" (http://larryferlazzo.edublogs.org/2013/07/15/the-best-video-clips-demonstrating-grit-help-me-find-more/); "The Best Videos Illustrating the Qualities of a Successful Language Learner" (http://larryferlazzo.edublogs.org/2011/07/22/the-best-videos-illustrating-qualities-of-a-successful-language-learner/) and "The Best Resources for Learning About the Importance of Grit" (http://larryferlazzo.edublogs.org/2011/05/17/the-best-resources-for-learning-about-the-importance-of-grit/) and a computer projector.

- Ideally, access to a computer lab or tablets and laptops for all students.

Student copies of "Students' View of Intelligence Can Help Grades" (http://www.npr.org/templates/story/story.php?storyId=7406521).

Common Core English Language Arts Standards

Reading:

- Determine central ideas or themes of a text and analyze their development; summarize the key supporting details and ideas.

- Read and comprehend complex literary and informational texts independently and proficiently.

Writing:

- Write arguments to support claims in an analysis of substantive topics or texts, using valid reasoning and relevant and sufficient evidence.

Speaking and Listening:

- Prepare for and participate effectively in a range of conversations and collaborations with diverse partners, building on others' ideas and expressing their own clearly and persuasively.

Language:

- Demonstrate command of the conventions of standard English grammar and usage when writing or speaking.

- Demonstrate command of the conventions of standard English capitalization, punctuation, and spelling when writing.

Procedure

1. As students walk in, have this written on the board: *Take out a sheet of paper and quietly watch the videos. Write down notes about what human qualities the videos show and how they show them.* Show two of the videos found on "The Best Video Clips Demonstrating Grit." Ask students to verbally (and quickly) share what they wrote with a partner. Circulate both during the video-watching time and during the sharing time to identify students who should be asked to share with the entire class. After partners have shared, call on one to three students to tell the entire class what they wrote. Most students will identify perseverance—perhaps using other words—and you should agree and explain another way of saying it is "grit."

2. Explain that sometimes we all hit bumps on the road towards achieving our goals. Share an example or two from your own life. Explain that this might happen with some of the goals students have identified in the goal-setting activities the class has been doing, and that they are going to spend a little time today talking about the importance of having "grit." Explain that a professor named Angela Duckworth has done research on this, and they're going to watch a short video of her discussing what she has found. While the class is watching the video, which is only six minutes long, ask them to take notes and be prepared to respond to the question, "What is grit and why is it important?" in one short paragraph. Give students time to respond to the question in an "ABC" paragraph—Answer the question; Back it up with evidence (for example, a story or a piece of information that Professor Duckworth gives); make a Comment or Connection relating it to your life or something else you have read or learned elsewhere. Examples of this type of paragraph can be found in Chapter 3 on reading and writing, and can be shown as an example.

3. Show Professor Duckworth's TED Talk on grit that can be found at "The Best Resources for Learning About the Importance of Grit." After watching the

video, give the students five to ten minutes to write their paragraph. Students should then divide into pairs and verbally share what they wrote, and one or two students can share with the entire class. Encourage students to read with prosody (with feeling) and model a sentence read with that kind of intonation and another in a monotone.

4. If time permits, and if laptops/tablets are available for all students, they can take Professor Duckworth's "grit survey" (http://www.authentichappiness. sas.upenn.edu/default.aspx). A link to it can also be found on "The Best Resources for Learning About the Importance of Grit" list. Students have to register first, and it's a short survey. Afterwards, students can share in partners or with the class if they agree or disagree with what the survey said about their level of "grit."

5. Professor Duckworth ends her TED Talk by saying that the best way to build grit is to have a growth mindset. Remind students of that, and explain that the class is going to spend a little time learning about what that means. Explain that you are going to give students a copy of a short article titled "Students' View of Intelligence Can Help Grades," and that they should read it with a partner (one way to inject a little levity into the "pairing up" procedure is by having students choose a partner with the same or different color socks, color hair, etc.), taking turns to read each paragraph aloud while the other student reads along silently. After students have completed reading it, ask them to work together to write a one- or two-sentence summary defining a growth mindset. Circulate during this activity, helping students and identifying those who have developed particularly good summaries. This activity should take about ten minutes.

6. Ask some students to share their summaries with the entire class.

7. Explain that you hope students will keep what they have learned today in mind as they work towards achieving their goals. End with two or three humorous and/or engaging videos on perseverance found at "The Best Videos Illustrating the Qualities of a Successful Language Learner" (http:// larryferlazzo.edublogs.org/2011/07/22/the-best-videos-illustrating-quali ties-of-a-successful-language-learner/).

Assessment

1. Review the response to the ABC writing prompt to see if students responded to the three elements of the prompt.

2. If you feel a more involved assessment is necessary, you can develop a simple rubric appropriate for your classroom situation. Free online resources to both find pre-made rubrics and to create new ones can be found at

http://larryferlazzo.edublogs.org/2010/09/18/the-best-rubric-sites-and-a-beginning-discussion-about-their-use/

Possible Extensions/Modifications

- Instead of writing a one- or two-sentence summary of the growth mindset article, students could write a full-fledged essay responding to this prompt:

  According to Carol Dweck, what is a "growth mindset" and why is it important? Do you agree with what Dweck is saying? To support your opinion you may use examples from your own experiences, your observations of others, and any of your reading.

- Students could create short skits demonstrating examples of grit, and video-tape them (see Ed Tech box in Goal-Setting Lesson Plan II). Students could also create online animations, instead.

Ed Tech

Students can make online animations demonstrating examples of grit using any of the tools at "The Best Ways for Students to Create Online Animations" (http://larryferlazzo.edublogs.org/2008/05/11/the-best-ways-for-students-to-create-online-animations/). Be sure to obtain parent permission prior to posting student work online. Information, including model permission slips, can be found at "The Best Teacher Resources for Online Student Safety and Legal Issues" (http://larryferlazzo.edublogs.org/2009/08/10/the-best-teacher-resources-for-online-student-safety-legal-issues/).

Deliberate Practice Mini-Lesson Plan

Procedure

1. Students enter the classroom and see the word "deliberate" written on the board or overhead. Ask the students to take out a piece of paper, copy the word down, and write what they think it means. Circulate around the room looking at what students are writing, and then call on students you have seen writing thoughtful responses. Write them up under the word "deliberate" on the board.

2. Next, write the word "practice" next to the word "deliberate" and ask students to copy the word down and write what they think it means, repeating the process for the word "deliberate."

3. Explain that in order to achieve our goals, it's not just a matter of mindlessly doing the same thing over and over again—grit is not enough. We also have to practice, and researchers have identified a specific kind of practice called "deliberate practice." A combination of what students had written should be a relatively accurate definition of it. If clarification is needed, quote dictionary definitions of the two words and further explain that it is not just mindless repetition of a task but instead, it involves regularly doing increasingly challenging tasks and reflecting on the progress made and the problems encountered. We accomplish our goals through this kind of practice.

4. Give an example or two from your own life. It could be the process you go through in becoming a better teacher as well as a non-school example.

5. Then display Figure 1.14, "Ray Allen Deliberate Practice Read Aloud," on the overhead and read it to the class.

6. Show the short "Ray Allen's Shooting Routine" video—there are many videos on what he does before the game if you search "Ray Allen Routine" (https://www.youtube.com/watch?v=N7KGG681Cd0).

7. Then project an image of myelin on the screen (an Internet search will yield many, but one can also be found at this site—along with additional background information on myelin: http://larryferlazzo.edublogs.org/2013/08/05/deliberate-practice-myelin-the-brain/). Explain that the image is of myelin, and say that myelin is white matter in the brain that forms layers that make nerve impulses faster and stronger and which a number of researchers suggest increases learning. The amount of myelin and its density seems to increase through practice and makes what you are learning to do more automatic. The idea of deliberate practice comes in

because we have to ensure that myelin forms to increase and strengthen the right impulses—if we keep on practicing something the wrong way, then we'll make the wrong actions automatic. Deliberate practice means continuous reflection to see if what we are doing is correct. See Fields, 2008 (http://www.scientificamerican.com/article/white-matter-matters/).

8. Explain that the students are now going to take a short assessment to determine how well they use deliberate practice in working towards their goals. They do not have to share their score with anyone else, including the teacher. Display Figure 1.15, "Learning Quotient Assessment" (developed by Daniel Coyle, 2009) on the overhead. Ask students to take out a sheet of paper (or make student copies of the assessment) and go over each item, rating themselves on each. After it is completed, students should total their score. After the points are totaled, say that a perfect Learning Quotient is 50, and Harold Coyle suggests that 25 or 30 is average.

9. Ask students to take out their goal sheets to review their action plans. In light of today's lesson, might they want to add some things from the Learning Quotient Assessment quiz? Give students a few minutes to make changes to their plans; have students share them, and then ask some students to let the entire class know about the changes they made.

Figure 1.14   Ray Allen Deliberate Practice Read Aloud

Ray Allen has hit more three-pointers than anyone ever has in the NBA. How did he do it?

There were the obvious tasks of shooting thousands of shots from each spot behind the arc so that any attempt from any angle would feel familiar, rote, routine. The more subtle groundwork centered on a regimented diet, a controlled sleeping pattern, an increased emphasis on his rigid conditioning habits to strengthen his core and challenge his body.

What was his response when a TV commentator said he was "born to shoot"?

"I've argued this with a lot of people in my life," Allen said. "When people say God blessed me with a beautiful jump shot, it really pisses me off. I tell those people, 'Don't undermine the work I've put in every day.' Not some days. Every day. Ask anyone who has been on a team with me who shoots the most. Go back to Seattle and Milwaukee, and ask them. The answer is me—not because it's a competition but because that's how I prepare."

Source: From MacMullan, J. (2011, February 11). http://sports.espn.go.com/boston/nba/columns/story?columnist=macmullan_jackie&id=6106450

How Do You Motivate Students?

Figure 1.15   Learning Quotient Assessment

Rate yourself from 0 to 5 on the following questions, where 0 is for strongly disagree; 5 is for strongly agree.

1. You work on your skills for an hour or more every day.
2. You are focused on process, not the immediate outcomes.
3. You have strong relationships with mentors/coaches, and use them as models and guidance.
4. You are keenly aware of how much you do not know, and the gap between your present abilities and your long-term goals.
5. You can accurately and precisely describe the skills you want to build.
6. You think about improving your skills all the time.
7. You approach your daily work with enthusiasm.
8. You are balanced between building with repetition and seeking innovations.
9. You are comfortable going outside of your comfort zone.
10. You are constantly adapting and refining your learning process.

A perfect LQ would be 50 . . . most of us would fall in the 25–30 range or so.

Source: Developed by Daniel Coyle and used with permission (http://thetalentcode. com/2013/07/01/whats-your-lq-learning-quotient/)

Student Engagement Assessment Mini-Lesson Plan

Procedure

1. During the first week of school, explain that one way you get to know your classes is by learning about their past experiences in school. Explain that you are going to pass out a sheet with ten statements, which you do not want students to put their names on. You want students to say honestly what their experiences in school have been.

2. Place the sheet on the overhead or document camera, and pass out Figure 1.16, "Beginning of School Year Student Engagement Assessment." Explain that you are going to go through it together so that everyone is clear on the questions. Students are to write either 1, 2, 3, 4 or 5 next to each statement—1 means "almost never" and 5 means "almost always." The other numbers—2, 3, and 4—mean somewhere in between.

3. Remind students again not to write their names on the sheets. Read each question aloud and help make it more clear by providing examples. For the first statement, you might say, "For example, were you given opportunities to read books that you wanted and did teachers ever let students decide how they wanted to choose groups or what they would study on a particular day?" After giving the example, ask the students to write the appropriate number, then move on to the next statement.

4. After students complete the assessment, thank them and collect the sheets. Later, you can tabulate them—perhaps finding the median and average response for each statement.

5. Later in the year: Both at the end of the first semester and at the end of the school year, repeat this lesson with Figure 1.17, "Semester and Year-End Student Engagement Assessment." At each of those times, however, you can explain that you want to get a sense of how students are feeling about the class so you can be a better teacher for them. After each assessment, you can do tabulations and compare the results with previous ones to determine if instruction should be changed. Ideally, you can discuss the results of each of these two surveys with the class after tabulations are complete, share your reflections, and perhaps ask students for their thoughts and suggestions.

    Note: Feel free to adjust, add, or delete any of the questions on the survey based on what *you* know about intrinsic motivation and student engagement.

Figure 1.16 Beginning of School Year Student
Engagement Assessment

Please Do Not Write Your Name on this Sheet

Using a scale of 1 to 5, with 1 being "almost never" to 5 being "almost always," please write the number that applies to your past experience in school next to the statement.

1. I've felt like I have had some control and choice about what I did in my classes.

2. I've been encouraged to explore things in my classes that I've been interested in.

3. I've felt like I have received the support I needed to be successful in my classes.

4. I've felt that students in my classes have wanted to help each other succeed.

5. I've felt encouraged by teachers to work with other students.

6. I've felt respected by my teachers.

7. I've liked my teachers.

8. I've believed my teachers cared about what happened to me.

9. I've believed the work we did in my classes has been valuable and interesting.

10. I've applied what I learned in one class to other classes and to my life outside of school.

Figure 1.17   Semester and Year-End Student
Engagement Assessment

Please Do Not Write Your Name on this Sheet

Semester and Year-End Student Engagement Assessment

Using a scale of 1 to 5, with 1 being "almost never" to 5 being "almost always," please write the number that applies to your experience in this class next to the statement.

1. I feel like I have some control and choice about what I do in this class.
2. I'm encouraged to learn things in this class that I'm interested in.
3. I feel like I receive the support I need to be successful in this class.
4. I think students in this class want to help each other succeed.
5. I feel encouraged to work with other students.
6. I feel respected by my teacher.
7. I like my teacher.
8. I believe the teacher cares about what happens to me.
9. I believe the work we do in this class is valuable and interesting.
10. I can apply what I learn in this class to other classes and to my life outside of school.

References

Assor, A., Kaplan, H., & Rogh, G. (2002). Choice is good, but relevance is excellent: Autonomy-enhancing and suppressing teacher behaviours predicting students' engagement in schoolwork. *British Journal of Educational Psychology, 72,* 261–278.

Back (n.d.). *Online etymology dictionary.* Retrieved from: http://www.etymonline.com/index.php?term=back&allowed_in_frame=0

Balfanz, R., & Byrnes, V. (2012, May 24). *The importance of being in school: A report on absenteeism in the nation's public schools.* Washington, DC: Thomas B. Fordham Institute.

Barcelona, V.C. (2008, August 15). *Woody Allen interview.* Retrieved from: http://collider.com/entertainment/interviews/article.asp/aid/8878/tcid/1/pg/2

Busteed, B. (2013, January 7). The school cliff: Student engagement drops with each school year. *The Gallup Blog.* Retrieved from: http://thegallupblog.gallup.com/2013/01/the-school-cliff-student-engagement.html

Caine, R.N., & Caine, G. (1994). *Making connections: Teaching and the human brain.* Menlo Park, CA: Addison Wesley.

CAST (n.d.). *Learning tools.* Retrieved from: http://www.cast.org/learningtools/index.html

Chamorro-Premuzic, T. (2013, April 10). Does money really affect motivation? A review of the research. *HBR Blog Network*. Retrieved from: http://blogs.hbr. org/cs/2013/04/does_money_really_affect_motiv.html

Cheung, T.T.L., Gillebaart, M., Kroese, F., & De Ridder, D. (2014, July 8). Why are people with high self-control happier? The effect of trait self-control on happiness as mediated by regulatory focus. *Frontiers in Psychology*. doi: 10.3389/fpsyg.2014.00722. Retrieved from: http://journal.frontiersin.org/ Journal/10.3389/fpsyg.2014.00722/pdf

Committee on Increasing High School Students' Engagement and Motivation to Learn (2003). *Engaging schools: Fostering high school students' motivation to learn*. Washington, DC: The National Academies Press.

Construction of individual meaning is improved when students make connections (n.d.). Retrieved from: http://www.dialogueonlearning.tc3.edu/model/construct ingmeaning/cm-connectionsgraphics.htm

Coyle, D. (2009). *The talent code: Greatness isn't born. It's grown. Here's how*. New York: Bantam Books.

Cranmer, D. (n.d.). Teaching the vocabulary of a text. *The Journal*, 58–61.

Davies, S. T. (2014, August 14). *A tiny, powerful idea: How to commit to your goals in the long-term*. Retrieved from: http://www.samuelthomasdavies.com/how-to-commit-to-your-goals-in-the-long-term

Deci, E.L., Koestner, R., & Ryan, R.M. (1999). A meta-analytic review of experiments examining the effects of extrinsic rewards on intrinsic motivation. *Psychological Bulletin*, 125(6), 627–668.

Donnelly, W.B., & Roe, C.J. (2010). Using sentence frames to develop academic vocabulary for English Learners. *The Reading Teacher*, 64(2), 131–136.

Ericsson, K.A., Krampe, R.T., & Tesch-Romer, C. (1993). The role of deliberate practice in the acquisition of expert performance. *Psychological Review*, 100(3), 363–406.

Farrington, C.A., Roderick, M., Allensworth, E., Nagaoka, J., Seneca Keyes, T., Johnson, D.W., & Beechum, N.O. (2012). *Teaching adolescents to become learners: The role of noncognitive factors in shaping school performance*. Chicago: University of Chicago Consortium on Chicago School Research.

Feed (n.d.). *Online etymology dictionary*. Retrieved from: http://www.etymonline. com/index.php?term=feed&allowed_in_frame=0

Feiler, B. (2013, January 11). Train a parent, save a child. *The New York Times*. Retrieved from: http://www.nytimes.com/2013/01/13/fashion/modifying-a-childs-behavior-without-resorting-to-bribes-this-life.html?pagewanted=all

Feiler, B. (2013, March 15). The stories that bind us. *The New York Times*. Retrieved from: http://www.nytimes.com/2013/03/17/fashion/the-family-stories-that-bind-us-this-life.html?pagewanted=1&smid=tw-share

Ferlazzo, L. (2008, May 11). The best ways for students to create online animations. *Larry Ferlazzo's websites of the day*. Retrieved from: http://larryferlazzo.edublogs.org/2008/05/11/the-best-ways-for-students-to-create-online-animations/

Ferlazzo, L. (2009, February 9). Not "The best," but "A list" of mindmapping, flow chart tools, & graphic organizers. *Larry Ferlazzo's websites of the day*. Retrieved from: http://larryferlazzo.edublogs.org/2009/02/09/not-the-best-but-a-list-of-mindmapping-flow-chart-tools-graphic-organizers/

Ferlazzo, L. (2009, May 25). The best resources for helping teachers use Bloom's Taxonomy in the classroom. *Larry Ferlazzo's websites of the day*. Retrieved from: http://larryferlazzo.edublogs.org/2009/05/25/the-best-resources-for-helping-teachers-use-blooms-taxonomy-in-the-classroom/

Ferlazzo, L. (2009, August 10). The best teacher resources for online student safety and legal issues. *Larry Ferlazzo's websites of the day*. Retrieved from: http://larryferlazzo.edublogs.org/2009/08/10/the-best-teacher-resources-for-online-student-safety-legal-issues/

Ferlazzo, L. (2010). *English language learners, teaching strategies that work*. Santa Barbara, CA: ABC CLIO.

Ferlazzo, L. (2010, March 30). Not the "best," but a list . . . of online video editors. *Larry Ferlazzo's websites of the day*. Retrieved from: http://larryferlazzo.edublogs.org/2010/03/30/not-the-best-but-a-list-of-online-video-editors/

Ferlazzo, L. (2010, April 2). The best sites for cooperative learning ideas. *Larry Ferlazzo's websites of the day*. Retrieved from: http://larryferlazzo.edublogs.org/2010/04/02/the-best-sites-for-cooperative-learning-ideas/

Ferlazzo, L. (2010, May 17). The best posts and articles on "motivating" students. *Larry Ferlazzo's websites of the day*. Retrieved from: http://larryferlazzo.edublogs.org/2010/05/17/my-best-posts-on-motivating-students/

Ferlazzo, L. (2010, September 18). The best rubric sites (and a beginning discussion about their use). *Larry Ferlazzo's websites of the day*. Retrieved from: http://larryferlazzo.edublogs.org/2010/09/18/the-best-rubric-sites-and-a-beginning-discussion-about-their-use/

Ferlazzo, L. (2011a). *Helping students motivate themselves: Practical answers to classroom challenges*. New York: Routledge.

Ferlazzo, L. (2011b). *Helping students motivate themselves*. Larchmont, NY: Eye on Education.

Ferlazzo, L. (2011, May 17). The best resources for learning about the importance of "grit." *Larry Ferlazzo's websites of the day*. Retrieved from: http://larryferlazzo.edublogs.org/2011/05/17/the-best-resources-for-learning-about-the-importance-of-grit/

Ferlazzo, L. (2011, July 22). The best videos demonstrating qualities of a successful language learner. *Larry Ferlazzo's websites of the day*. Retrieved from: http://larryferlazzo.edublogs.org/2011/07/22/the-best-videos-illustrating-qualities-of-a-successful-language-learner/

Ferlazzo, L. (2011, September 11). The best MATH sites that students can use independently and let teachers check on progress. *Larry Ferlazzo's websites of the day*. Retrieved from: http://larryferlazzo.edublogs.org/2011/09/11/the-best-math-sites-that-students-can-use-independently-and-let-teachers-check-on-progress/

Ferlazzo, L. (2012, January 9). The best resources on differentiating instruction. *Larry Ferlazzo's websites of the day*. Retrieved from: http://larryferlazzo.edublogs.org/2012/01/09/the-best-resources-on-differentiating-instruction/

Ferlazzo, L. (2012, January 17). Response: Several ways to differentiate instruction. *Education Week Teacher*. Retrieved from: http://blogs.edweek.org/teachers/classroom_qa_with_larry_ferlazzo/2012/01/response_ways_to_differentiate_instruction.html

Ferlazzo, L. (2012, June 4). You cannot make a plant grow—You can provide the conditions for growth. *Larry Ferlazzo's websites of the day*. Retrieved from: http://larryferlazzo.edublogs.org/2012/06/04/you-cannot-make-a-plant-grow-you-can-provide-the-conditions-for-growth/

Ferlazzo, L. (2013). *Self-driven learning: Teaching strategies for student motivation*. New York: Routledge.

Ferlazzo, L. (2013, February 17). Teachers as "persuaders": An interview with Daniel Pink. *Education Week Teacher*. Retrieved from: http://blogs.edweek.org/teachers/classroom_qa_with_larry_ferlazzo/2013/02/teachers_as_persuaders_an_interview_with_daniel_pink.html

Ferlazzo, L. (2013, March 13). The best resources for doing a "One sentence project." *Larry Ferlazzo's websites of the day*. Retrieved from: http://larryferlazzo.edublogs.org/2013/03/13/the-best-resources-for-doing-a-one-sentence-project/

Ferlazzo, L. (2013, April 3). Writing prompts—Feel free to contribute your own! *Larry Ferlazzo's websites of the day*. Retrieved from: http://larryferlazzo.edublogs.org/2013/04/03/writing-prompts-feel-free-to-contribute-your-own/

Ferlazzo, L. (2013, July 11). The best video clips on goal setting—Help me find more. *Larry Ferlazzo's websites of the day*. Retrieved from: http://larryferlazzo.edublogs.org/2013/07/11/the-best-video-clips-on-goal-setting-help-me-find-more/

Ferlazzo, L. (2013, July 15). The best video clips demonstrating "grit"—Help me find more. *Larry Ferlazzo's websites of the day*. Retrieved from: http://larryferlazzo.edublogs.org/2013/07/15/the-best-video-clips-demonstrating-grit-help-me-find-more/

Ferlazzo, L. (2013, August 5). Deliberate practice, myelin, and the brain. *Larry Ferlazzo's websites of the day*. Retrieved from: http://larryferlazzo.edublogs.org/2013/08/05/deliberate-practice-myelin-the-brain/

Fields, R.D. (2008, March). White matter. *Scientific American*, 54–61. Retrieved from: https://docs.google.com/viewer?a=v&q=cache:k75C_CFOHDkJ:www.cs.unc.edu/~styner/public/DTI_tutorial/1%2520Scientific%2520American%25202008%2520Fields.pdf+&hl=en&gl=us&pid=bl&srcid=ADGEESiibZ5C2YpL0d6kSy5e9Pxdlh6d6w3ZiLi4jDHSVKnEpZwPVu6L6bMaIrb8WLlmMq33fUpy2d5vIkeb7US_l4A8Wgv9LmZRPR2CWHj9ChZvtXP8f_nAOxqgzikKBYTCx5Xg5bBn&sig=AHIEtbTMhUJ9jN1ESn40ZklTT90WPJI3EQ&pli=1

Freeman, T.M., Anderman, L.H., & Jensen, J.M. (2007). Sense of belonging in college freshmen at the classroom and campus levels. *The Journal of Experiential Education, 75*(3). Retrieved from: http://www.tandfonline.com/doi/abs/10.3200/JEXE.75.3.203–220?journalCode=vjxe20

Gallo, A. (2011, February 7). Making sure your employees succeed. *HBR Blog Network*. Retrieved from: http://blogs.hbr.org/2011/02/making-sure-your-employees-suc/

Gladwell, M. (2012, July 30). Slackers: Alberto Salazar and the art of exhaustion. *The New Yorker*. Retrieved from: http://www.newyorker.com/reporting/2012/07/30/120730fa_fact_gladwell?currentPage=2

Goal setting theory overview (n.d.). Retrieved from: https://wikispaces.psu.edu/display/PSYCH484/6.+Goal+Setting+Theory

Hacker, D. J., Dunlosky, J., & Graesser, A. C. (Eds.) (2009). *Handbook of metacognition in education*. New York: Routledge.

Hall, T., & Strangman, N. (2002). *Graphic organizers*. Wakefield, MA: National Center on Accessing the General Curriculum. Retrieved from: http://aim.cast.org/learn/historyarchive/backgroundpapers/graphic_organizers

Halvorson, H. G. (2011, February 25). Nine things successful people do differently. *HBR Blog network*. Retrieved from: http://blogs.hbr.org/cs/2011/02/nine_things_successful_people.html

Hattie, J. (2011). *Visible learning for teachers: Maximizing impact on learning*. New York: Routledge.

Heacox, D. (2012, July 27). Author spotlight on Diane Heacox, author of *Differentiating instruction in the regular classroom*. *YouTube*. Retrieved from: http://www.youtube.com/watch?v=9AmpPtePnoE

Hogan, K., & Pressley, M. (1997). *Scaffolding student learning: Instructional approaches and issues*. Brookline, MA: Brookline Books.

Hotz, R. L. (2012, May 7). Science reveals why we brag so much. *The Wall Street Journal*. Retrieved from: http://online.wsj.com/article/SB10001424052702304451104577390392329291890.html

Huebner, T. (2010). What research says about . . . differentiated learning. *Educational Leadership, 67*(5), 79–81.

Hulleman, C. S., Godes, O., Hendricks, B. L., & Harackiewicz, J. M. (2010). Enhancing interest and performance with a utility value intervention. *Journal of Educational Psychology, 102*(4), 880–895.

Hulleman, C. S., & Harackiewicz, J. M. (2009, December). Promoting interest and performance in high school science classes. *Science*. Retrieved from: http://www.sciencemag.org/content/326/5958/1410

Kirk, K. (n.d.). *Motivating students*. Retrieved from: http://serc.carleton.edu/NAGTWorkshops/affective/motivation.html

Klass, P. (2012, December 10). Understanding how children develop empathy. *The New York Times*. Retrieved from: http://well.blogs.nytimes.com/2012/12/10/understanding-how-children-develop-empathy/

Kluger, J. (2013, March 7). How hope works: Wishing won't make it so, but hoping—and knowing how to do it—might. *Time*. Retrieved from: http://healthland.time.com/2013/03/07/this-is-your-mind-on-hope

Konnikova, M. (2012, April 30). On writing, memory, and forgetting: Socrates and Hemingway take on Zeigarnik. *Scientific American*. Retrieved from: http://blogs.scientificamerican.com/literally-psyched/2012/04/30/on-writing-memory-and-forgetting-socrates-and-hemingway-take-on-zeigarnik/

Latham, G. (2004). The motivational benefits of goal-setting. *Academy of Management Executive, 18*(4).

Locke, E. A. (1996). Motivation through conscious goal setting. *Applied Preventive Psychology, 5*, 117–124.

Locke, E. A., & Latham, G. P. (2006). New directions in goal-setting theory. *Current Directions in Psychological Science, 15*(5), 265–268. Retrieved from: http://home.ubalt.edu/tmitch/642/Articles%20syllabus/Locke%20et%20al%20New%20dir%20goal%20setting%202006.pdf

Lubin, J., & Sewak, M. (2007). *Enhancing learning through the use of graphic organizers: A review of the literature.* Retrieved from: http://www.lynchburg.edu/Documents/GraduateStudies/Lynchburg%20College%20Journal%20of%20Special%20Education/Volume%201-4%20PDF%20Articles/LubinJand SewakM%20-%20Enhancing%20Learning%20Through%20the%20Use%20of%20Graphic%20Organizers.pdf

MacMullan, J. (2011, February 11). Preparation is key to Ray Allen's 3s. *ESPN Boston.* Retrieved from: http://sports.espn.go.com/boston/nba/columns/story?columnist=macmullan_jackie&id=6106450

Markman, A. (2012, March 8). It is motivating to be part of a group. Being part of a group—any group—is motivating. *Psychology Today.* Retrieved from: http://www.psychologytoday.com/blog/ulterior-motives/201203/it-is-motivating-belong-group

Marzano, R. J., & Marzano, J. S. (2003). The key to classroom management. *Educational Leadership, 61*(1), 6–13.

Marzano, R. J. (2009). The art and science of teaching/Six steps to better vocabulary instruction. *Educational Leadership, 67*(1), 83–84.

Marzano, R. J. (2011a). Art and science of teaching/Relating to students: It's what you do that counts. *Educational Leadership, 68*(6), 82–83.

Marzano, R. J. (2011b). Art and science of teaching/The perils and promises of discovery learning. *Educational Leadership, 69*(1), 86–87.

McGrath, H., & Noble, T. (2007). *The big picture of positive peer relationships: What they are, why they work and how schools can develop them.* Paper presented at the 3rd Annual National Centre Against Bullying Conference, Melbourne.

Montalvo, G. P., Mansfield, E. A., & Miller, R. B. (2007). Liking or disliking the teacher: Student motivation, engagement and achievement. *Evaluation and Research in Education, 20*(3), 144–158. Retrieved from: http://dx.doi.org/10.2167/eri406.0

Nussbaum, D. (2013, May 21). *Narrative transportation.* Retrieved from: http://www.davenussbaum.com/narrative-transportation

Peer-to-peer support and other motivators at work (n.d.). Retrieved from: http://www.globoforce.com/teresa_amabile_interview

Perkins, D. (2003, December). Making thinking visible. *New Horizons for Learning.* Retrieved from: http://www.newhorizons.org/strategies/thinking/perkins.htm

Pink, D. H. (2009). *Drive: The surprising truth about what motivates us.* New York: Riverhead Trade.

Pozen, R. C. (2013, March 28). The delicate art of giving feedback. *HBR Blog*. Retrieved from: http://blogs.hbr.org/cs/2013/03/the_delicate_art_of_giving_fee.html

Prince, M., & Felder, R. (2007, March/April). The many faces of inductive teaching and learning. *Journal of College Science Teaching*. Retrieved from: http://www3.nsta.org/main/news/stories/college_science.php?news_story_ID=53403

Ray Allen's shooting routine. (2013, June 18). *YouTube*. Retrieved from: https://www.youtube.com/watch?v=NK8Hq7bO3dc

Rebora, A. (2008, September 10). Making a difference: Carol Ann Tomlinson explains how differentiated instruction works and why we need it now. *Education Week Teacher PD Sourcebook*. Retrieved from: http://www.edweek.org/tsb/articles/2008/09/10/01tomlinson.h02.html

Rock, D. (2011, November 10). Praise leads to cheating? *Harvard Business Review*. Retrieved from: http://blogs.hbr.org/cs/2011/11/praise_leads_to_cheating.html?referral=00563&cm_mmc=email-_-newsletter-_-daily_alert-_-alert_date&utm_source=newsletter_daily_alert&utm_medium=email&utm_campaign=alert_date

Ryan, R. M., & Deci, E. L. (2000). Intrinsic and extrinsic motivations: Classic definitions and new directions. *Contemporary Educational Psychology, 25*, 54–67. Retrieved from: http://mmrg.pbworks.com/f/Ryan,+Deci+00.pdf

Schechtman, N., DeBarger, A. H., Dornsife, C., Rosier, S., & Yarnall, L. (2013). *Promoting grit, tenacity, and perseverance: Critical factors for success in the 21st century*. Washington, DC: U.S. Department of Education, Office of Educational Technology. Retrieved from: http://www.ed.gov/edblogs/technology/files/2013/02/OET-Draft-Grit-Report-2–17–13.pdf

Schwartz, T. (2013, June 14). Overcoming your negativity bias. *DealBook*. Retrieved from: http://dealbook.nytimes.com/2013/06/14/overcoming-your-negativity-bias/?smid=tw-nytimes&_r=0

Sedita, J. (2005). Effective vocabulary instruction. *Insights on Learning Disabilities, 2*(1), 33–45.

Seligman, M. (2011). *Flourish*. New York: Free Press.

Seppala, E. (2012, December 25). Share your good news, and you will be better off: Psychologists document the joys of sharing joy. *Scientific American*. Retrieved from: http://www.scientificamerican.com/article.cfm?id=share-your-good-news-and-you-will-be-better-off

Sparks, S. D. (2013, July 10). "Active" student engagement goes beyond class behavior, study finds. *Education Week*. Retrieved from: http://blogs.edweek.org/edweek/inside-school-research/2013/07/pittsburgh—a_student_who_show.html

Stefanou, C. R., Perencevich, K. C., DiCintio, M., & Turner, J. C. (2004). Supporting autonomy in the classroom: Ways teachers encourage student decision making and ownership. *Educational Psychologist, 39*(2), 97–110.

Sutton, B. (2010, August 28). It isn't just a myth: A little thanks goes a long way [blog post]. Retrieved from *Work Matters* at: http://bobsutton.typepad.com/my_weblog/2010/08/it-isnt-just-a-myth-a-little-thanks-goes-a-long-way.html

Szalavitz, M. (2013, May 20). 10,000 hours may not make a master after all. *Time*. Retrieved from: http://healthland.time.com/2013/05/20/10000-hours-may-not-make-a-master-after-all/

Tomlinson, C.A. (2003). Deciding to teach them all. *Educational Leadership, 61*(2), 6–11.

Tomlinson, C.A. (2011, October 5). Carol Tomlinson on differentiation: Proactive instruction. *YouTube*. Retrieved from: http://www.youtube.com/watch?v=mpy6rDnXNbs

Tomlinson, C.A. (n.d.). What is differentiated instruction? *Reading Rockets*. Retrieved from: http://www.readingrockets.org/article/263

Trudeau, M. (2007, February 15). *Students' view of intelligence can help grades*. Retrieved from: http://www.npr.org/templates/story/story.php?storyId=7406521

Tugend, A. (2012, October 5). Experts' advice to the goal-oriented: Don't overdo it. *The New York Times*. Retrieved from: http://www.nytimes.com/2012/10/06/your-money/the-perils-of-setting-goals.html?pagewanted=all&_r=0

Tugend, A. (2013, April 5). You've been doing a fantastic job. Just one thing . . . *The New York Times*. Retrieved from: http://mobile.nytimes.com/2013/04/06/your-money/how-to-give-effective-feedback-both-positive-and-negative.html?utm_source=dlvr.it&utm_medium=twitter

Usher, A., Kober, N., Jennings, J., & Rentner, D.S. (2012). *What is motivation and why does it matter?* Washington, DC: Center on Education Policy, George Washington University. Retrieved from: www.cep-dc.org/cfcontent_file.cfm?Attachment=UsherKober%5FBackground3%5FMotivation%5F5%2E22%2E12%2Epdf

Virginia Tech. (2011). Easy to visualize goal is powerful motivator to finish a race or a task. *Science Daily*. Retrieved from: http://www.sciencedaily.com/releases/2011/08/110815143935.htm

Wait time (n.d.). *P-16 science education at the Akron Global Polymer Academy*. Retrieved from: http://www.agpa.uakron.edu/p16/btp.php?id=wait-time

Ward, A.F. (2013, July 16). The neuroscience of everybody's favorite topic: Why do people spend so much time talking about themselves? *Scientific American*. Retrieved from: http://www.scientificamerican.com/article.cfm?id=the-neuroscience-of-everybody-favorite-topic-themselves&utm_source=feedburner&utm_medium=feed&utm_campaign=Feed%3A+sciam%2Fmind-and-brain+%28Topic%3A+Mind+%26+Brain%29

Washburn, K. (2009, June 9). Learning from mistakes takes the right feedback. *Edurati Review*. Retrieved from: http://www.eduratireview.com/2009/06/i-slammed-my-foot-and-to-my-surprise.html

Washburn, K. (2013, August 5). Teaching by modeling: A tale of basketball & mirror neurons. *Clerestory learning*. Retrieved from: http://blog.clerestorylearning.com/teaching-by-modeling-a-tale-of-basketball-mirror-neurons

What's an easy way to strengthen your relationships? (2010, August 2). Retrieved from: http://www.bakadesuyo.com/whats-an-easy-way-to-strengthen-your-relation?utm_source=feedburner&utm_medium=feed&utm_campaign=Feed:+bakadesuyo+(Barking+up+the+wrong+tree

Willingham, D. (2013, June 3). *Storify: Make science tell a story*. Retrieved from: http://www.danielwillingham.com/1/post/2013/06/storify-make-science-tell-a-story.html

Willingham, D. (2013, July 8). *Better studying = less studying. Wait, what?* Retrieved from: http://www.danielwillingham.com/1/post/2013/07/better-studying-less-studying-wait-what.html

Willis, J. (2006). *An ASCD study guide for research-based strategies to ignite student learning*. Alexandria, VA: ASCD.

Yaeger, D. S., Henderson, M., Paunesku, D., Walton, G. M., Spitzer, B. J., & Duckworth, A. L. (2014, March). *Boring but important: A self-transcendent purpose for learning fosters academic self-regulation*. Retrieved from: http://www.stanford.edu/~gwalton/home/Publications_files/Yeager_etal_inpress.pdf

Yong, E. (2010, March 19). Requests work better than orders, even when we're asking or ordering ourselves [blog post], Science Blogs: Not Exactly Rocket Science. Retrieved from: http://scienceblogs.com/notrocketscience/2010/03/19/requests-work-better-than-orders-even-when-were-asking-or-or/

Chapter 2

I Still Want To Know

How Can You Best Handle Classroom Management?

I really liked the "positive not punitive" classroom management strategies that you recommended in your previous books. Do you have any more ideas I can use to help students want to better manage their own behavior?

Each of the books in this series have had mostly different chapters, but they've all had ones explicitly on motivation and classroom management—always full of many different strategies. The reason is that these two topics are "mysteries" and not "puzzles."

Let me explain.

Security expert Gregory F. Treverton (2007) originally developed the frame of "puzzles" and "mysteries" and applied it to foreign policy challenges like the Cold War, the Iraq War, and terrorism. In effect, he describes puzzles as problems that follow some type of logical analysis that typically lead to clear conclusions. It's usually a puzzle to trace back to the causes of an action once it has taken place.

Mysteries, on the other hand, are composed of far more fast-moving parts and ambiguities. The individual uniqueness of the key actors' self-interests and how they might change and interact with others need to be identified. Treverton suggests that we can be far more effective at preventing an unwanted action from taking place by approaching many challenges as mysteries instead of as puzzles.

We generally find the flow-chart clarity of puzzles more satisfying than the messiness of mysteries—it echoes the old saying of how much more simple life can look when "if the only tool you have is a hammer, then every problem looks like a nail." Treverton cites numerous examples showing that our bias towards looking through the lens of a "puzzle" has often led us down a disastrous path of not only not preventing actions we wanted stopped, but even making situations worse.

Motivation and classroom management are, indeed, mysteries—there are countless moving parts in a classroom every day, and the trials of adolescence often make them change every minute! Looking at them as a puzzle will typically lead to frustration and disappointment. Research-based or not, not all of the strategies shared in my books are going to work all the time with all of my—or your—students. And, because of that challenge, we can never have too many strategies in our back pocket to help with student motivation and classroom management.

My previous books share many ideas for "immediate" actions teachers can take in promoting a positive classroom environment, and I won't restate them here. However, I will quickly summarize what I consider to be the two most important elements of an effective classroom management strategy—building relationships and being positive—and recent research behind those beliefs. In addition, this chapter includes a substantial "Setting the Stage" section with three new mini-lessons—on dealing with feeling bored, learning about gratitude, and identifying long-term dangers of being involved in physical fights. One full lesson—on poverty's effect on self-control—is also included here. All of these lessons are designed to help students *want* to become more committed and respectful members of a classroom and school-wide learning community.

The Foundations of an Effective Classroom Management Strategy: Building Relationships and Being Positive

Building relationships with students is a cornerstone of effective teaching, including classroom management (Ferlazzo, 2011, p. 6). By emphasizing this practice, educators can, at the same time, model that behavior for their students and demonstrate that relationship-building is also a critical skill for *living*.

Chapter 1 contains many concrete suggestions for how teachers can make those connections and help students develop intrinsic motivation for learning. In fact, most—if not all—of the strategies needed to develop intrinsic motivation are also required to develop and maintain a positive, well-ordered and supportive classroom environment so that learning can flourish. Though this is important for all students, researchers have recently found that the quality of the relationship boys in particular have with their teachers is important for learning. In an international study, researchers found that when boys were asked to describe lessons in school that they thought were particularly effective, most were unable to do so without at the same time talking about the relationship they had with their teacher: "For so many of the boys, the issue was not what subject or instructional approach engaged them, but rather for whom they might risk engagement and effort" (Reichert & Hawley, 2014). And, to apply this finding to the classroom management context, another quote—this one from author Mark Goulston (2013) in *The Harvard Business Review*—summarizes it well: "You don't win on the strength of your argument. You win on the strength of your relationship."

It's difficult, if not impossible, to develop a positive relationship with a student by utilizing a strategy of anger, threats, and intimidation. Recent research has reinforced extensive previous studies (Ferlazzo, 2013, p. 67) that have found it takes acting positive in order to develop that kind of a relationship and in order to have positive results in the classroom. Two studies concluded that shouting at children, as opposed to reasoning with them, actually tends to make behavior problems worse (Paton, 2014; Waldman, 2013); a follow-up to the famous Marshmallow Experiment (Ferlazzo, 2011, p. 56) identified that feelings of trust towards the adult in charge has a large impact on children's practice of self-control (Ferlazzo, 2012); and one research project found that students performed worse on exams when reminded of the consequences of failure as opposed to those who were given a more positive message by their teachers (Teachers' scare tactics, 2014). Another produced the same results along with some intriguing observations that one of the researchers, Tali Sharot, offered to NPR:

> The study findings square with neuroscience showing that positive information is processed in many parts of the brain, while negative information tends to be centered in the prefrontal cortex, Sharot says. That's the part of the brain that matures last, into the 20s in many cases. It's the area in charge of judgment and problem-solving.
>
> "We learn better from good news than from bad news," Sharot says. (Shute, 2013)

Of course, we are not super-human, and it's doubtful that any of us can maintain a positive attitude 100 percent of the time in our classrooms—especially in the face of the challenges that confront us daily.

One way I attempt to remind myself of the need for positivity is by taping a sheet on the computer screen in my classroom featuring a sentence

I've modified from a ubiquitous online saying: "My student is not giving me a hard time. My student is **having** a hard time."

Setting the Stage

This section contains three mini-lessons that should each take less than 30 minutes, and one full-fledged lesson that might take up to two-and-a-half 55-minute periods but could be modified to take less time.

Boredom

The first short mini-lesson is on boredom. There are few teachers who have not heard a student in their class proclaim "This is boring!" or have not had many students who thought it in their minds even though they did not share it out loud. That type of reaction can also often be a prelude to a classroom management problem. This short lesson acknowledges that teachers need to prepare engaging lessons, but also helps students develop strategies that they can use to help, too.

Gratitude Mini-Lesson

The human mind's desire to respond to temptation is considered by neuro-scientists to be a part of our "hot" emotional system that harks back to our ancient ancestors' need to react quickly to dangers and opportunities in order to survive (Mischel, 2014, p. 44). This "hot" system contrasts with the mind's "cool" system, which is more cognitive and focuses on self-control and the future implications of actions (Mischel, 2014, p. 46).

Recently, however, researchers have begun to explore what effect pro-voking other strong emotions besides fear and temptation could have on self-control—instead of trying to cool down a hot emotion like impatience and working to suppress it, could another equally strong or stronger "hot" feeling with more positive effects be encouraged to "drown out" the nega-tive one? Studies now show that cultivating the emotion of happiness has little impact on self-control, while fostering feelings of sadness and disgust not only do not help generate a stronger sense of self-control but actually make it worse. However, generating feelings of gratitude have the very different result of people generating greater levels of patience (DeSteno et al., 2014, p. 6).

The emotion of gratitude has long been found to be tied to feelings of positive well-being, and a short mini-lesson found in *Self-Driven Learning* (Ferlazzo, 2013, p. 33) demonstrates how simple activities like writing a "gratitude letter" can help students develop a more positive attitude toward school and learning. The mini-lesson in this book instead focuses more on how students can use feelings of gratitude to foster their levels of self-control. Each of these two gratitude lessons stand alone and, if desired, both mini-lessons could easily be taught. I have used this particular mini-lesson (co-developed by my colleague Katie Hull Sypnieski) around the Thanksgiving holiday, though it could be done at any time.

Fighting Mini-Lesson

A recent study has found that adolescent boys who are in two fights, and adolescent girls who are in one fight, suffer the loss of IQ equal to one full year of school (Schwartz & Beaver, 2013). This mini-lesson is an attempt to push students to think twice about the consequences of getting into a physical fight in a different way from what may often sound to them as "preachy."

Poverty and the Adolescent Brain Lesson

"Pounding" students about why they need to have grit and self-control can only go so far. Depending on the classroom environment and the dispositions of individual students, when students are unsuccessful—and even the most motivated students will have their off-days—they might look at themselves as failures. I know from personal experience that some students are truly sincere in wanting to develop more self-control and perseverance, and intellectually understand all of the lessons in Social Emotional Learning (SEL) they've experienced, but still fall back into their unproductive patterns. I've had more than one student say to me, "Mr. Ferlazzo, I just don't know why I can't . . . (stop talking to others during class, stay more focused, etc.)."

As plenty of research has shown, we teachers only have control of between 10 and 30 percent of the factors that influence student academic achievement (Berliner, 2014), and obviously many of those other forces contribute to the inability of some of our students to successfully overcome grit and self-control issues (along with many other challenges).

Many—if not most—of Social Emotional Learning lessons (including the ones I teach and are in my books) tend to gloss over these outside factors that complicate self-control and perseverance abilities, including the recently discovered impact that poverty has on a person's self-control (Ferlazzo, 2013, August 30) and the challenges presented by the changes going on in the adolescent brain. This doesn't make them bad lessons and, in fact, many students still gain a great deal from them. But they clearly don't "hit the mark" for *all* students.

So, could there be a way for students to learn about some of these "extra" obstacles they face in developing more self-control and grit, yet at the same time not make them further depressed about the steep climb they might have to make? (Of course, we also have to recognize that some students might need far more support than we are able to provide, no matter what we do in the classroom.) After all, the changes going on in the teenage brain are not going to go away, and the number of low-income students in our schools is only increasing. Almost half of the students in US public schools are low-income, and children from poor families now comprise a majority of the students in public schools in the South and in the West (Layton, 2013).

A recent project focusing on first-generation college students might hold some hints about how middle- and high-school educators might be able to approach this question. Researchers narrowed the achievement gap between first-generation college students and continuing generation students by 63 percent in the first year of college. Researchers had believed that the major causes of first-year problems for first-generation students included a lack of self-confidence in their academic ability and low self-esteem, and the fact that, because of their lack of family background with how college worked, they didn't come with that type of prior knowledge and couldn't seek it out from family members. They believed that by having veteran students, many who shared similar backgrounds, discuss the obstacles they faced in college, how they overcame them, and how experiences in their pasts helped them to be successful, would assist the incoming students to feel more motivated and prepared. The project had these veteran students speak to incoming freshmen for 45 minutes and then had the new students create a one- or two-minute video in the next 25 minutes summarizing what they felt they had learned from the panelists (Stephens et al., 2014).

This lesson uses that experiment as its inspiration, though makes major modifications to ensure that is more relevant and practical for a middle- or high-school class environment. To summarize the lesson plan, students work individually, in pairs, and in small groups to read and react to short pieces on:

- the benefits of self-control
- changes in the teenage brain and their effect on self-control
- the impact of poverty on self-control and grit
- ways to develop more self-control and grit despite these challenges
- stories of other young people who grew up in poverty and/or other challenging situations and what they learned from it that helped them become successful.

After the readings and their presentations, students have the option of writing about the key lessons they learned or creating an online presentation (video, PowerPoint, animation, etc.) about the main lessons they felt they learned.

This lesson tries to duplicate the key elements of the research project—it acknowledges the obstacles that students are facing, provides strategies to overcome them, and presents stories of success by their peers. In addition, students summarize what they have learned.

There is also a lesson on self-control in *Helping Students Motivate Themselves* (Ferlazzo, 2011, p. 56). This lesson is very different, and both can be done independently of the other and in any order.

A central element of that first self-control lesson is the famous Marshmallow Test, originated by Professor Walter Mischel. In that test, children entered a room, were given a marshmallow, and told that if they didn't eat it until a researcher returned in 15 minutes that they would be given a second one. The approximately 30 percent of children who were able to wait until the researcher returned had much more successful life outcomes years later.

I interviewed Professor Mischel and asked him his opinion about a lesson such as the one in this book that would inform students about some of the particular self-control challenges they might face because of issues such as poverty. Here is his response:

> Helping students to see the external factors in their lives that diminish their self-control capacity, reduce their trust, and undermine their lives is important . . . They also need to see what they can do to cope with the distressing conditions in which they are living through no fault of their own. Empathy for the realities that are making their lives so difficult needs to be combined with teaching strategies and alternative ways of thinking that enable success at least within school. (W. Mischel, July 17, 2014 http://blogs.edweek.org/teachers/classroom_qa_with_larry_ferlazzo/2014/09/the_marshmallow_test_an_interview_with_walter_mischel.html)

Boredom Mini-Lesson Plan

Procedure

1. Explain that we're going to begin a lesson by watching a short video. Tell students that as they are watching the video, you want them to think about times they might have had similar experiences.

2. Show the well-known scene in the movie *Ferris Beuller's Day Off* where Ben Stein portrays a boring economics teacher (http://www.youtube.com/watch?v=dxPVyieptwA&feature=player_embedded).

3. Ask the students to take a minute to think of similar experiences they have had and, without saying the name of the teacher, have them quickly share their stories with a partner.

4. Tell the class that yes, sometimes we teachers can be boring. However, it may not always be the teachers' fault. Distribute copies of Figure 2.1, "This is Boring!" (note that it refers to Bloom's Taxonomy—that can be removed if your students are not familiar with it), and tell students they are to read it aloud to a partner (each students reads three paragraphs and then switch). While they are reading, they should annotate the text at least four times by using each of these reading strategies once—ask a question, visualize by drawing an image and writing a sentence describing it and its connection to the text, evaluate by agreeing or disagreeing with something in the text, and making a connection between the text and something else they have read or their own life. You may want to model doing it in the first paragraph. Circulate to identify work you would like to highlight.

5. Invite a few students to quickly share their annotations with the entire class.

6. Ask students to write a short paragraph using the ABC format—Answer the question, Back it up with evidence such as a quotation from the text, and make a Connection or Comment. The question is, "What do you think is the best thing you can do the next time you feel bored in a classroom?"

7. After ten minutes, students can verbally share their paragraphs with partners. Ask one or two students to share with the entire class and then collect all the paragraphs.

Figure 2.1   "This is Boring!"

We have all experienced times as a student when we have felt bored. Sometimes, it's because a teacher hasn't done a very good job of preparing a lesson or teaching it. Teachers can make mistakes or get lazy.

Sometimes, though, there are other reasons why students can get bored.

Studies have shown that stress students might be feeling about their lives outside the classroom can make them more likely to feel bored by school.

Researchers have also found that the first time we do something or even hear something (a song, for example), we tend to find it pretty interesting. However, as time goes on, and we do the same thing (or hear the same thing) often, it's easy to get bored by it.

They call it "satiation."

Scientists suggest that, in addition to teachers working hard at creating and teaching more interesting lessons, students can also take responsibility for slowing their "rate of satiation."

They suggest that students can acknowledge their negative feelings as they start to get bored (though they don't necessarily have to say it out loud in class). At the same time, they can try to focus on positive learning opportunities.

Researchers had people listen to a boring piece of music. Participants who learned the importance of distinguishing details of the music, and how to look for them, enjoyed the music much more than others. In other words, when they started feeling bored by just the "surface" of what they were listening to, they were able to become more interested in it by looking at it at a deeper level.

In our class, for example, if you start feeling bored, you could try to think of ways to apply what we're doing in class to life outside of school, or you could remember what we learned about Bloom's Taxonomy and start making a list of questions about what we're doing that are at the higher levels.

Researchers also suggest that if you are feeling bored, another way to deal with it is by physically moving—either changing seats, standing up, going to the restroom, getting a drink of water, etc.

None of this research means that it's not the teacher's responsibility to create a positive learning environment. However, the next time students begin to feel bored, they might want to take a moment to consider what they could do about it, too.

Sources: Markman, A. (2012). http://www.huffingtonpost.com/art-markman-phd/boredom_b_2000662.html?utm_hp_ref=tw
Sparks, S. D. (2012). http://www.edweek.org/ew/articles/2012/10/10/07boredom_ep.h32.html?tkn=ULOFaySCEpgZDh3jcqorzemuHbC0xtOAa6VS&cmp=SOC-EDIT-GOO
Konnikova, M. (2012). http://www.bostonglobe.com/ideas/2012/12/02/could-boredom-curable/Mz1W0a5jfyrtTH9wZgdFVI/story.html?s_campaign=sm_tw

Gratitude and Self-Control Mini-Lesson Plan

Procedure

1. Announce at the beginning of class that you are going to show a seven-minute video titled "The Science Of Happiness: An Experiment In Gratitude" (https://www.youtube.com/watch?v=oHv6vTKD6lg#t=18) and want students to sit and watch it quietly.

2. After the video has ended, display this writing prompt on a document camera or whiteboard:
   Close your eyes and think of somebody who is really influential in your life and/or who matters to you. Why is this person so important? Please write your response.

3. Share a model that you wrote about a person in your life, and then give students ten minutes to work on their own short paragraph/essay.

4. Students then share with partners what they wrote.

5. Invites students to call the person they wrote about and tell them—either privately or in public. You can model by doing it on a speakerphone with the topic of your paragraph. Typically, at least a few students will then follow that example, and it can become quite an emotional experience.

6. Depending on the class atmosphere at this time, this next activity can be done during the same class or on the following day. Ideally, a lesson on self-control from this volume or from one of the previous books in this series has already been taught. If that has occurred, you can explain that we've already learned about the importance of self-control in achieving our goals, and the class is now going to learn about another strategy we can all use to strengthen our self-control. Display the Read Aloud in Figure 2.2 and read it to the class.

7. Then ask the students to write down three events they are grateful for that occurred over the past week and have them share these with a partner. Ask some students to give examples to the entire class.

8. End the lesson by either telling the class that this activity will be a regular weekly one and/or explain to students that this is one tool they can implement on their own if they want to develop more self-control.

Figure 2.2 Gratitude and Self-Control Read Aloud

The human mind's desire to respond to temptation is considered by neuroscientists to be a part of our "hot" emotional system that is related to our ancient ancestors' need to react quickly to dangers and opportunities in order to survive. This "hot" system contrasts with the mind's "cool" system, which thinks more about the future implications of actions and practices self-control.

One way to control our "hot" emotions is to work at "cooling" it down by saying "no" to it a lot. For example, if you're often tempted to talk at inappropriate times in the classroom, you can continually reminding yourself to be quiet. Doing this can certainly be effective.

Researchers have also found that another way to build up your self-control is by encouraging a different emotion that is also considered a "hot" one—gratitude. This strong positive emotion then tends to "drown out" the feeling of wanting to give in to temptation. So, in addition to helping people feel happier, practicing gratitude regularly has also been shown to help strengthen self-control.

Researchers suspect that a simple activity of writing down three to five events that happen each day or each week that people are grateful for could be one way to increase feelings of self-control.

Sources: Mischel, W. (2014). *The marshmallow test.* New York: Little Brown and Company, p. 44.
DeSteno, D. et al. (2014). https://static.squarespace.com/static/52853b8ae4b0a6c35d3f8e9d/t/531f8140e4b03eb27337b156/1394573632883/gratitude-a-tool-for-reducing-economic-impatience.pdf
Emmons, R. A. & McCullough, M. E. (2003). http://greatergood.berkeley.edu/pdfs/Gratitude PDFs/6Emmons-BlessingsBurdens.pdf

Fighting Mini-Lesson Plan

Procedure

1. Show a one-minute video titled "Cutest Karate Kids Taekwondo Fight Ever—Martial Artist Battle" (https://www.youtube.com/watch?v=4kPophWJKhk).

2. Next, ask the class if whether when they see a fight at school, or if they are involved in one, it looks like the one in the video. Students will most likely laugh, as they will when watching the video. Ask students to describe what they see happen in fights or what they have experienced. Then ask students to share reasons that they or others they know have gotten into a fight—"looked at me wrong," "threw a piece of paper at me," etc. If someone says they were "disrespected," try to find specifically what was done. Make a list of these reasons on a document camera or on the whiteboard.

3. Then explain that you are going to distribute copies of a Read Aloud (Figure 2.3) summarizing a study on how one or two fights affect adolescents and that you will place it on a document camera and read it aloud. Tell all students to read silently as you read. When you are finished ask students to take a couple of minutes and use a reading strategy to write a simple one- or two-sentence response to the Read Aloud—it could be a summary, how the information makes them feel, if it reminds them of something they saw or experienced, or a question. Circulate and identify students who have written comments to highlight.

4. Invite students to share their comments, and calls on students you have noted who had written down particularly thoughtful ones.

5. Write this prompt on the document camera or whiteboard: *"Look at the list of reasons that fights have started. Based on what you read, do you think that they are worth losing one year's worth of learning in your mind? Why or why not?"* Ask students to write a simple paragraph responding to this question in the next ten minutes.

6. Divide students into pairs in which they verbally share what they wrote with each other. You can also invite certain students to share with the entire class.

7. Ask students for ideas on how to solve conflicts differently and make a list on the whiteboard or document camera.

8. To end the lesson, ask students to write down what they thought was the most important thing they learned from the lesson and hand it in to you as an "exit slip."

Figure 2.3 Teen Fighting

A recent study of 20,000 middle- and high-school students that lasted eight years found that adolescent boys who get hurt in two fights lose IQ points that are equivalent to missing one year of school. Girls suffer the same loss after just one fight because their physical bodies are less able to withstand being hit.

Because the study data involved all fight-related injuries, the researchers felt that the IQ loss would be even greater if the research had only considered head injuries.

About 4 percent of high-school students are injured as a result of a physical fights each year, in addition to injuries from contact sports and bullying.

Source: Schwartz, J. A., & Beaver, K. M. (2013). http://www.jahonline.org/article/S1054–139X(13) 00333–9/abstract

Building a Community of Self-Motivated Learners

Poverty and the Adolescent Brain—What Are Their Impacts on Self-Control and Grit?: Lesson Plan

Instructional Objectives for Students

- Further develop their ability to practice reading strategies to help comprehend a text.

- Learn about research demonstrating the effect both adolescence and poverty has on the brain, and specific strategies they can use to improve self-control.

- Articulate—either in writing or visually in digital form—what they have learned from the lesson.

Duration

Two 55-minute class periods and 30 minutes of a third day, depending on modifications made by the teacher.

Materials

- Access to the Internet and a computer projector to show one of the two choices for introductory videos—"Chicken or the Egg" (https://www.you tube.com/watch?v=nfYPktsd9bs) or "Sesame Street: Me Want It (But Me Wait)" (https://www.youtube.com/watch?v=9PnbKL3wuH4#t=55).

- Student copies of the following short stories by teenagers who have overcome adversity (depending on the number of students in the class, you might want to make two or three copies of each for the same number of students to read the same story):

  — The essay "Controlling My Temper," which can be found at http://youth today.org/2001/04/controlling-my-temper/ or http://www.cyc-net.org/cyc-online/cycol-0902-temper.html (you might want to make copies of this particular essay for all students).

  — The website "Stage of Life: Teen Challenges" (http://www.stageoflife. com/Teen_Challenges.aspx) has scores of stories by teens writing about "Challenges with School: Teachers, Grades, Graduation, Bullying." These stories are particularly applicable to the lesson:

    "I Overcame the Total Hate I Had for School"

"I Overcame My Preconceived Notions"

"I Overcame the Challenges of Surviving My New and Difficult High School"

"I Overcame My Grades"

"I Overcame High School"

"I Overcame the Obstacles of High School"

"I Overcame Getting Through High School"

— The website "Youth Communication" has an equal number of similar stories (http://youthcomm.codehorse.com/topics/index.html). In the topic index click on "School." These stories are particularly applicable to the lesson:

"Super Senior"

"Why I Failed the 9th Grade"

"Hiding My Talent No More"

— This class blog post, Challenge I Overcame ("http://theoryofknowledge. edublogs.org/2014/11/02/challenge-i-overcame-essay/" \l "comments" http://theoryofknowledge.edublogs.org/2014/11/02/challenge-i-over came-essay/#comments) has many similar stories that can be used in this lesson

- Copies of Figures 2.4 (Benefits of Self-Control), 2.5 (Teen Brains and Self Control), and 2.6 (Poverty and Self-Control) for all students.

- Copies for all students of "Six Scientifically Proven Ways to Boost Your Self Control" (Teen Brains and Self Control), http://www.fastcompany.com/3032513/ work-smart/6-scientifically-proven-ways-to-boost-your-self-control?part ner=newsletter

- Construction or legal size paper and color markers.

- Optional: Student access to laptops or tablets.

Common Core English Language Arts Standards

Reading:

- Determine central ideas or themes of a text and analyze their development; summarize the key supporting details and ideas.

- Read and comprehend complex literary and informational texts independently and proficiently.

Writing:

- Write arguments to support claims in an analysis of substantive topics or texts, using valid reasoning and relevant and sufficient evidence (only if the teacher decides the lesson's culminating project will be in written form).

Speaking and Listening:

- Prepare for and participate effectively in a range of conversations and collaborations with diverse partners, building on others' ideas and expressing their own clearly and persuasively.

- Integrate and evaluate information presented in diverse media and formats, including visually, quantitatively, and orally (only if the teacher decides to have students digitally create the lesson's culminating project).

- Make strategic use of digital media and visual displays of data to express information and enhance understanding of presentations (only if the teacher decides to have students digitally create the lesson's culminating project).

Language:

- Demonstrate command of the conventions of standard English grammar and usage when writing or speaking.

- Demonstrate command of the conventions of standard English capitalization, punctuation, and spelling when writing.

Procedure

First Day

1. Tell the students you want them to watch a three-minute video. You can choose to show either "The Chicken or the Egg" or the *Sesame Street* video (my students tend to think watching *Sesame Street* is "cool"). After watching it, ask the students to write down what they think was the main message or theme in the video and then ask them to share what they wrote with a partner.

2. Call on some students to share; most will probably say something along the lines of "the video is about self-control." Write "self-control" on the board, and explain that the class is going to learn about it today and probably into the next day. (Note: If you have already taught the self-control lesson from *Helping Students Motivate Themselves*, explain that the first Read Aloud is a "refresher" or just ask students to write down what they remember from that lesson and discuss, instead of distributing this new Read Aloud.)

3. Distribute copies of Figure 2.4, Benefits of Self-Control, and explain that you would like students to read in pairs—one paragraph per person—and use one reading strategy for each of the two paragraphs—either a one-sentence summary, visualize by drawing an image, make a connection to their own personal experience or something else they have read, write a question they have about what they read, or evaluate by agreeing or disagreeing and

explain why. In addition, ask the students to write one sentence summarizing the most important points in the article at the bottom of the sheet. Remind students that you would like them to read with prosody (with feeling). Model reading one sentence with intonation and another in a monotone. Students are given five minutes to complete the assignment. Circulate while students are reading to identify particularly thoughtful comments you may want to highlight later.

4. Call on certain students to share one of their reading strategies, and then call on them to share their summary sentences. Next, point out that self-control isn't easy all the time and provide one or two specific examples from your own life. Say that self-control might even be more difficult for teenagers than adults, and the class is going to learn why, along with ways to develop more of it. These activities should take approximately five minutes.

5. Pass out copies of Figure 2.5, Teen Brains and Self-Control, and also place it on the document camera. Tell students you are going to read it to the class, and you want them to read along silently. As you are reading, the students should underline or highlight two or three of the most interesting pieces of information in the Read Aloud, and after you are done write down a few words either about why they think each piece is interesting or how it connects to a personal experience.

6. After you have completed the reading, give students a few minutes to write down their reasons for picking at least two pieces of information as interesting to them. Then ask students to work with a different partner and quickly share what they picked and wrote.

7. After three minutes of sharing with a partner, invite a few students to share with the entire class.

8. Explain that before the class discusses a number of ways to develop self-control, we are going to learn about another issue that might make having self-control consistently more difficult—a lack of money. Say that students are again going to read a short passage with a partner, but it has to be with a person they have yet to work with today (you can assign partners or introduce a little levity by having students choose a classmate with different color hair, the same color shirt, etc.). Distribute Figure 2.6, Money and Self-Control, and ask students to take turns reading portions of it and use three different reading strategies somewhere on the text, choosing from these: visualize by drawing an image, make a connection to their own personal experience or something else they have read, write a question about what they read, or evaluate by agreeing or disagreeing and explain why. In addition, ask students to write one sentence summarizing the most important point in the article at the bottom of the sheet. Give students ten minutes to complete the assignment. Circulate during this period to identify particularly thoughtful comments you would like shared with the entire class.

9. Ask particular students to share what they wrote, spending no more than five minutes on sharing.

10. Then say that even though there are challenges to maintaining self-control, researchers have found that there are actions people can take to strengthen it. Show the article, "Six Scientifically Proven Ways to Boost Your Self Control," on the document camera, and explain that you are going to assign each student to read two of the "ways" in the article and some will read the introduction of the article. Explain that this process is called a "jigsaw"—different students read different parts of a text and then later share what they learned with their classmates. They are first going to read it on their own and, on a piece of scratch paper, make a draft of a poster they will make summarizing in two to four sentences the most important parts of what they read. They will also have to draw two simple pictures illustrating their points. They will be making these posters so that they can teach what they learn to their classmates. But, first, they will share their rough ideas with everyone else who is assigned the same passages so they can see if they want to make any changes to improve their final poster. This kind of exercise has a number of advantages, one being that research shows that students expecting to have to teach content enhances their learning (Expecting to Teach, 2014, http://www.sciencedaily.com/releases/2014/08/140808163445.htm).

11. Have students count off by fours (1, 2, 3, 4; 1, 2, 3, 4; etc.). Write on your copy at the document camera that the "ones" will read the introduction; the "twos" will read "ways" one and two; etc. Pass out the article, makes sure that every student has a piece of scratch paper, and give them ten minutes to read silently on their own and compose their draft poster.

12. Students should complete reading their assigned portions of the text and create a rough draft for their poster by the end of the period. If they are not done, it can be assigned as homework. It is important to provide enough time to ensure that students have at least read their portions by the end of the period—we want students to end the day seeing that there are actions they can take to improve self-control, and not end the day focusing on the obstacles to doing so.

Second Day

1. You have two choices as to how you start the day:
   - One way would be by immediately reminding students what number they are, having them take out their draft posters and having the "ones" meet

in one corner; the "twos" in another, etc., and telling them that in their four groups they should each quickly show their draft and say their summary, and take notes if people have done or said something that they want to "steal" for their final draft (this activity should only take five minutes).

- Another way to begin would be to show the introductory video you didn't show the previous day as a reminder/summary about the focus of the lesson. After the video, you could divide students into groups to share their drafts.

2. Next, tell the students they have eight minutes to complete their posters and practice their presentations. While they are working on their posters, you can go around and assign a "one," "two," "three," and "four" to a group. I have found the easiest way to do this is to give each integrated group a letter and have the four students all write down their letter on their poster so they don't forget.

3. At the end of eight minutes, show where each letter group will meet in the room, explain that they should present in order, says that each student should try to ask a least one question during the presentation time (not to each presenter—just ask at least one question to one presenter). Write these instructions on the whiteboard or document camera so students can refer to them. List one additional instruction—at the end of the presentations, the group should decide which one or two of the "ways" they think are most effective and why, and decide on one person who is going to report their answer to the class. Give students one minute to be in their section in a circle and begin to present. Say they will have ten minutes in their group.

4. Students teach each other while you circulate among the groups.

5. At the end of ten minutes, ask everyone to return to their seats, call out the letter of each group and ask for their spokesperson to stand at their seat and report on which one or two ways they chose as best and why. Move through these reports quickly.

6. Next, tell the students that taking these kinds of actions to improve ourselves are not easy—we all face challenges and we learned about some of them yesterday. But people are able to do it. Say you want the class to read a story together, put the story "Controlling My Temper" on the document camera, and pass out copies to students. On the whiteboard, write three questions:

   1. *What was the problem?*
   2. *How was it resolved?*
   3. *What did he/she learn?*

   Ask students to read silently as you read the story, and underline the answers to those three questions.

7. Read the story, give students a minute to make sure they have answered the questions, and ask them to share their answers with a partner. Call on one or two students to answer them to the entire class.

8. Say you are going to distribute copies of very short stories that students wrote about overcoming adversity and most, but not all, students will receive different ones. Most stories are just two to four paragraphs. Give the students eight minutes to read and answer the same three questions.

9. If there are at least ten minutes remaining, explain that the class will be arranged in a "speed-dating" style, with half of the class moving their seats so they are facing the other half (because of room size constraints, there will probably have to be two of these types of lines). Say that each side will have 30 seconds to share their answers about their story with the person across from them. At the end of 30 seconds, their partner will share. Then you will yell "Switch" and everyone in one row will move down to the next desk and repeat. If there is not time to do this in class, but there are a few minutes left, you can just quickly assign students to groups of three or four and have them share within those groups the answers to their stories.

Third Day

1. Explain that they are going to complete the lesson on self-control today. If there was no time the previous day for students to share the answers to questions about the stories, spend a few minutes having them do so at the beginning of class today.

2. The "culminating project" for this lesson is having students share the two or three most important things they feel they learned during the previous two days and why they think those points are important. There are several options for how students can complete this project:

   - Students could write a short essay structured as an "ABC"—Answer the question, Back it up with Evidence (a quotation from what they have read), and make a Connection and/or Comment connecting it to their personal experience or something else they have read or seen, and explaining why it is important. The prompt could be:

     What do you think are the two or three most important things you have learned over the past two days and why do you think they are important?

   - Students could share important lessons they learned in a digital form—either through a video or other means. See the Ed Tech box for ideas. Doing it digitally would probably take more time than writing the essay.

3. End the lesson by having students share verbally or online their essays or projects.

Assessment

1. Collect all hand-outs to review the quality of student annotation.

2. Review the culminating project, which will either be a short essay or a digital representation of what students felt they learned.

3. If you feel a more involved assessment is necessary, develop a simple rubric appropriate for your classroom situation. Free online resources to both find pre-made rubrics and to create new ones can be found at http://larryferlazzo.edublogs.org/2010/09/18/the-best-rubric-sites-and-a-beginning-discussion-about-their-use/

Possible Extensions/Modifications

- Students could write their own short stories about a self-control, perseverance, or other challenging experience they have faced in their lives using the outline of explaining what the problem was, how it was resolved, and what they learned from it.

- If teaching in a high school, you could make arrangements to identify and prepare Seniors to make short presentations about challenges they faced, how they overcame them, and what they learned.

- You could have students read another very accessible article on strategies to develop self-control: "5 Quick Tips to Boost Your Willpower" (http://www.fastcompany.com/3034507/work-smart/5-quick-tricks-to-boost-your-willpower?utm_source=mailchimp&utm_medium=email&utm_campaign=colead-weekly-newsletter&position=2&partner=newsletter).

Ed Tech

Students can create a digital representation of two or three of the most important things they learned through a variety of tools, ranging from a video on YouTube, a PowerPoint, an online slideshow, comic strip, or an animation. There are many such free tools available, and lists of them can be found at:

The Best Ways to Create Online Slideshows
http://larryferlazzo.edublogs.org/2008/05/06/the-best-ways-to-create-online-slideshows/

The Best Ways to Create Comic Strips Online
http://larryferlazzo.edublogs.org/2008/06/04/the-best-ways-to-make-comic-strips-online/

> The Best Ways for Students to Create Online Animations
> http://larryferlazzo.edublogs.org/2008/05/11/the-best-ways-for-students-to-create-online-animations/

One way to easily share these student creations is through a class blog. Information on how to easily create one can be found at:

> The Best Sources for Advice on Student Blogging
> http://larryferlazzo.edublogs.org/2008/12/26/the-best-sources-for-advice-on-student-blogging/

Be sure to obtain parent permission before posting student work online. You can learn more at:

> The Best Teacher Resources for Online Student Safety and Legal Issues
> http://larryferlazzo.edublogs.org/2009/08/10/the-best-teacher-resources-for-online-student-safety-legal-issues/

Figure 2.4   Benefits of Self-Control

"First, self-control—like intelligence—has lifelong benefits. It is a better predictor of exam results among adolescents than IQ scores. Students with more self-control are more likely to turn up to school on time, do their homework and watch less television . . . all of which translated into better grades. A more recent study, which followed 1000 children in New Zealand from birth to 32 years old, found that those who exhibited greater self-control in childhood grew into healthier, more emotionally stable adults. They were also better off financially.

This mirrors a famous observation by the psychologist Walter Mischel, now at Columbia University in New York City. In the late 1960s, Mischel offered young children a choice between eating one treat immediately, or holding off for 15 minutes and getting two. Years later, Mischel discovered that the children who had managed to wait did better at high school than those who had succumbed to temptation. As adults, those able to delay gratification were also more popular with their peers, less likely to be overweight and earned higher salaries."

Source: Bond, M. (2014) http://www.newscientist.com/article/mg22129590.600-the-science-of-success-blood-or-sweat-and-tears.html, p. 33

Figure 2.5 Teen Brains and Self-Control

The good news is that the teenage brain is set up for "peak learning"—in other words, to learn a lot of things quickly. It's also set up as part of our evolution to want to take risks because that is required to begin to make moves towards independence, like thinking about life outside of home.

The bad news is that the teenage brain is not fully developed, particularly the area called the pre-frontal cortex near the front of their head. That is where self-control, judgment, goal-setting, understanding consequences—all elements of what is called executive function—is controlled. It generally isn't fully developed until the age of 25.

In other words, for teens, the "emotional center" of the brain tends to move directly into action before it passes through the pre-frontal cortex, where, as an adult, impulsive urges tend to be evaluated first.

The reward function of the teen brain is also set up to more strongly desire peer acceptance and approval, which is why some teens act one way when they are alone talking with a teacher and show less self-control in a classroom full of students.

More good news is that it's not a matter of teens never using the pre-frontal cortex—it's an issue of having difficulty using it consistently.

One way to visualize what is going on in the teen brain is that the accelerator is on, but the brakes are low on fluid.

And there are things that teens can do to change that situation.

Sources: Boston Children's Hospital (2008). https://www.youtube.com/watch?v=RpMG7vS9pfw&index=1&list=PLG-SfEe9uWHUGi9MyVCrk6AEN6T5Srbao
Castagna, K. (2014). http://blogs.plos.org/neuroanthropology/2014/05/16/facts-fictions-teen age-brain-gasoline-brakes/
Cahalan, S (2013). http://nypost.com/2013/12/07/why-is-your-teen-crazy/
What Kids Can Do (n.d.). http://www.howyouthlearn.org/research_teenagebrain.html#sthash. mLVmYubL.dpuf
Shute, N. (2008). http://health.usnews.com/health-news/family-health/brain-and-behavior/articles/2008/11/26/how-to-deploy-the-amazing-power-of-the-teen-brain?page=2
Hofmann, W. et al. (2012). http://www.cell.com/trends/cognitive-sciences/abstract/S1364–6613(12)00028–9?cc=y?cc=y

Figure 2.6   Money and Self-Control

Recent studies have found that the specific burden and stress of being low-income can reduce people's capacity for self-control. In other words, the pressure of not having much money and being concerned about its impact now and in the future takes away energy that would ordinarily be used for self-control and perseverance.

Researchers call it the brain's "bandwidth." When we concentrate on one thing, let's say playing a video game, then we don't pay as much attention to other things around us. It's the same with money pressures—we can get preoccupied with them and not pay as much attention to other issues, like self-control and other things we might need to focus on to do well. The difference between playing a video game and not having needed financial resources, however, is that you can turn off the video game easily. It's not as easy for a person to change their financial situation.

Here's what one researcher says:

> *"When your bandwidth is loaded, in the case of the poor," [Princeton professor] Eldar Shafir says, "you're just more likely to not notice things, you're more likely to not resist things you ought to resist, you're more likely to forget things, you're going to have less patience . . . It's not the person, it's the context they're inhabiting."*
> [http://www.citylab.com/work/2013/08/how-poverty-taxes-brain/6716/]

> *"It's not the person, it's the situation they're in and anyone could find themselves there," says Shafir.*
> [http://healthland.time.com/2013/08/30/how-financial-woes-change-your-brain-and-not-for-the-better/?iid=hl-main-lead]

Doing well in school is one action students can take to help create a better economic situation for themselves and create more "bandwidth" space for self-control and perseverance. Working to improve our communities by advocating for public policies is another.

There are also specific things students can do on their own to boost their self-control right now.

Sources: Maron, D. F. (2013). http://www.scientificamerican.com/article/poor-choices-financial/
Badger, E. (2013). http://www.citylab.com/work/2013/08/how-poverty-taxes-brain/6716/
Bond, M. (2014). http://www.newscientist.com/article/mg22129590.600-the-science-of-success-blood-or-sweat-and-tears.html
Szalavitz, M. (2013). http://healthland.time.com/2013/08/30/how-financial-woes-change-your-brain-and-not-for-the-better/?iid=hl-main-lead

References

The Awesome People Channel (2013, March 19). Cutest karate kids Taekwando fight ever—Martial arts battle. *YouTube*. Retrieved from: https://www.you tube.com/watch?v=4kPophWJKhk

Badger, E. (2013, August 29). How poverty taxes the brain. *The Atlantic Citylab*. Retrieved from: http://www.citylab.com/work/2013/08/how-poverty-taxes-brain/6716

Berliner, D.C. (2014, June 5). Morality, validity, and the design of instructionally sensitive tests. *Education Week*. Retrieved from: http://blogs.edweek.org/edweek/assessing_the_assessments/2014/06/morality_validity_and_the_design_of_instructionally_sensitive_tests.html?cmp=SOC-SHR-TW

Bogle, C.A. (2001, April 1). Controlling my temper. *Youth Today*. Retrieved from: http://youthtoday.org/2001/04/controlling-my-temper/

Bond, M. (2014, March 6). The science of success: Blood, sweat or tears? *New Scientist*. Retrieved from: http://www.newscientist.com/article/mg22129590.600-the-science-of-success-blood-or-sweat-and-tears.html

Boring economics teacher (n.d.). *YouTube*. Retrieved from: http://www.youtube.com/watch?v=dxPVyieptwA&feature=player_embedded

Boston Children's Hospital (2008). The teenage brain part 1. *YouTube*. Retrieved from: https://www.youtube.com/watch?v=RpMG7vS9pfw&index=1&list=PLG-SfEe9uWHUGi9MyVCrk6AEN6T5Srbao

Cahalan, S. (2013, December 7). Mystery solved: Why teens are nuts. *New York Post*. Retrieved from: http://nypost.com/2013/12/07/why-is-your-teen-crazy/

Castagna, K. (2014, May 16). Facts or fictions about the teenage brain: Is it all gasoline, no brakes? *Neuroanthropology*. Retrieved from: http://blogs.plos.org/neuroanthropology/2014/05/16/facts-fictions-teenage-brain-gasoline-brakes/

Challenge I Overcame (2014). Theory of knowledge. Retrieved from http://theoryofknowledge.edublogs.org/2014/11/02/challenge-i-overcame-essay/#comments

Chicken or the egg (2013, June 9). Retrieved from: https://www.youtube.com/watch?v=nfYPktsd9bs

Cooper, B.B. (2014, July 1). 6 scientifically proven ways to boost your self-control. *Fast Company.com*. Retrieved from: http://www.fastcompany.com/3032513/work-smart/6-scientifically-proven-ways-to-boost-your-self-control?partner=newsletter

DeSteno, D., Li, Y., Dickens, L., & Lerner, J.S. (2014). *Gratitude: A tool for reducing economic impatience*. Retrieved from: https://static.squarespace.com/static/52853b8ae4b0a6c35d3f8e9d/t/531f8140e4b03eb27337b156/1394573632883/gratitude-a-tool-for-reducing-economic-impatience.pdf

Emmons, R.A., & McCullough, M.E. (2003). Counting blessings versus burdens: An experimental investigation of gratitude and subjective well-being in daily life. *Journal of Personality and Social Psychology, 84*(2), 377–389.

Expecting to teach enhances learning, recall (2014, August 8). *Science Daily*. Retrieved from: http://www.sciencedaily.com/releases/2014/08/140808163445.htm

Ferlazzo, L. (2008, May 6). The best ways to create online slideshows. *Larry Ferlazzo's websites of the day*. Retrieved from: http://larryferlazzo.edublogs.org/2008/05/06/the-best-ways-to-create-online-slideshows/

Ferlazzo, L. (2008, May 11). The best ways for students to create online animations. *Larry Ferlazzo's websites of the day*. Retrieved from: http://larryferlazzo.edublogs.org/2008/05/11/the-best-ways-for-students-to-create-online-animations/

Ferlazzo, L. (2008, June 4). The best ways to make comic strips online. *Larry Ferlazzo's websites of the day*. Retrieved from: http://larryferlazzo.edublogs.org/2008/06/04/the-best-ways-to-make-comic-strips-online/

Ferlazzo, L. (2008, December 26). The best sources for advice on student blogging. *Larry Ferlazzo's websites of the day*. Retrieved from: http://larryferlazzo.edublogs.org/2008/12/26/the-best-sources-for-advice-on-student-blogging/

Ferlazzo, L. (2009, August 10). The best teacher resources for online student safety and legal issues. *Larry Ferlazzo's websites of the day*. Retrieved from: http://larryferlazzo.edublogs.org/2009/08/10/the-best-teacher-resources-for-online-student-safety-legal-issues/

Ferlazzo, L. (2010, September 18). The best rubric sites (and a beginning discussion about their use). *Larry Ferlazzo's websites of the day*. Retrieved from: http://larryferlazzo.edublogs.org/2010/09/18/the-best-rubric-sites-and-a-beginning-discussion-about-their-use/

Ferlazzo, L. (2011). *Helping students motivate themselves*. Larchmont, NY: Eye on Education.

Ferlazzo, L. (2012, November 12). Marshmallows and trust. *Larry Ferlazzo's websites of the day*. Retrieved from: http://larryferlazzo.edublogs.org/2012/11/12/marshmallows-trust/

Ferlazzo, L. (2013). *Self-driven learning: Teaching strategies for student motivation*. New York: Routledge.

Ferlazzo, L. (2013, August 30). The best articles about the study showing social emotional learning isn't enough. *Larry Ferlazzo's websites of the day*. Retrieved from: http://larryferlazzo.edublogs.org/2013/08/30/the-best-articles-about-the-study-showing-social-emotional-learning-isnt-enough

Gillett, R. (2014, August 19). *5 quick tips to boost your will power*. Retrieved from: http://www.fastcompany.com/3034507/work-smart/5-quick-tricks-to-boost-your-willpower?utm_source=mailchimp&utm_medium=email&utm_campaign=colead-weekly-newsletter&position=2&partner=newsletter

Goulston, M. (2013, July 1). Practical tips for overcoming resistance. *Harvard Business Review Blog Network*. Retrieved from: http://blogs.hbr.org/2013/07/practical-tips-for-overcoming-r/

Hoffman, W., Schmeichel, B.J., & Baddeley, A.D. (2012). Executive functions and self-regulation. *Trends in Cognitive Sciences*, 16(3), 174–180. Retrieved from: http://www.cell.com/trends/cognitive-sciences/abstract/S1364–6613(12)00028–9?cc=y?cc=y

How teens feel about real world issues (n.d.). *Stage of Life*. Retrieved from: http://www.stageoflife.com/Teen_Challenges.aspx

Konnikova, M. (2012, December 2). Could boredom be curable? An elusive human annoyance may finally be yielding its secrets. *The Boston Globe*. Retrieved from: http://www.bostonglobe.com/ideas/2012/12/02/could-boredom-curable/Mz1W0a5jfyrtTH9wZgdFVI/story.html?s_campaign=sm_tw

Layton, L. (2013, October 16). Study: Poor children are now the majority in American public schools in South, West. *The Washington Post*. Retrieved from: http://www.washingtonpost.com/local/education/2013/10/16/34eb4984–35bb-11e3–8a0e-4e2cf80831fc_story.html

Markman, A. (2012, October 22). Staving off boredom by focusing on it. *HuffPost: The Blog*. Retrieved from: http://www.huffingtonpost.com/art-markman-phd/boredom_b_2000662.html?utm_hp_ref=tw

Maron, D. F. (2013, August 29). Poor choices: Financial worries can impair one's ability to make sound decisions. *Scientific American*. Retrieved from: http://www.scientificamerican.com/article/poor-choices-financial/

Mischel, W. (2014). *The marshmallow test*. New York: Little Brown and Company.

Paton, G. (2014, April 8). Shouting at children "increases their behavior problems." *The Telegraph*. Retrieved from: http://www.telegraph.co.uk/education/educationnews/10750525/Shouting-at-children-increases-their-behaviour-problems.html

Reichert, M., & Hawley, R. (2014, May 6). What relationships mean in educating boys. *Education Week*. Retrieved from: http://www.edweek.org/ew/articles/2014/05/07/30reichert.h33.html

Schwartz, J. A., & Beaver, K. M. (2013, July 26). Serious fighting-related injuries produce a significant reduction in intelligence. *Journal of Adolescent Health* [online]. Retrieved from: http://www.jahonline.org/article/S1054–139X(13)00333–9/fulltext

Sesame Street (2013, August 5). Sesame Street: Me want it (but me wait). *YouTube*. Retrieved from: https://www.youtube.com/watch?v=9PnbKL3wuH4#t=55

Shute, N. (2008, November 26). How to deploy the amazing power of the teen brain. *US News*. Retrieved from: http://health.usnews.com/health-news/family-health/brain-and-behavior/articles/2008/11/26/how-to-deploy-the-amazing-power-of-the-teen-brain?page=2

Shute, N. (2013, September 10). Even when told true risks, kids often misjudge them. *NPR Online*. Retrieved from: http://www.npr.org/blogs/health/2013/09/09/220737817/even-when-told-true-risks-kids-often-misjudge-them

SoulPancake (2013, July 11). The science of happiness: An experiment in gratitude. *YouTube*. Retrieved from: https://www.youtube.com/watch?v=oHv6vTKD6lg#t=18

Sparks, S. D. (2012, October 9). Studies link students' boredom to stress. *Education Week*. Retrieved from: http://www.edweek.org/ew/articles/2012/10/10/07boredom_ep.h32.html?tkn=ULOFaySCEpgZDh3jcqorzemuHbC0xtOAa6VS&cmp=SOC-EDIT-GOO

Stephens, N.M., Hamedani, M.G., & Destin, M. (2014, February 19). Closing the social-class achievement gap: A difference-education intervention improves first-generation students' academic performance and all students' college transition. *Psychological Science*, doi: 10.1177/0956797613518349. Retrieved from: https://edpolicy.stanford.edu/sites/default/files/publications/closing-social-class-achievement-gap.pdf

Szalavitz, M. (2013, August 30). How financial woes change your brain (and not for the better). *Time*. Retrieved from: http://healthland.time.com/2013/08/30/how-financial-woes-change-your-brain-and-not-for-the-better/?iid=hl-main-lead

Teachers' scare tactics may lead to lower exam scores (2014, April 21). *Science Daily*. Retrieved from: http://www.sciencedaily.com/releases/2014/04/140 421093728.htm

Treverton, G.F. (2007, June). Risks and riddles: The Soviet Union was a puzzle. Al Qaeda is a mystery. Why we need to know the difference. *Smithsonian. com*. Retrieved from: http://www.smithsonianmag.com/people-places/risks-and-riddles-154744750/

Waldman, K. (2013, November 6). Stop yelling at your kids. It's bad for them. *Slate. com*. Retrieved from: http://www.slate.com/blogs/xx_factor/2013/11/06/yelling_at_your_kids_don_t_do_it_oops_you_just_did.html

What Kids Can Do (n.d.). *The teenage brain: Research highlights*. Retrieved from: http://www.howyouthlearn.org/research_teenagebrain.html#sthash.mLVmYubL.dpuf

Youth communication website (n.d.). Retrieved from: http://youthcomm.codehorse.com/topics/index.html

Chapter 3

I Still Want to Know

How Can You Get Students More Interested in Reading and Writing?

You had great ideas in your last book about how to cultivate a desire among students to improve their reading and writing skills. Do you have anything else up your sleeve?

Chapter 1 discussed the key qualities needed to nurture intrinsic motivation. Activities suggested in this chapter will reinforce all of them in the area of teaching and learning literacy skills. Let's begin with a review of those essential qualities in the context of reading and writing:

♦ **Autonomy.** A major Pew Research Center report (Lenhart et al., 2008) found that choice has an equally important role in teens feeling a desire to write (the story in Chapter 1 of my student who was energized by writing about football illustrates this point). Likewise, in reading, extensive research documents that teachers encouraging students to read books of their choice for pleasure is a major contribution towards students developing a positive attitude towards reading and a life-long interest in it (Leisure Reading Task Force, 2014, p. 2).

♦ **Competence.** A scene from the HBO series *The Leftovers* (http://www.hbo.com/the-leftovers) succinctly explains why this quality is so important for intrinsic motivation. In it, two FBI agents were sitting in an office, and one told the other that his child wanted to quit soccer and wanted to know if he should let him do it. The other agent asked him, "Is he any good at it?" The first agent responded, "Nobody quits what they're good at," and much research backs him up (Tsioulcas, 2013; Yuhas, 2012). Providing scaffolding like writing frames and strategies/tools such as graphic organizers (student- or teacher-created) for responding to prompts (Ferlazzo, 2013, p. 144) can assist students' developing confidence as writers. The Progress Principle, which highlights that intrinsic motivation can be driven by people seeing meaningful progress in their work, was mentioned in the first chapter and in previous titles in this series (Ferlazzo, 2013, p. 10). Creating structured opportunities for students to see their progress in reading and writing by comparing work (preferably emphasizing tools like "improvement rubrics" that focus more on what they have successfully done and less on their deficits [Ferlazzo, 2011, p. 79]) done at the beginning of the school year with accomplishments later in the year can also support student feelings of competence. In fact, at our school English folders are passed up through the grades and students can see and reflect on their progress over the *years*!

♦ **Relatedness.** The Pew Research Center found that teens say the most important factor for them to feel motivated to write is using it as a way to connect with, and receive feedback from, teachers, family members, and friends (Lenhart et al., 2008). Opportunities for students to discuss what they are reading with their teachers and with their peers in low-or-no-stakes environments has been found to promote a greater interest in reading (Leisure Reading Task Force, 2014, p. 4).

♦ **The work is seen as interesting, and valuable for future goals.** In other words, as mentioned in Chapter 1, students should see it as relevant to their present lives and/or hopes and dreams for the future.

A slight "qualifier" should be attached to the second part of this last element—the one about it being seen as helpful to hopes and dreams for the future. As mentioned in Chapter 1, some researchers suggest that teachers explicitly pointing out how skills being taught in the classroom can be used in the future by students can be damaging to intrinsic motivation, particularly if they do not feel confident in their abilities or have little interest in the subject (Hulleman et al., 2010, p. 881). This issue is particularly relevant to a discussion on reading and writing since a significant percentage of students, particularly boys, often say that English is not a favorite subject (Wiggins, 2014) and multiple surveys have found that decreasing percentages of young people say they enjoy reading (Leisure Reading Task Force, 2014, p. 3). As a result of these negative attitudes, many of us teachers may tend to use a motivational strategy of emphasizing to students how important literacy will be to any of their future goals (Ferlazzo, 2013, p. 147).

Is this a bad strategy? The slightly "qualified" answer is yes, no, and possibly maybe . . . Other researchers also suggest that we need to be particularly careful when we focus on relevance towards a student's goals, though they also see potential benefits. Motivation researchers Edward Deci and Richard Ryan call slightly different versions of it "regulation through identification" and "integrated regulation." They believe the motive of wanting to do something less for the joy it brings and more for its *instrumental* value towards achieving a goal is a less harmful form of extrinsic motivation that—on a continuum—is as close as you can get to intrinsic motivation without being there (Ryan & Deci, 2000, p. 61). They also point out, however, that its promotion can still bring many benefits, including greater engagement and learning as well as increasing the potential that those tasks can be moved to the final step of intrinsically motivated, as long as the other three elements—autonomy, competence, and relatedness—are present (Ryan & Deci, 2000, pp. 63, 65). Indeed, organizers of the 2012 international PISA test in 2012 found that, over the previous ten years, countries where students reported an increase in intrinsic motivation also reported an increase in students reporting this kind of instrumental motivation (Organization for Economic Cooperation and Development [OECD], 2012, p. 74).

So, what does this "qualifier" mean practically for our classroom practice? Is it a group of academicians arguing about how many angels can dance on the head of a pin (What's the historical origin, n.d.)? Or is it a meaningful nuance we should seriously consider?

I would suggest that teachers explicitly connecting what is being taught in school to student goals—by pointing it out themselves or by drawing it out of students (which, as Chapter 1 pointed out, appears to have less damaging potential)—can have a place in class, but also has to be kept in its place. In my experience, we will get fewer "Why are we learning this?" questions in learning environments that promote autonomy, competence, relatedness, or are connected to student interest. But when we do, I don't see anything wrong in helping students make those connections to their personal and professional goals or periodically having teacher-initiated lessons with that focus, such as several in this book and in previous ones (Ferlazzo, 2013, p. 147). On the other hand, constantly getting "Why are we learning this?" or "How are we going to use this?" questions might be an important indicator that we are not doing as good a job as we could be on implementing those other important conditions necessary for the development of intrinsic motivation.

In confronting these kinds of challenges, it is important to keep in mind the passage attributed to Voltaire: "Perfect is the enemy of good" (Perfect is the enemy of good, n.d.). *Self-Driven Learning* (Ferlazzo, 2013) included many immediate suggestions and lesson plans for teachers to use to help students develop intrinsic motivation around writing and reading, including creating "authentic audiences" for student writing, encouraging students to read books of their choice, and helping them learn how reading strengthens the brain (p. 135). This chapter will include several more classroom ideas, including two mini-lessons and two full lesson plans.

Writing

Technology and Writing Motivation

When we write, we're transcribing what is in our mind to paper or a screen through either handwriting, typing, or dictation. Though many of us may be able to work well through any one of those three modes, researchers have found that there are advantages to having students with writing difficulties type instead (there are also other benefits when using effective voice recognition software): "Compared to handwriting, typing (or word-processing) involves simpler graphemic processing and motor sequences and so may impose less transcription load on text generation, all else being equal" (Deane et al., 2008, p. 8). Studies have found "significantly higher" improvement for "less-skilled writers" when they are word processing instead of handwriting (Deane et al., 2008).

Since feeling a sense of competence is an essential element of intrinsic motivation, the availability of a desktop, laptop, or tablet for, if not all students, at least for some, could be an important option for teachers to have available. Being able to just have one student sit at my desk and use my computer has had a dramatic impact in my classroom at times—one, the student has been more engaged and done a much better job than she/he would have if she/he had needed to stay at a desk and handwrite an essay and, two, it creates a much better environment for the entire class since that student is less likely to be distracting (as we all know, many behavior issues are the way students choose to mask their academic shortcomings).

It should be pointed out that this word-processing recommendation is primarily for older students who are writing compositions. Research is fairly clear that learning writing by hand is important for children who are just beginning to understand literacy and for students of all ages who are learning a second (or third) language (Bounds, 2010). In addition, research has found that students taking notes by hand during lectures are more effective in learning and remembering content than those who do it by keyboard—since handwriting is slower, they tend to summarize and digest the content while typists tend to write what they are hearing verbatim (May, 2014).

Using Student-Created Prompts as a Differentiation Strategy

Chapter 1 reviewed a number of differentiation strategies. Many of the ideas suggested there focused on assisting students who are facing academic challenges. Unfortunately, it is not uncommon for students on the other end—who are ready for more complex tasks—not to receive a similar amount of attention (DeNisco, 2014; Even gifted students, 2013).

Building on an idea from my talented colleague Jeff Johnson, I've successfully adapted a "student-created prompt" activity that supports the key elements required for intrinsic motivation—autonomy, choice, competence, and relevance to student interest—and also provides opportunities to differentiate throughout the entire spectrum.

After students have completed a goal-setting activity like one of the examples shared in Chapter 1, I approach each student individually to see if they might be interested in doing more intellectually challenging assignments that are tied to their goals (which, in my classes, often includes "become a better writer") and interests. If they are willing to give it a try, I then ask them to make a list of their interests and say that we'll talk again soon about the next steps.

It's ideal, though not absolutely necessary, if students have learned about Bloom's Taxonomy (Ferlazzo, 2011, p. 142) and about the value of asking good questions (Ferlazzo, 2013, p. 109) prior to the next step. If not, the teacher can explain what Bloom's is when engaging in individual conversations.

After students have compiled their list of interests, I remind them that we talked a lot about how good readers often ask questions when they are reading, and also remind them about discussions we had about Bloom's Taxonomy (Ferlazzo, 2009, May 25). I give them a copy of a list of question-starters from Bloom (Bloom's Taxonomy Wheel/Circle, 2003, is one example, but many are available online) and tell them that sometimes I might ask them to create their own writing prompt using one of the higher-order question-starters of their choice. One example I used was if we were reading about tornadoes and they were done early with an assignment, they could choose the question-starter "How can you improve . . . ?" and they might fill in the blank with "tornado shelters." They would then write a one-paragraph response to that prompt using the "ABC" outline (Answer the question; Back it up with evidence like a quotation; make a

Comment/Connection). I also tell them there would be times I would ask them to create a prompt from the list of things they listed as interests. I also make it clear that it would always be an optional activity, and they should only pursue it if they believe it would help them achieve one of their goals.

Not all students agree to my initial proposition, and not all of those who do agree choose to follow through. But there are always a number of students who do, and I work hard at making sure that among their number is at least one person who their classmates look up to as a leader. I'm usually successful at "co-conspiring" with him/her to use his/her influence to gradually bring others on board after a period of time.

Setting the Stage for Writing

The "Why Do We Write?" lesson plan invites students to think about times they have felt good about their writing, consider ways they think writing well could be beneficial to them, explore how writing physically affects the brain, and learn about how writing well is important in many professional occupations. After considering all these reasons, students identify which one is most important to them. *Self-Driven Learning* (Ferlazzo, 2013) has a longer lesson on scenarios where reading and writing well could be useful (p. 147), but this shorter lesson plan is different and can be used at another time of the year to reinforce a similar message. Either lesson plan can be used first.

"Why Do We Write?" Lesson Plan

Instructional Objectives for Students

- Further develop their ability to practice reading strategies to help comprehend a text.

- Explore different ways the ability to write well can be beneficial to them.

- Articulate—either in writing and/or visually in digital form—what they identify as their most important personal reason for developing their writing skills.

Duration

One 55-minute class period.

Materials

- Access to the Internet and a computer projector to show the video "The Power of Words" (https://www.youtube.com/watch?v=Hzgzim5m7oU); other videos that include short testimonials from different professionals on how they use writing in their work (http://larryferlazzo.edublogs.org/2014/07/13/the-best-video-clips-on-the-benefits-of-writing-well-help-me-find-more/), and an image of the caudate nucleus (http://www.sciencedirect.com/science/article/pii/S1053811914004613).

- Access to a whiteboard, blackboard, or document camera.

- Student copies of the one-and-a-half-page summary at the beginning of "Writing: A Ticket to Work . . . or a Ticket Out: A Survey of Business Leaders" (http://www.collegeboard.com/prod_downloads/writingcom/writing-ticket-to-work.pdf).

Common Core English Language Arts Standards

Reading:

- Determine central ideas or themes of a text and analyze their development; summarize the key supporting details and ideas.

- Read and comprehend complex literary and informational texts independently and proficiently.

Writing:

- Write arguments to support claims in an analysis of substantive topics or texts, using valid reasoning and relevant and sufficient evidence.

Speaking and Listening:

- Prepare for and participate effectively in a range of conversations and collaborations with diverse partners, building on others' ideas and expressing their own clearly and persuasively.

- Integrate and evaluate information presented in diverse media and formats, including visually, quantitatively, and orally (only if the teacher decides to have students digitally create the lesson's culminating project).

- Make strategic use of digital media and visual displays of data to express information and enhance understanding of presentations (only if the teacher decides to have students digitally create the lesson's culminating project).

Language:

- Demonstrate command of the conventions of standard English grammar and usage when writing or speaking.

- Demonstrate command of the conventions of standard English capitalization, punctuation, and spelling when writing.

Procedure

1. Students enter the room and see these two questions on the whiteboard or document camera:

   - *Try to think of a time when you really felt good about something you wrote. What was it, and why did you feel good about it? It could have been a paper for school, a card for a friend, a Facebook post, etc.*

   - *How do you think writing well will help you in your present life or future one? List as many ways as you can. If you don't think it can help you, please explain why.*

   Explain that they have five minutes to write a response to the questions, and that students don't have to worry about their writing being perfect.

2. Ask students to share their lists in pairs, and then compile a class list on easel paper or on the document camera. This activity should take five to seven minutes.

3. Explain that, as students know, we spend a lot of time writing in this class. We're going to spend some time today talking about why we make it a priority.

4. Show the two-minute video "The Power of Words" (https://www.youtube.com/watch?v=Hzgzim5m7oU). After the video, show students these two

questions, and asks them to write down quick responses to both in a minute:

Why do you think the change in words made such a difference?
What do you think the woman did in the past that helped her think of the change?

Ask students to quickly share their responses with a different partner, and then ask them to share with the entire class.

5. Highlight the fact that the woman probably had practiced a lot as a writer (with luck, students will have made that point with one of their responses to the second question)—she came up with the effective revision pretty quickly. Explain that researchers have found that people who become more experienced writers use a part of the brain that is inactive for people who don't try to improve. It's called the caudate nucleus. The more you practice anything, including writing, the more activity there is in that part of the brain and the easier things become for you; they're more natural, more automatic (http://www.nytimes.com/2014/06/19/science/researching-the-brain-of-writers.html?_r=3). Show an image of the caudate nucleus to the class (http://www.sciencedirect.com/science/article/pii/S1053811914004613).

6. Point out that some students wrote that they felt writing would help them at work (assuming that some students did list that at the beginning—if not, just say that it will). Then distribute copies of the one-and-a-half-page summary at the beginning of "Writing: A Ticket to Work . . . or a Ticket Out: A Survey of Business Leaders" (http://www.collegeboard.com/prod_down loads/writingcom/writing-ticket-to-work.pdf) for students to read in pairs—taking turns reading each paragraph aloud—and highlight or underline five to seven words in each paragraph that they believe illustrate the most important points. Explain that it's important to just highlight a few words, and discuss how being selective can be a tool to help in future high-school and college classes so that when students need to review they don't have to re-read an entire text, only what they have highlighted. Ask students to put a star next to what they feel is the most important piece of information they learned from the text and to write a few words about why they think it is most important. Give students ten minutes for this activity. Explain the importance of reading with prosody (with feeling) and model reading a sentence with intonation and another in a monotone.

7. Invite some students to share what they thought were the most important pieces of information with the entire class.

8. Show one of the short videos from "The Best Videos Clips on the Benefits of Writing Well" (http://larryferlazzo.edublogs.org/2014/07/13/the-best-video-clips-on-the-benefits-of-writing-well-help-me-find-more/) that include

Building a Community of Self-Motivated Learners

short testimonials from different professionals on how they use writing in their work. Depending on time, you could either have students read the text or show the video instead of doing both.

9. Quickly review with students that they've discussed when they've enjoyed or felt good about their writing; they brainstormed why writing could be important to their lives; they learned about writing's impact on the brain; and heard how writing is used in different jobs. Then ask students to write a short paragraph answering these questions:

What do you think is the most important reason for you to learn to write well? Why?

Tell the students you would like them to write an ABC response (Answer the Question; Back it up with evidence from their experience, what they saw on the videos, or what they read—if they read the report summary; and then make a Connection and/or Comment about their experience or goals).

10. Again, depending on time, you can just collect the paragraphs or ask students to share them with a partner, followed by inviting contributions from the whole class.

Assessment

1. Collect all hand-outs to review the quality of student annotation.
2. Review the ABC paragraph.
3. If you feel a more involved assessment is necessary, you can develop a simple rubric appropriate for your classroom situation. Free online resources to both find pre-made rubrics and to create new ones can be found at http://larryferlazzo.edublogs.org/2010/09/18/the-best-rubric-sites-and-a-beginning-discussion-about-their-use/

Possible Extension/Modification

- You could extend the lesson to a second day by having students create a digital representation of their paragraph. See the Ed Tech box for additional suggestions.

Reading

Reading Socially

As mentioned earlier, promoting "relatedness" is an important element of intrinsic motivation, and substantial research has found that it relates to reading, as well. Connecting reading to social interaction has been shown both to help students feel motivated to read and to also increase reading comprehension (Cambria & Guthrie, 2010, p. 27). One way to make this type of interaction happen is a version of a literature circle.

Literature circles are a well-known concept that, done well, can meet several of the criteria for developing intrinsic motivation. I do a version with my students that seems to target all those elements at a high level, and students who appear to be among the least motivated readers often become much more engaged as a result of their participation in what I call "book clubs."

Having the cooperation of a school librarian, assuming you have one (which is, appallingly, a much rarer case than in the past), is a key to these book clubs' success. I announce to students that groups of them can decide on a book they would like to read together and/or have a conversation with our librarian or me about potential books (the books have to be classroom appropriate) and also visit our school's bookroom to explore what is available. Sometimes the librarian has multiple copies or can get them, and sometimes we contribute our own funds to buy the copies and then have them available in future years.

Picking a book of their choice and the people with whom they want to read are key "selling points" behind the book clubs. Another is that autonomy is encouraged because they get to go to the library and read and discuss their book once a week during the 15 minutes at the beginning of our class when everyone is silently reading. Though the librarian is there and "keeping an eye" on things, they are basically on their own. When visiting the library, students follow the guidelines found in Figure 3.1 (note that

Figure 3.1   Book Discussion Group Guidelines

1. When you arrive at the library, please check-in with the librarian. Make sure she/he has a seating chart with your names.

2. Each person shares the one- or two-sentence summary they wrote about the chapter or chapters they were to read. Discuss which one you like the best and why.

3. Each person shares the connection ("This makes me remember . . .") they wrote about the chapter or chapters they were to read. Please ask at least one question about each connection.

4. Each person shares the question they wrote about the chapter. Discuss what you think the answers might be to each one.

5. Each person shares what their favorite part or parts of the chapter was/were, and why they liked it.

6. Each person makes a prediction. What do you think will happen next in the story and why? Do you agree?

7. Each person answers the Bloom's Taxonomy question that you chose for this week.

8. Decide as a group what chapters you will read by the next meeting and which Bloom's Taxonomy question you will answer then.

9. Thank the librarian and return to class.

students can use resources mentioned earlier for the Bloom's Taxonomy question). Students are required to write answers to the questions on the "Guidelines" sheet (and show them to me) prior to going to the library for their period of discussion, and they generally complete them during one of the other days in class during silent reading time or on their own.

Usually one or two small groups will begin these book clubs and over a period of weeks others decide that they, too, want to create their own.

Student Self-Accountability

I have students in my ESL classes complete a simple "Reading Log" every Friday. It has five columns—one each for the day, title of the book, the number of minutes read, space for a student signature, and space for a parent signature (see Figure 3.2). Though I leave it on for a reason, the "parent signature" box has remained blank for years.

Figure 3.2 Weekly Reading Log

Name _____

Date	Book Title	Minutes Read	Student Signature	Parent Signature

I tell students at the beginning of the year that I expect that they will read a book of their choice at least two hours each week, and that if they promise to me that they will tell the truth on the log—even if they read less some weeks—then I will eliminate the requirement of a parent signature. Students always agree and make a public commitment, as well as shaking hands on it with me. I think seeing the "parent signature" column is a reminder of that commitment.

Each Friday, they quickly complete the sheet and, if they haven't read for two hours during the previous four days, they write a few words at the bottom of the sheet with specific plans about when they will read that Friday night or over the weekend ("I'll read for 20 minutes after we get home from our cousin's barbeque," etc.). I check with students on Monday (during the first ten minutes of class, which is always silent reading time) if they followed through and, if not, they tell me how they're going to make up the time that week. And we talk about how things do come up, and that there's always flexibility.

I'm confident that the vast majority—at least 90 percent—of students are genuinely honest, and make that determination by seeing how far they're getting in the books they read during our silent reading time and by the progress they make during cloze and fluency formative assessments (see the next section, "Measuring Reading Progress"). Based on my previous experience, I'm also confident in saying that it's a much higher percentage than years ago when I required parent signatures, which are easily faked.

Yes, I talk with parents about the reading expectation, but between multiple home languages, regularly changing phone numbers and moves, and other difficulties in making parent contact, there is a large percentage of parents that I just can't communicate with—despite my obvious commitment to parent engagement (Ferlazzo & Hammond, 2009).

Of course, this accountability strategy is combined with a strong emphasis on relationship-building and with life-skills lessons focused on helping students develop intrinsic motivation. So, let's say 10 percent of my students might not be entirely truthful with me. I'll take 90 percent student engagement over 100 percent "compliance" any day.

You might still be wondering about the accuracy of that 90 percent figure. In addition to the ways I came to that figure that I mentioned earlier, there is one other tactic I use to determine that percentage. Periodically, I hand out a blank piece of paper to each student and tell them not to put their name on it. I say I want them to write "yes" if they tend to be honest in the reading log or "no" if they are not. I make it very clear that I will not change the procedure no matter what they answer—I want to minimize the odds that students will write "yes" because they're afraid I might start requiring parent signatures. I tell them to fold their papers so no one can see what they wrote and have a student collect them. While they're doing something else later in the class period, I'll tabulate the sheets (sometimes I'll have a student do it). Usually, I have two students who write "no" in each class. I'll announce the results and tell them I'm impressed, though not surprised. I sometimes also jokingly announce that I will have the "no" papers analyzed for fingerprints and track that person down.

This does serve as another way to check up on them. More importantly, though, it reinforces to students that they are in a genuine community of learners comprised of people who keep their word. And the one or two students who are not following through also feel some peer pressure that they, too, need to step up to the plate.

Trust can have a powerful impact in the classroom.

Measuring Reading Progress

As mentioned earlier in this chapter and in Chapter 1, one way to help students develop a sense of competence is by providing opportunities for them to see concrete progress in improving their abilities. One way to accomplish this in the context of reading is by periodically having students complete clozes (short texts with words missing that students have to complete—two or three to find an average. They are also known as "fill-in-the-blanks" or "gap-fills") and by having them read various texts for one minute each (usually at grade level and, again, two or three for averaging purposes). We do this three times a year at our school under the supervision of respected literacy consultant Kelly Young at Pebblecreek Labs: http://pebblecreeklabs.com/. Students complete the same clozes and read the same texts each time. Clozes are effective at measuring reading comprehension (Bormuth, 1969; Nielsen, 2011) and reading texts for a minute is a useful way to measure reading fluency levels—in other words, reading with accuracy, at an appropriate rate of speech, and with expression (also called prosody) (Hasbrouck, n.d.).

Teachers can give students the results of their assessments and they can use them to inform their goal-setting plans (see Chapter 1). Of course, an essential element of ensuring it's effective in the development of intrinsic motivation is by being aware of how teachers talk to students about their scores—all too often we worship at the altar of being "data-driven" instead of operating like we're "data-informed" (Ferlazzo, 2011, January 28)—in other words, we need to consider these assessment results as just one part of everything else we know about this student and his/her situation. One important consideration that this has to include is that the focus should not necessarily be on maximizing the number of words each student can read each minute—we don't need oral speed readers. We want to, instead, encourage our students to read with prosody—with expression, intonation, and at a reasonable speed.

These assessments are about much more than data. Those few minutes when students read to teachers are also opportunities for us to check in with them to learn how they're doing in multiple aspects of their lives. In addition, individual conversations teachers have with each student about the results of the assessments are good opportunities to talk about their future hopes and goals. These conversations help us connect genuinely useful data to genuine student self-interests. This, in turn, helps students develop intrinsic motivation to achieve goals that they set for themselves—with some teacher assistance.

First, I'll share general guidelines I use in conversations with students about any kind of assessment data, and that prioritize the development of intrinsic motivation. Second, I'll share in more detail what that looks like in the talks we have specifically about cloze and reading fluency scores.

These are the elements that guide conversations I have about most assessments (talks about standardized test results are a little different, and I discuss them in *Self-Driven Learning* [Ferlazzo, 2013, p. 181]):

♦ The conversation needs to start with authentic data that is reliable and valid—in other words, it measures something worth measuring, and consistently measures it accurately (Reliability and validity, n.d.).

♦ *Students* need to believe that it is reliable and valid, and measures something that is important to them.

♦ A relationship is present between the teacher and student that appreciates honesty and caring.

♦ A clear connection can be made to the skills being measured and the hopes and dreams of the student. It is much better if the student can make that connection on their own, though some guidance from the teacher might be needed.

♦ The emphasis needs to be on student assets and potential, not on deficits. This doesn't mean challenges are "sugar-coated." Instead, it means that they are discussed in the context of next steps, an "action plan," and encouragement. These plans need to be realistic, and there must be student "buy-in." There is an old community organizing saying that "If you don't give a person a chance to say 'no,' then you don't give them a chance to say 'yes,' either." If it looks like students are committing to an action plan because of pressure from a teacher, they are unlikely to follow through on it. It's always an option to give students time to think and return to the conversation at a later date.

Here is how a conversation about cloze and fluency scores looks like using the above criteria.

First, I begin by telling the student I'm going to ask them a question, and that I'm going to ask that they answer it honestly. I promise I won't react negatively to anything they say, and there won't be any grade consequences at all. "How much time do you read most nights?" I ask (students are supposed to read for half an hour several nights each week). Almost universally, I'm convinced that students answer candidly.

Next, I take one of three roads—depending on their fluency and cloze scores (of course, it's not always as clear-cut).

If students have not made much progress: When this is the case, almost always students have answered my question by telling me they don't spend much time reading. I tell them that it shows in their scores. We talk about how they are going to have to do a lot of reading in high school, and it's going to be hard to keep up if they can't read faster—homework will take a lot longer. The student and I might take a few seconds to calculate how much time they would be able to save if they could increase their reading by 10, 20, 30, or even 40 words a minute. Through the relationship we have built, I know the interests of each student (and if I don't remember, I can ask them during our talk), and what they say they want to do after high school, so I might ask them how much reading they think they'll have to do to study for that profession or to actually do the profession. I'll ask if they are having a hard time finding books they find interesting, and we'll discuss ways to find them. I'll end by asking them to think about what they want their fluency and cloze goal to be at the end of the year so they can be prepared to complete a goal sheet (see Chapter 1) the next week, and ask them to think about specific things they can do to achieve it.

If students have made good progress, but are still not reading at the appropriate level: When this is the case, I'll tell them that the average student increases their reading fluency by between 15 and 18 words per minute in a full year and their cloze score by 10 to 12 percent (though the higher score they have, the less gain is expected [email from Kelly Young to author, 7/19]), and that they've already exceeded that goal. After that pat on the back, I'll say something like, "Boy, if you were able to make that amount of progress in half a year by reading . . . minutes each night (whatever amount they told me initially), imagine the progress you could make if you increased that amount—even a little bit—or read a little more challenging book?" Then we'll have a conversation similar to the one I recounted in the first instance—doing a little calculation, talking about its impact on their future, and asking them to think about their goal and action plan.

If students have made progress and are already reading well: When this is the case, I'll tell them that I'm going to be honest with them—they're doing fine and will do fine in school. I'll also ask them if they want to settle for "fine" or do they want to go for "great"? We'll then have a conversation about their hopes for the future. I'll tell them that one thing they need to remember, though, is that it can sometimes take more work to go from reading 190 words per minute to 200 than to go from 100 to 110. It's like a competitive runner—it can be harder for someone to go from running a four-minute mile to someone running a 3:55-mile than someone going from a ten-minute mile to running a mile in nine minutes. A person might go from 100 to 110 words per minute reading a Goosebumps book for 30 minutes a night, but it's unlikely someone is going to go from 190 to 200 by doing the same thing. They'd need to look at reading more challenging books and reading for a longer time.

Building a Community of Self-Motivated Learners

Ed Tech

There are several ways students can measure their own reading fluency progress online. There are many free audio tools that students can use to record their reading of texts so they can evaluate their prosody—how clearly and expressively they read. It would be easy to have students take a text of their choosing, pick a tool from "The Best Sites to Practice Speaking English" (http://larryferlazzo.edublogs.org/2008/03/17/the-best-sites-to-practice-speaking-english/), record themselves reading the passage, and paste the link to it on a class blog. Periodically during the year students can record themselves reading the same text and evaluate the progress they have made.

In addition, new websites, such as Literably (https://literably.com/) and FluencyTutor (http://www.fluencytutorforgoogle.com/), are developing software that can evaluate students' fluency after they record themselves reading a passage found on the site. Though it will never be a substitute for students reading face-to-face directly to a teacher, it can be another way for students to track their own reading progress.

Setting the Stage for Reading

This section contains two mini-lessons related to reading—one on the physical impact reading has on the brain and the other on the role of deliberate practice in reading. In addition, a full lesson plan on the "summer slide" and the importance of continuing to read during that vacation time is included.

Reading and the Brain Mini-Lesson

There is a mini-lesson on the physical changes reading can produce in the brain in *Self-Driven Learning* (Ferlazzo, 2013, p. 138). Here is another one that is different and based on research that has been done since that book's publication. Both lessons can be done during a school year, and either one can be done first. Helping students see that learning has a direct and positive impact on what physically goes on in their brain can provide students with a greater sense of autonomy and competence—they are in control of, and can manipulate, what is called "the most complex object in the known universe" (Decoding "the most complex object," 2013).

LeBron James Mini-Lesson

This mini-lesson includes a text about LeBron James as a basketball player and as a reader. There is evidence that James is an excellent athlete—one who engages in Deliberate Practice to master the skill of basketball. This passage shows that James also practices his reading skills, indeed, that he uses his reading skills to help him focus and relax before a game.

This mini-lesson may be used to introduce the "Deliberate Practice" lesson in *Self-Driven Learning* (Ferlazzo, 2013, p. 155), or before or after the deliberate practice mini-lesson in Chapter 1, or it may be used on its own at another time of the year. There are multiple connections that the teacher might help students make to their own lives and their own literacy journey. Questions teachers might ask before this lesson are "Does mastery in one skill motivate a person to become expert in other areas?"; "How is it possible that our literacy skills help us become smarter in other skills?"

This mini-lesson was developed by my talented colleague, Dana Dusbiber, and is shared here with her permission.

Summer Slide Lesson

Summer learning loss is a major factor in the achievement gap. As Professor Andrew McEachin wrote in *Education Week*: "The research . . . shows us that . . . students learn at roughly the same rate during the school year. This means that the gaps do not grow significantly while students are in school . . . achievement gaps widen during the summer period" (Summer Break, 2014).

In fact, on average, all students lose about a month's worth of learning due to summer vacation (Garland, 2012), but low-income students are affected the most and two-thirds of the achievement gap is due to summer learning loss (Strauss, 2009).

This lesson plan, which for obvious reasons should be taught near the end of the school year, is designed to help students see the advantages of participating in learning activities over the summer, explore different options, and encourage them to make a plan of what they can do over that time.

Reading and the Brain
Mini-Lesson Plan

Procedure

1. Students enter the classroom seeing an image of the human brain pro-jected on the screen—ideally, an image that students might find somewhat "icky"—the image should grab their attention. Explain that the class is going to spend the next 30 minutes learning what reading can physically do to the brain, and how our actions can control what happens there.

2. Tell the class that you are going to number them off by "threes" (1, 2, 3; 1, 2, 3, etc.). The "ones" are going to read Figure 3.3, "Reading, Writing and Alzheimer's"; the "twos" are going to read Figure 3.4, "This is Your Brain on Reading"; and the "threes" are going to read an article from *The Telegraph* newspaper, "Reading Can Help Reduce Stress" (http://www.telegraph.co.uk/health/healthnews/5070874/reading-can-help-reduce-stress.html). You need to make enough copies of the student hand-outs prior to class time.

3. Give each student a paper and markers to make a simple poster about their article. The poster has to list three important points from the article and include a drawing illustrating the article's main idea. Tell students they will have ten minutes to read and complete their posters on their own.

4. While students are working on their posters, go around and assign a letter to each group of one, two, and three that are near each other and tell the three members of each group to write down their letter. In other words, make sure that there will be many groups of three students, and that each group should contain a student with a poster for each of the different hand-outs.

5. When ten minutes are done, announce that each student will be present-ing their poster to two other students. Assign locations in the classroom for each letter group. After each student presents, they should decide as a group which piece of information they thought was the most interesting and why, and decide on one person who will say it to the class when you call on their group. Explain that they will have six minutes to get into their groups, present, and decide on the most interesting piece of information.

6. Students present in small groups.

7. After six minutes, explain that you are going to point to each group and that as you point at each group, the spokesperson should stand up immediately and announce the group's decision about the most interesting piece of informa-tion and why they chose it. The reporting process should take five minutes.

8. Collect the posters and, after class, put a representative sample of them on the classroom walls as reminders.

Figure 3.3   Reading, Writing, and Alzheimer's

Research has found that early reading and writing in childhood can slow the development of Alzheimer's in old age. It found that reading later in life helps, but it was able to independently confirm that reading earlier in life helped even more. As a summary of the research said:

It's never too late to start, but earlier is better.

The study found "that mental exercise during learning boosts brain function and rewires connections in neural circuits to enhance memory and mental performance." Starting learning activities like reading and writing in childhood and continuing them as an adult builds those connections that can fight against mental diseases like Alzheimer's.

"Reading gives our brains a workout because comprehending text requires more mental energy than . . . processing an image on a television screen . . . Writing can be likened to practice: the more we rehearse the perfect squat, the better our form becomes . . . Writing helps us consolidate new information for the times we may need to recall it, which boosts our memory skills."

Sources: Fields, R. D. (2013). http://blogs.scientificamerican.com/mind-guest-blog/2013/07/03/school-work-prevents-senile-dementia/

Jacobs, T. (2013). http://www.psmag.com/navigation/health-and-behavior/lifetime-of-reading-slows-cognitive-decline-61800/?utm_source=feedburner&utm_medium=feed&utm_campaign=Feed%3A%20miller-mccune%2Fmain_feed%20%28Pacific%20Standard%20-%20Main%20Feed%29

Koren, M. (2013). http://www.smithsonianmag.com/science-nature/being-a-lifelong-bookworm-may-keep-you-sharp-in-old-age-6786112/?utm_campaign=20130703&utm_medium=social media&utm_source=twitter.com&utm_content=surprisingsciencebookworm2

Figure 3.4 This is Your Brain on Reading

Stanford researchers have found a "dramatic and unexpected increase in blood flow" to the brain when we read. Stanford researcher Natalie Phillips said "the global increase in blood flow during close reading [if you were reading a text for a class] suggests that paying attention to literary texts requires the coordination of multiple complex cognitive functions. Blood flow also increased during pleasure reading, but in different areas of the brain."

As brain researcher Eric Jensen writes: "Oxygen is essential for brain function, and enhanced blood flow increases the amount of oxygen transported to the brain." The more blood flow we have to the brain, the better we learn.

Reading is one way to increase that blood flow, and movement is another. That's one reason we read, and one reason we physically move to get into small groups.

Sources: Goldman, C. (2012). http://news.stanford.edu/news/2012/september/austen-reading-fmri-090712.html
Jensen, E. (n.d.). http://www.ascd.org/publications/books/104013/chapters/Movement-and-Learning.aspx

LeBron James Mini-Lesson Plan

Procedure

1. Show students the YouTube video "LeBron Focuses by Reading" (http://www.youtube.com/watch?v=e3EOsMgzRbg). Allow students to simply enjoy the video. Provide a few minutes for them to talk about what they viewed.

2. Distribute the passage *LeBron James, Open Book* (http://espn.go.com/nba/playoffs/2012/story/_/id/8080433/lebron-james-read-nba-finals). You have the option of distributing it in one of two forms:

   - One way is to distribute the text as it appeared originally, and ask students to annotate it using various reading strategies like making a connection, visualizing (drawing), asking questions, summarizing, evaluating, etc.

   - The other way is for you to reformat the entire text the way the first paragraph is formatted in Figure 3.5. In this form, the text is in the left column and you write literal (e.g. What color are my shoes?) and interpretative (e.g. How do you think I'm feeling today?) questions—these are also known as "right there" and "think about" questions, see *Self-Driven Learning*, p. 109)—on the right for students to answer. Students can also be challenged to write their own questions and answers on the sheet, possibly including Bloom's Taxonomy question-starters.

3. Students work individually or in pairs to complete the reading and annotation. Bring the class back together for a few minutes and elicit from students samples of their annotations (it is not necessary to review every single paragraph in the story).

4. Next, ask students to write a simple ABC (Answer the question, Back it up with a quotation, and make a Connection/Comment) paragraph in response to the question: "Why do you think James began to read so much?"

5. Depending on the time available, you can either immediately collect the paragraphs or first have students verbally share what they wrote with a partner.

Figure 3.5 LeBron James, Open Book

June 21, 2012; Michael Wilbon ESPN.com

The most noticeable thing LeBron's done so far, besides average nearly 30 points and drag Oklahoma City to the brink of elimination, is turn his locker stall into a library cubicle. **This is related to his performance on the basketball court, trust me.**	How is LeBron's reading related to his performance on the basketball court?

Summer Slide Lesson Plan

Instructional Objectives for Students

- Further develop their ability to practice reading strategies to help comprehend a text.

- Learn about summer learning loss and its disadvantages.

- Develop an individual summer learning plan.

Duration

Two 55-minute class periods.

Materials

- Access to the Internet and a computer projector to show images and play sounds, as well as to show potential summer learning websites.

- Access to a whiteboard, blackboard, or document camera.

- Student copies of "How Summer Increases the Achievement Gap" (http://hechingered.org/content/how-summer-increases-the-achievement-gap_5072/).

- Access to a computer lab or multiple laptops or tablets during the second day.

Common Core English Language Arts Standards

Reading:

- Determine central ideas or themes of a text and analyze their development; summarize the key supporting details and ideas.

- Read and comprehend complex literary and informational texts independently and proficiently.

Speaking and Listening:

- Prepare for and participate effectively in a range of conversations and collaborations with diverse partners, building on others' ideas and expressing their own clearly and persuasively.

Language:

- Demonstrate command of the conventions of standard English grammar and usage when writing or speaking.

- Demonstrate command of the conventions of standard English capitalization, punctuation, and spelling when writing.

Procedure

First Day

1. Students enter the class seeing an image of water pouring out of a faucet on the screen (search for "water coming out of faucet" on the Web) and hearing the sound of water pouring (search for "sound of water pouring out of faucet" on the Web).

2. Above the sound of the pouring water, say that school is like water coming from a faucet—everyday students are encouraged and challenged to learn, to read, to think—and that they react to the water in various ways (you and students can have some fun with brainstorming things students do with it—drink it, mix it with their own ingredients, etc.). Then, turn off the sound of the pouring water and show an image of a faucet turned off and say that this is what can happen in the summer—that faucet gets turned off. All students then are not necessarily receiving something challenging every day to which they have to react.

3. Distribute copies of the article, "How Summer Increases the Achievement Gap" (http://hechingered.org/content/how-summer-increases-the-achievement-gap_5072/). Explain that you want the students to work with a partner to read the first nine paragraphs of the article (students don't have to read the last six paragraphs). You want them to demonstrate reading strategies while they write, and they can choose from visualizing (drawing a picture); asking a question; writing a summary; evaluating (agreeing or disagreeing; liking or not liking); or making a connection to their own experience or something else they have read. List the strategies on the board, and tell students they have to use one of them for each paragraph, and that they have to use each of the strategies at least once. In addition, you want students to write a one-sentence summary of the article at the bottom. Explain that you want students to read with prosody (with feeling) and model reading a sentence with intonation and then in a monotone.

4. Students read in pairs and annotate the text over the next ten minutes.

5. Call on various students to share the strategies they used and their one-sentence summaries.

6. Explain that with the summer approaching, you would like students to think about if they want to take control of the faucet and turn it on for themselves. Say that you want students to take a minute and think about what things they could do over the summer to learn and write them down at the bottom of the article. After a minute, ask students to tell a nearby student

what they wrote down. Then ask students to share with the entire class and write ideas on the whiteboard or document camera.

7. Affirm what will, with luck, be good suggestions shared by the class. Share some ideas of your own, too (depending on the situation, these could be lending books from the classroom library, bringing in a city librarian or going on a field trip to get library cards, explaining summer school enrichment offerings, etc.). In addition, explain that you have set-up online virtual classrooms on the Web (see the Ed Tech box below), where students can do many interesting activities. You might even say that you have made arrangements with their teachers next year for them to receive extra credit for the work they do there (as mentioned in Chapter 1, extrinsic motivation is not always bad). Use the computer projector to quickly review the different sites, and explain that the entire class will be going to the computer lab the next day to register at the sites and try them out. Say that even if students don't think they want to do them over the summer, you still want all students to register so they can see how they work.

Second Day

1. Bring the class to the computer lab, or provide students with laptops or tablets, for students to try out the different activities (see the Ed Tech box below) which, ideally, have links to them listed on a web page or on a class blog.

2. Near the end of the period, distribute blank pieces of paper and review with students the list of activities they and you developed the previous day about summer learning activities. Ask students to write on the paper their name, and what they think they can commit to doing over the summer (it can be more than one activity and can include the computer sites) and in a few words say why they have decided to do them. Students share their plans in small groups.

Assessment

1. Collect all hand-outs to review the quality of student annotation.

2. Collect the plans students have made.

3. If you feel a more involved assessment is necessary, you can develop a simple rubric appropriate for your classroom situation. Free online resources to both find pre-made rubrics and to create new ones can be found at http://larryferlazzo.edublogs.org/2010/09/18/the-best-rubric-sites-and-a-beginning-discussion-about-their-use/

Possible Extension/Modification

- Extend the lesson to a third day or even a fourth day to give students plenty of time to get comfortable using the sites.

Ed Tech

There are many free and very low-cost websites that allow teachers to easily create virtual classrooms where students can register and where teachers can keep track of their progress. A list of 11 that I used one summer can be found at "Here Are the Eleven Sites I'm Using for My Summer School Virtual Classroom" (http://larryferlazzo.edublogs. org/2014/05/26/here-are-the-eleven-sites-im-using-for-my-summer-school-virtual-classroom/). Many more such sites are listed at "The Best Sites that Students Can Use Independently and Let Teachers Check on Progress" (http://larryferlazzo.edublogs. org/2008/05/21/the-best-sites-that-students-can-use-independently-and-let-tea chers-check-on-progress/). More information on the effect of summer learning loss can be found at "The Best Resources on the Summer Slide" (http://larryferlazzo.edublogs. org/2011/06/26/the-best-resources-on-the-summer-slide/).

References

Bloom's taxonomy wheel/circle. (2003). Retrieved from: http://www.in2edu.com/resources/thinking_resources/blooms_taxonomy_chart.pdf

Bormuth, J.R. (1969). Factor validity of cloze tests as measures of reading comprehension ability. *Reading Research Quarterly*, 4(3), 358–365. Retrieved from: http://www.jstor.org/stable/747144

Bounds, G. (2010, October 5). How handwriting trains the brain: Forming letters is key to learning, memory, ideas. *Wall Street Journal*. Retrieved from: http://online.wsj.com/news/articles/SB10001424052748704631504575531932754922518?mod=WSJ_LifeStyle_LeadStoryNA&mg=reno64-wsj&url=http%3A%2F%2Fonline.wsj.com%2Farticle%2FSB1000142405274870463150457553193275 4922518.html%3Fmod%3DWSJ_LifeStyle_LeadStoryNA

Cambria, J., & Guthrie, J.T. (2010). Motivating and engaging students in reading. *The NERA Journal*, 46(1), 16–29. Retrieved from: http://literacyconnects.org/img/2013/03/Motivating-and-engaging-students-in-reading-Cambria-Guthrie.pdf

Deane, P., Odendahl, N., Quinlan, T., Fowles, M., Welsh, C., & Bivens-Tatum, J. (2008, October). *Cognitive models of writing: Writing proficiency as a complex integrated skill.* Retrieved from: http://origin-www.ets.org/Media/Research/pdf/RR-08-55.pdf

Decoding "the most complex object in the universe" (2013, June 14). *NPR.org*. Retrieved from: http://www.npr.org/2013/06/14/191614360/decoding-the-most-complex-object-in-the-universe

DeNisco, A. (2014, February). Are gifted students slighted in schools? *District Administration*. Retrieved from: http://www.districtadministration.com/article/are-gifted-students-slighted-schools

Erhard, K., Kessler, F., Neumann, N., Ortheil, H.-J., & Lotze, M. (2014). Professional training in creative writing is associated with enhanced fronto-striatal activity in a literary text continuation task. *NeuroImage, 100*, 15–23. Retrieved from: http://www.sciencedirect.com/science/article/pii/S1053811914004613

Even gifted students can't keep up. (2013, December 14). *New York Times*. Retrieved from: http://www.nytimes.com/2013/12/15/opinion/sunday/in-math-and-science-the-best-fend-for-themselves.html

Ferlazzo, L. (2008, March 17). The best sites to practice speaking English. *Larry Ferlazzo's websites of the day*. Retrieved from: http://larryferlazzo.edublogs.org/2008/03/17/the-best-sites-to-practice-speaking-english

Ferlazzo, L. (2008, May 21). The best sites that students can use independently and let teachers check on progress. *Larry Ferlazzo's websites of the day*. Retrieved from: http://larryferlazzo.edublogs.org/2008/05/21/the-best-sites-that-students-can-use-independently-and-let-teachers-check-on-progress

Ferlazzo, L. (2009, May 25). The best resources for helping teachers use Bloom's Taxonomy in the classroom. *Larry Ferlazzo's websites of the day*. Retrieved from: http://larryferlazzo.edublogs.org/2009/05/25/the-best-resources-for-helping-teachers-use-blooms-taxonomy-in-the-classroom/

Ferlazzo, L. (2010, September 18). The best rubric sites (and a beginning discussion about their use). *Larry Ferlazzo's websites of the day*. Retrieved from: http://larryferlazzo.edublogs.org/2010/09/18/the-best-rubric-sites-and-a-beginning-discussion-about-their-use/

Ferlazzo, L. (2011). *Helping students motivate themselves*. Larchmont, NY: Eye on Education.

Ferlazzo, L. (2011, January 28). The best resources showing why we need to be "data informed" & not "data driven." *Larry Ferlazzo's websites of the day*. Retrieved from: http://larryferlazzo.edublogs.org/2011/01/28/the-best-resources-showing-why-we-need-to-be-data-informed-not-data-driven/

Ferlazzo, L. (2011, June 26). The best resources on "the summer slide." *Larry Ferlazzo's websites of the day*. Retrieved from: http://larryferlazzo.edublogs.org/2011/06/26/the-best-resources-on-the-summer-slide

Ferlazzo, L. (2013). *Self-driven learning: Teaching strategies for student motivation*. New York: Routledge.

Ferlazzo, L. (2014, February 23). The "all-time" best ways to create online content easily & quickly. *Larry Ferlazzo's websites of the day*. Retrieved from: http://larryferlazzo.edublogs.org/2014/02/23/the-all-time-ways-to-create-online-content-easily-quickly/

Ferlazzo, L. (2014, May 26). Here are the eleven sites I'm using for my summer school 'virtual classroom'. *Larry Ferlazzo's websites of the day*. Retrieved from:

http://larryferlazzo.edublogs.org/2014/05/26/here-are-the-eleven-sites-im-using-for-my-summer-school-virtual-classroom

Ferlazzo, L. (2014, July 13). The best video clips on the benefits of writing well—Help me find more. *Larry Ferlazzo's websites of the day*. Retrieved from: http://larryferlazzo.edublogs.org/2014/07/13/the-best-video-clips-on-the-benefits-of-writing-well-help-me-find-more/

Ferlazzo, L., & Hammond, L. (2009). *Building parent engagement in schools*. Santa Barbara, CA: Linworth.

Fields, R.D. (2013, July 3). School work prevents senile dementia. *Scientific American*. Retrieved from: http://blogs.scientificamerican.com/mind-guest-blog/2013/07/03/school-work-prevents-senile-dementia/

Gardner, A. (2010, February 23). The power of words. *YouTube*. Retrieved from: https://www.youtube.com/watch?v=Hzgzim5m7oU

Garland, S. (2012, May 24). How summer increases the achievement gap. *Hechinger Ed*. Retrieved from: http://hechingered.org/content/how-summer-increases-the-achievement-gap_5072

Goldman, C. (2012, September 7). This is your brain on Jane Austen, and Stanford researchers are taking notes. *Stanford News*. Retrieved from: http://news.stanford.edu/news/2012/september/austen-reading-fmri-090712.html

Hasbrouck, J. (n.d.). Understanding and assessing fluency. *Reading Rockets*. Retrieved from: http://www.readingrockets.org/article/27091

Hulleman, C.S., Godes, O., Hendricks, B.L., & Harackiewicz, J.M. (2010). Enhancing interest and performance with a utility value intervention. *Journal of Educational Psychology*, *102*(4), 880–895. Retrieved from: http://psycnet.apa.org/journals/edu/102/4/880

Jacobs, T. (2013, July 3). Lifetime of reading slows cognitive decline. *Pacific Standard*. Retrieved from: http://www.psmag.com/navigation/health-and-behavior/lifetime-of-reading-slows-cognitive-decline-61800/?utm_source=feedburner&utm_medium=feed&utm_campaign=Feed%3A%20miller-mccune%2Fmain_feed%20%28Pacific%20Standard%20-%20Main%20Feed%29

Jensen, E. (n.d.). Movement and learning. *ASCD.org*. Retrieved from: http://www.ascd.org/publications/books/104013/chapters/Movement-and-Learning.aspx

Koren, M. (2013, July 3). Being a lifelong bookworm may keep you sharp in old age. *Smithsonian.com*. Retrieved from: http://www.smithsonianmag.com/science-nature/being-a-lifelong-bookworm-may-keep-you-sharp-in-old-age-6786112/?utm_campaign=20130703&utm_medium=socialmedia&utm_source=twitter.com&utm_content=surprisingsciencebookworm2

LeBron focuses by reading (2012, June 15). *YouTube*. Retrieved from: http://www.youtube.com/watch?v=e3E0sMgzRbg

Leisure Reading Task Force (2014). *Leisure reading*. International Reading Association. Retrieved from: http://www.reading.org/Libraries/position-statements-and-resolutions/ps1082_leisure_reading.pdf

Lenhart, A., Arafeh, S., Smith, A., & Macgill, A. (2008, April 24). What teens tell us encourages them to write. *Pew Research Internet Project*. Retrieved from: http://

www.pewinternet.org/2008/04/24/what-teens-tell-us-encourages-them-to-write/

May, C. (2014, June 3). A learning secret: Don't take notes with a laptop. *Scientific American*. Retrieved from: http://www.scientificamerican.com/article/a-learning-secret-don-t-take-notes-with-a-laptop/

Nielsen, J. (2011, February 28). *Cloze test for reading comprehension*. Retrieved from: http://www.nngroup.com/articles/cloze-test-reading-comprehension

Organization for Economic Cooperation and Development (2012). *PISA 2012 results: Ready to learn: Students' engagement, drive and self-beliefs (Volume III)*. Retrieved from: http://www.oecd.org/pisa/keyfindings/pisa-2012-results-volume-iii.htm

Perfect is the enemy of good (n.d.). *Wikipedia.com*. Retrieved from: http://en.wikipedia.org/wiki/Perfect_is_the_enemy_of_good

Reading 'can help reduce stress' (2009, March 30). *The Telegraph*. Retrieved from http://www.telegraph.co.uk.health/healthnews/5070874/reading-can-help-reduce-stress.html

Reliability and validity (n.d.). *Classroom assessment*. Retrieved from: http://fcit.usf.edu/assessment/basic/basicc.html

Ryan, R. M., & Deci, E. L. (2000). Intrinsic and extrinsic motivations: Classic definitions and new directions. *Contemporary Educational Psychology, 25,* 54–67. Retrieved from: http://mmrg.pbworks.com/f/Ryan,+Deci+00.pdf

Strauss, V. (2009, June 15). 'Summer brain drain' robs some students of skills gained during the year. *The Washington Post*. Retrieved from: http://www.washingtonpost.com/wp-dyn/content/article/2009/06/14/AR2009061402427.html?hpid=topnews&sid=ST2009061402437

Summer break and the achievement gap (2014, May 30). *Education Week*. Retrieved from: http://blogs.edweek.org/edweek/rick_hess_straight_up/2014/05/summer_break_and_the_achievement_gap.html

Tsioulcas, A. (2013, February 15). Can you learn to like music you hate? *NPR.org*. Retrieved from: http://www.npr.org/blogs/deceptivecadence/2013/02/15/172120886/can-you-learn-to-like-music-you-hate

What's the historical origin and meaning of how many angels can dance on the head of a pin? (n.d.). *Askville.com*. Retrieved from: http://askville.amazon.com/historical-origin-meaning-angels-dance-head-pin/AnswerViewer.do?requestId=184400

Wiggins, G. (2014, May). *The typical HS: Student survey, part 3*. Retrieved from: http://grantwiggins.wordpress.com/2014/05/27/the-typical-hs-student-survey-part-3

Writing: A ticket to work . . . or a ticket out. A survey of business leaders (2004, September). The College Board. Retrieved from: http://www.collegeboard.com/prod_downloads/writingcom/writing-ticket-to-work.pdf

Yuhas, D. (2012, October 18). Three critical elements sustain motivation. *Scientific American*. Retrieved from: http://www.scientificamerican.com/article/three-critical-elements-sustain-motivation/

Zimmer, C. (2014, June 20). This is your brain on writing. *New York Times*. Retrieved from: http://www.nytimes.com/2014/06/19/science/researching-the-brain-of-writers.html?_r=3

How Can You Get Students to Transfer Their Knowledge and Skills from One Class to Other Classes and Outside-of-School Situations?

I've been hearing a lot about the need for students to be able to transfer what they learn in my class and apply it to new and different situations. That sounds easier said than done. Do you have any suggestions to help?

"Transfer of learning" is the term used to describe applying what one has learned in one situation to another in a different context. This kind of extension could take place during a school year within an individual class when applying what is learned about one problem to another, to different and future classes, to home situations, and to a workplace situation (now and in the future) (Bransford et al., 2000, p. 51). Of course, most of the learning we do is built upon our existing knowledge and skills. This chapter focuses on how teachers can encourage students to become more conscious of, and interested in, "transferring their learning" to more challenging and higher-order thinking contexts (in many ways, comparable to the application stage of Bloom's Taxonomy).

There are a number of kinds of "transfer," most notably ones categorized in a continuum as "near" and "far" (it's also been called "nearer" and "farther," Shank, 2004). *Near transfer* tends to be focused on procedures or a routine where learned skills in one area are more easily applied consistently to a somewhat similar situation (Dadgar, n.d.). For example, students might apply the essay writing skills they learn in English class to writing essays in Social Studies courses, or we apply much of what we learn about driving a car to driving a bus or a truck. As we move a little further on the continuum, once students studying history have learned about the American Revolution, they can begin to explore the similarities and differences between that event and revolutions in other countries and at other times. These kinds of near transfers are easier to encourage and have a higher likelihood of success than what's at the other side of the continuum—*far transfer*.

In the more difficult area of far transfer, students use their judgment about applying their skills and knowledge from one context to a substantially different one. For example, a chess player might apply the strategies they have learned to understanding and perhaps even running a political campaign, or someone might learn about concepts related to wind flow from studying windmills and relate them to using a sail on a boat (Dadgar, n.d.).

Near and far transfer can go two ways: forward-thinking and backward-reaching (*Backward-Reaching Transfer*, 2006; *Forward-Thinking Transfer*, 2006). In forward-thinking, we think about what we have learned and how we can apply it in the future; in backward-reaching, we remember what we learned in the past and apply it to a challenge we're facing now. In a TEDx Talk on deeper learning and transfer, Marc Chun uses two examples to illustrate these two perspectives: James Bond has to do forward-thinking when he is given all sorts of deadly gadgets prior to his missions and he considers when and how he'll use them; TV hero MacGyver always does a lot of backward-reaching when he's stuck in almost inescapable situations and has to apply his previous knowledge to figuring out how to use the items at hand to save everyone (*Diving into Deeper Learning*, 2013). For two classroom-related examples, forward-thinking could be illustrated by students considering how and when they would apply what they learn from the lessons in the next chapter about healthy eating, and backward-reaching could be demonstrated in completing the "What I Know" column in a K-W-L chart introducing a new lesson.

There are two other terms worth keeping in mind when thinking about transfer—"hugging" and "bridging." Researchers David Perkins and Gavriel Salomon use the word "hugging" to describe instructional strategies commonly used for near transfer—again, applying known skills and concepts to similar situations—and the word "bridging" for ways of teaching far transfer—applying their existing skills to situations that are different from the context in which the original was learned (Perkins & Salomon, n.d., p. 7). Though one or two instructional strategies listed later in this chapter are particularly useful to one or the other kind of transfer (and those particular applications will be highlighted), many are helpful for both.

Transfer is *a*, if not *the*, primary purpose of schooling. We want our students to be able to apply the knowledge and skills they learn with us to other challenges inside and outside of school—the goal of our English class is not to have students pass the exam, but to be competent and critical life-long writers and readers; the goal of studying history is not to memorize the dates of major battles, but to develop a broad historical perspective that they can apply to understanding the world around them today and in the future. Unfortunately, however, at times the pressure of high-stakes testing does not support or encourage teachers prioritizing those purposes (Dewitz & Graves, 2014, p. 2).

Many teachers operate under the assumption that transfer happens automatically and, in a number of cases, it does—using basic reading skills in multiple contexts is one example (Dewitz & Graves, 2014, p. 6). However, studies show that many students have difficulties in applying knowledge they learned in one class to another and to outside situations (Sousa, 2006, p. 138). How often in our own classes will students learn new words on a quiz or vocabulary review but not use them in their writing, or second language learners will know grammatical written forms but are unable to use them in conversation? Assuming automatic transfer of learning will more likely lead us to live out the supposed Chinese proverb that says "people have to stand still for a long time with their mouths open before roast chickens will fly into them" (*Welcome to My Favorite*, n.d.).

Transfer will not happen magically. This chapter will share many actions teachers can take on a regular basis to increase the chances of both near and far transfer occurring, and will also include a full lesson plan designed to help students understand what transfer is and why it is in their self-interest to engage in it.

Teachers should also keep in mind that consistently applying the key elements needed to help students develop intrinsic motivation—autonomy, competence, relatedness, and interest/relevance—at any classroom opportunity has also been found to be key in encouraging transfer (Pugh & Bergin, 2006, p. 156). Transfer, especially far transfer, is a difficult task that requires motivation (Dewitz & Graves, 2014, p. 7). In particular, research has found that self-efficacy, the belief in one's ability to be successful and that success is generated by effort (see Chapter 1), promotes transfer, as does an emphasis on learning goals (as opposed to performance goals—again, see Chapter 1) and having a strong interest in the topic being studied (Pugh & Bergin, 2006, p. 150). In other words, all of the other suggestions and lesson plans in this book and in previous titles should also have a positive impact on student transfer—if students know what it is, see it as valuable and interesting, and teachers make a priority of creating opportunities for it to happen.

Immediate Actions

Maximizing the Initial Learning Experience for Transfer

It should go without saying that in order for transfer to occur, students need to gain a good understanding of the concepts that we wish them to be able to apply to new problems. As Nobel-Prize-winning physicist Richard Feynman said, it's "the difference between knowing the name of something and knowing something" (Richard Feynman, 2008). Memorizing a list of facts or a list of procedures is unlikely to promote sufficient understanding of a concept for students to be able to apply it in a new situation.

For example, a National Academy of Sciences report shares a story of students learning that arteries are elastic but not learning why they have that property. Without that knowledge, students are then unable to construct an artificial artery (Bransford et al., 2000, p. 55). Another well-known example describes how two groups of children practiced throwing darts at a target 12 inches underwater and both became good at it with practice. The target was then moved to four inches below the surface, but just one group was instructed on how light refraction can cause a deceptive appearance of the target's location. Even though both groups had become good over time at the first dart-throwing practice, it was the group that received instruction that was able to quickly adjust its experience to a new situation (Bransford et al., 2000, p. 56).

Activate Prior Knowledge

One strategy researchers suggest using in an effective initial learning experience to maximize transfer potential is building upon the knowledge students already bring to a topic, which can enhance the likelihood of developing a genuine understanding of concepts. In addition to relating a lesson to familiar contexts, it strengthens and models the idea of transfer (Bransford et al., 2000, p. 68). As neurologist and teacher Judy Willis writes, "memories with personal meaning are most likely to become . . . long-term memories available for later retrieval" (Willis, 2006, p. 20). The example cited in the first chapter about connecting the lives of migrant children to the history of feudalism shows how activating prior knowledge can accomplish both goals. They related their stories with a critical eye to the textbook's declaration that feudalism ended hundreds of year earlier and developed a new interpretation. It's a critical thinking lesson that, with luck, will make them want to look for more evidence behind the claims made by the authors of textbooks, newspapers, and news shows they read and watch in the future. I say "with luck" because I could have done a much, much better job at explicitly helping students think about how they could use the lessons they learned from that experience in the future.

Create Time for Learning

That shortcoming in the feudalism lesson is directly connected to another element researchers suggest is critical during the initial and follow-up lessons: time. As a National Academy of Sciences report on deeper learning and transfer says:

> Attempts to cover too many topics too quickly may hinder learning and subsequent transfer because students (a) learn only isolated sets of facts that are not organized and connected or (b) are introduced to organizing principles that they cannot grasp because they lack enough specific knowledge to make them meaningful. (Bransford et al., 2000, p. 58)

Deliberate Practice

The pressure to "cover" the curriculum, especially prior to annual standardized tests, does not encourage teachers to often make the time needed to create the necessary conditions for transfer to occur. This time is needed for, among other things, students to utilize deliberate practice to increase understanding, discussed in both Chapters 1 and 3. This type of practice, which includes active monitoring of one's learning and regular receiving of feedback, is critical for maximizing the possibility of transfer. There are many ways time could be used for deliberate practice that would enhance student understanding of concepts so that transfer could be promoted. For example, after students learn the qualities of a successful presentation, instead of giving one presentation in front of the entire class, they could give it multiple times in small groups with time for both structured feedback from classmates and revision.

Explain in Their Own Words

Another important use of time to promote greater understanding of key concepts is to have students explain in their own words—to others or to themselves (called "self-explanation")—what they are learning (Williams & Lombrozo, 2010, p. 777). Substantial research has shown that not only does this type of explaining help students identify their incorrect assumptions, but it also helps them to generalize concepts for future applications (Sparks, 2013).

Other Ways to Promote Understanding

Other subsections in this chapter highlight instructional strategies that have been shown to specifically increase the chances of transfer. In addition, there are many other elements researchers have found to be useful in promoting understanding, including teacher modeling, using sufficient "wait time" for students to respond to questions, showing visuals related to the learning topic, encouraging physical movement, and providing formative assessment (Ferlazzo, 2011, p. 115).

Explicit Teaching of Transfer Situations

A number of studies conclude that transfer is more likely to occur if the teacher explicitly points out the transfer possibilities of what is being learned (Bransford et al., 2000, p. 60) or, even better, draws them out from the students themselves. The "Learning Transfer" lesson plan provides some specific tools to use to accomplish this goal.

One example is the use of inductive data sets (Ferlazzo, 2011, p. 139). Teaching inductively uses the brain's natural inclination to seek and generate patterns out of what it reads, sees, and hears. With inductive data sets, students are presented with perhaps 20 to 30 short passages on a topic—let's say China—and then have to annotate key points and categorize the passages into five subsections—let's say Geography, Economy, History, People, Culture (the topic and subsections are just examples—this process could be used for just about any lesson). After students categorize, they can find additional information that fits into each subsection and then turn them into individual paragraphs and, ultimately, into an essay.

Students could do text data set after text data set and get very skilled at all aspects of the inductive process. However, the key transfer that needs to take place is that they are learning an organized way to research and write an essay or article about any topic for any class or for any other reason. The process of reading, annotation, categorization, and writing is a simple and effective writing strategy.

In my first years of using inductive data sets, I believe few—if any—of my students transferred the process into their future writing. Since I began making that explicit connection, many students have told me they have used this writing process regularly in subsequent years and have shown me what they've produced.

Explicitly teaching students to look at problems or situations from multiple perspectives has also been shown to increase transfer—it can increase future student flexibility to deal with new information and events, and encourage them to make fewer assumptions (Dolmann et al., 2005, p. 733).

A simple introductory lesson to this idea can be having a student stand in the middle of the room in a classroom-appropriate pose of his/her choosing and have his/her classmates draw for a few minutes only the portion of the model that they see. A subsequent discussion about why no one could draw a complete picture because they only had a narrow view can be connected (by the teacher or, ideally, by students) to multiple future lessons about the value of looking at problems from all angles.

The hope, however ideal it might be, is that after enough times of explicit teacher encouragement about transfer, students will begin to initiate it themselves: "Once their minds are set for transfer, they will begin spontaneously to look for the connections that earlier had to be provoked" (Perkins & Salomon, n.d., p. 9).

Simulations

Simulations are especially recommended for "hugging"—promoting near transfer to similar future situations. They put students in the kinds of roles that they may very well find themselves in at a future date. Students can role-play job interviews instead of just talking about appropriate interview responses and behavior, or play different roles in complex racial or union-management negotiations (Perkins & Salomon, 1992; Perkins & Salomon, n.d., p. 10).

Student use of online computer simulations has also been found to have a positive effect on learning transfer (Rey, 2010, p. 677). See the Ed Tech box below for more information.

 Ed Tech

Many free online learning simulations are available on the Web, including role-playing job interviews, conflict resolution, life-saving techniques, financial decisions, and bullying situations. Many can be found at "The Best Online Learning Simulation Games and Interactives" (http://larryferlazzo.edublogs.org/2014/07/23/the-best-online-learning-simulation-games-interactives-help-me-find-more/).

Group Learning

The National Academy of Sciences examined how school environments tend to compare to the settings in other aspects of everyday life. They found that schools are much more focused on individualized work than most other non-school situations. For successful transfer to occur to non-classroom situations, they recommend that schools place a greater emphasis on shared learning (Bransford et al., 2000, p. 74).

A second report on transfer from the National Academy of Sciences specifically suggests that problem-based learning, discussed in *Helping Students Motivate Themselves* (Ferlazzo, 2011, p. 154), is a particularly effective small-group learning experience that promotes transfer (Pellegrino & Hilton, 2012, p. 166). In problem-based learning, students research and solve a real-world problem (see Ed Tech box below). Of course, one of the other advantages of working in small groups is it enhances intrinsic motivation (remember the "relatedness" element discussed in Chapter 1).

Ed Tech

There are many very practical online resources available on problem-based learning. Visit "The Best Sites for Cooperative Learning Ideas" (http://larryferlazzo.edublogs.org/2010/04/02/the-best-sites-for-cooperative-learning-ideas/) to see a few of them.

Metacognition

The use of metacognitive strategies—which help students reflect on their thinking about their learning, consider what other ways they might think about it, and determine what the best way to think might be (Ferlazzo, 2013, p. 98)—have been shown to help with transfer (Darling-Hammond & Austin, n.d., p. 195).

There are many ways to apply metacognition to improve learning, and a full lesson plan can be found in *Self-Driven Learning* (Ferlazzo, 2013, p. 98). Some researchers suggest that this question, or a variation of it, could be specifically applicable to encouraging transfer: "How is this example or problem similar to or different from others I have encountered?" (Darling-Hammond & Austin, n.d., p. 195). Teacher modeling of responding to this type of question, and also sharing other elements of his/her thinking process in approaching a text or challenge, can be an effective way to help students begin to develop metacognitive skills (Wiggins, 2012). Students can then demonstrate it on their own orally or in writing to receive constructive feedback. Note that these kinds of "self-explanations" are different from the kind mentioned in the first subsection of this chapter—Maximizing the Initial Learning Experience for Transfer. In that situation, students are self-explaining their understanding of a lesson being taught. In this context, they are explaining the thinking process they are going through to arrive at that understanding. The former is emphasizing the correct answer; the latter is focusing on the problem-solving process.

The "Learning Transfer" lesson plan includes graphic organizers that students can use to both prompt and document their use of these kinds of metacognitive strategies.

Analogies and Metaphors

An example of "backward-reaching" for knowledge transfer is using an analogy or metaphor—we can use what was known previously and apply it to a new situation to make it better understood—such as comparing how a heart works to a pump (Perkins & Salomon, 1992). When discussing the importance of providing evidence to support one's position, we can point to a chair and ask, "What would happen if its legs were removed?" After students respond that it would fall down, a teacher can say that the legs are like evidence and the seat is like a thesis statement—without it, it can't stand up.

One well-known experiment using analogy for transfer, and which also highlighted the importance of explicitly teaching its use, used a war story. Researchers first explained a situation to students where an army wanted to overcome a fortress that had its defenses organized so that the only way it could be successfully attacked was by a general who divided his forces so that smaller units of his army attacked it from all sides simultaneously. Afterwards, students were asked to solve the problem of how to effectively treat a tumor with rays that would not affect the tumor at a low intensity and would also destroy healthy tissue if used at a high level. Over 90 percent of the students figured out a solution of treating it with multiple small doses of rays targeting the tumor—but only if they were reminded of the fortress story. Only a small number solved the problem without the prompt (Bransford et al., 2000, p. 64).

I have used Plato's Allegory of the Cave in a similar fashion. A very crude and short summary of the allegory is that a group of prisoners are in a cave facing a wall for their entire lives with a fire and walkway behind them. All they see of the world are shadows. Then one is released and discovers what the real world is like and returns to tell his former fellow prisoners. However, they choose not to believe him and threaten to kill him if he tries to take them outside. After discussing the allegory and considering questions about its meaning and what might be our, and greater society's, "caves" today, students create short skits applying the allegory to modern life. It is then frequently brought up by students the rest of the year when we explore problems that are contributed to by people refusing to move from entrenched ideological positions.

Ed Tech

Accessible resources on Plato's Allegory of the Cave can be found at "Videos of the Allegory of the Cave" (http://theoryofknowledge.edublogs.org/2012/04/15/videos-of-allegory-of-the-cave/). The web page includes examples of students applying it to modern life.

Generalizing

Grant Wiggins suggests that regularly pushing students to generalize from specific situations to broader principles is another effective strategy for transfer. He makes this suggestion:

> After studying westward expansion, ask, "What big generalizations about human migration does this movement west suggest? Can you support your generalizations by other evidence you know of?" Then, ask the same question after studying early 20th-century immigration. (Wiggins, 2012)

Another opportunity could come after studying the early women's rights movement and the suffragists, asking students what are the generalizations they think could be made about the essential elements of a successful social change movement? The same question could then be asked following a study of the American Civil Rights Movement.

Setting the Stage

Learning Transfer Lesson

As mentioned earlier, explicitly discussing the idea of transfer—how it's done and why it's important—with students can be an effective strategy to have them actually do it. The "Learning Transfer" lesson plan provides a simple explanation of basic ideas about transfer in an engaging way, and introduces graphic organizers that can be reused throughout the year to help students apply it in class, in other classes, and in their lives outside of school.

Learning Transfer Lesson Plan

Instructional Objectives for Students

- Learn about the concept of transfer of learning and its importance.

- Be introduced to graphic organizer tools they can use to implement the concept.

- Demonstrate a use of learning transfer.

Duration

One 55-minute class period, plus ten minutes during various future classes to introduce, and have students use, new graphic organizers.

Materials

- Access to the Internet and a computer projector to show videos from "The Best Movie Scenes, Stories, and Quotations About Transfer of Learning" (http://larryferlazzo.edublogs.org/2014/07/21/the-best-movie-scenes-stories-quotations-about-transfer-of-learning-help-me-find-more/comment-page-1/).

- Access to a whiteboard, blackboard, or document camera.

- Student copies of transfer learning graphic organizers and transfer home-work assignment.

Common Core English Language Arts Standards

Writing:

- Write routinely over extended time frames (time for research, reflection, and revision) and shorter time frames (a single sitting or a day or two) for a range of tasks, purposes, and audiences.

Speaking and Listening:

- Prepare for and participate effectively in a range of conversations and collaborations with diverse partners, building on others' ideas and expressing their own clearly and persuasively.

Language:

- Demonstrate command of the conventions of standard English grammar and usage when writing or speaking.

- Demonstrate command of the conventions of standard English capitalization, punctuation, and spelling when writing

Procedure

1. Students enter the classroom seeing this instruction on the whiteboard or document camera:

Please write your response to this question: What is the purpose of your attending classes seven hours each day? In other words, what do you think is the primary reason society values school so highly that it spends billions of dollars each year on them and requires that you attend?

Tell the students they have five minutes to write a response to the question. During this time, walk around the room identifying who is writing responses that you want to highlight to the entire class.

2. After five minutes, ask the students to quickly verbally share their responses with partners and then begin to call on people to tell the entire class what they wrote. You might get responses like "to get an education"; "to learn"; "to be able to get a job"; "to have us stay off the streets." You don't have to respond to each one, but you do want to dig deeper on certain responses that could eventually get to the fact that the purpose of school is to help students learn skills and knowledge that they can use in the outside world. For example, a dialogue could go like this:

Student: *The primary reason is that society wants us to learn.*

Teacher: *Learn what?*

Student: *To read, write, know stuff.*

Teacher: *What stuff?*

Student: *You know, history of our country and the world, math . . .*

Teacher: *Why does society want you to know that stuff? Is it because society wants you to know the answers to test questions?*

Student: *I guess . . .*

Teacher: *What might be other reasons that society wants you to learn these things?*

Student: *So we can get a job.*

Teacher: *How do you think knowing these things will help you in a job?*

Student: *We'll be able to do the job better.*

Teacher: *Oh, so society wants you to be able to apply what you learn in school to situations outside of school.*

Student: *Yeah, that's it.*

Obviously, every teacher will have a different type of discussion, and it can be with the entire class—not just a dialogue with one student. But the aim is to get students to understand that the primary purpose of school is not so they can memorize all the facts. Instead, the primary purpose is to help them learn concepts that they can apply at home, in their neighborhoods, and at work. This discussion could take five to seven minutes.

3. Explain that the idea of applying what you learn in school to non-school situations, as well as applying what you learn in this class to other classes, is called "transfer of learning" (write it on the whiteboard or document camera). Explain that if it's the primary purpose of schooling, then it's obviously important. Go on to say it makes things more interesting, too—it's not going to be very engaging to learn something that you'll never use or think about again. Say that sometimes you may not think what you're learning is useful, but if you get in the habit of thinking about how it could be helpful, you may find learning to be much more interesting.

4. Then explain that you're going to show a series of short videos that will last ten minutes. The clips are from the original *Karate Kid* movie, where a teacher has agreed to teach a boy karate. Go to "The Best Movie Scenes, Stories, and Quotations About Transfer of Learning" (http://larryferlazzo. edublogs.org/2014/07/21/the-best-movie-scenes-stories-quotations-about-transfer-of-learning-help-me-find-more/comment-page-1/) and play, without commentary, the four *Karate Kid* clips that show the boy being told by the teacher to wax his car, sand the floor, and paint a fence as part of his training. The boy becomes very frustrated until he sees clearly in the final clip how those tasks were, in fact, helping him learn karate (to save time, you can show the car waxing clip and just tell students he was also required to sand and paint, and then show the entire final clip).

5. Explain that what they saw was an example of transfer of learning—the boy was able to apply what he had learned to an entirely new situation. Imagine how less frustrated he would have been if he had known this when he was waxing the car, sanding the floor, and painting the fence. Tell the class that you are going to ask them a question and want them to think about a response without shouting it out. Students can write their response on the same paper as they used for the opening question. This question is: *"Should the teacher have told the boy when he was doing each task why he was having him do it? Why or why not?"* After two minutes of working silently, ask students to share with a partner (a different one than earlier). You might want to suggest that, since the class just spent several minutes in the dark watching a video, you want people to get up and moving, so all students have to get up and move to another seat to talk with their new partner. After a minute, call on people to respond. After a few minutes of students sharing their opinions, say that you think since the boy was unfamiliar with the idea of transfer of learning, you think the teacher should

have told him. But the point of transfer is that eventually people need to be very conscious about doing it on their own—teachers aren't always around and that students will need to take personal responsibility and show creativity in figuring out how to transfer their knowledge to new situations.

6. Say that one reason students will need to reach the point of doing it on their own is because it just makes learning more interesting if you're constantly trying to figure out how to use information or a concept that you're learning (if the class has previously had lessons on how learning strengthens the brain [Ferlazzo, 2011, p. 7] you can also say it will make your brain stronger). You could give an example (one that I give is when I watch movies or read comics, I'm always trying to think about how I can use a scene or a comic strip as part of a lesson). Say that there is also another reason—it's important to employers. Say that the Association of American Colleges and Universities hired a group to survey employers to find out what they thought were the most important qualities in potential employees and some of the top ones were (you can write these on the board):
   Critical thinking and analytical reasoning skills
   The ability to analyze and solve complex problems
   The ability to apply knowledge and skills to real-world settings
   (https://www.aacu.org/leap/documents/2013_EmployerSurvey.pdf, p. 8)

7. Say that you'd like students to understand two types of learning transfer. There is the kind they saw in the *Karate Kid*—when people are confronted with a new task or problem, they think about how they can apply what they learned in the past to help them. That's called "backward-reaching" (you can model it with a physical movement with your arm). The other kind of learning transfer happens at the time you are learning something new, and you have to imagine how you can use it to solve a problem in the future—that's called "forward-thinking."
   Ask students who have heard of James Bond, 007, to raise their hand. Explain that you are going to show a short video of James Bond using forward-thinking learning transfer. Show a few minutes of a James Bond video from the "Best Film Scenes . . ." list where the scientist named Q is giving Bond deadly gadgets to use on his next mission. After the video, explain that when Q is giving Bond the gadgets, Bond has to be thinking about the different kinds of situations he could use them in—he's getting prepared in his mind for anything. After all, he's putting his life on the line.

8. Ask students to think of a time when they either used backward-reaching or forwarding-thinking learning transfer—when they either used something they had learned in school previously to help solve a problem or complete a task, or a time when during a lesson they thought of how they could use it in the future to complete a task or solve a problem. Give your

own examples (**Backward-reaching:** "I was upset one day with another teacher who wouldn't give me the help I wanted and was going to confront her, but then I remembered a story I learned in school about Abraham Lincoln during the Civil War. He made a deal with the Mormons in Utah that he wouldn't bother them if they didn't make any trouble for him, and told a story to justify it. He said when he was young, he was trying to clear a field for planting, and there was a big tree in the middle of it. He said instead of putting all the time and effort into removing it, he just went around it. When I remembered that story, I decided that it wasn't really necessary to deal with the hassle of confronting her—I could just go around her and get what I wanted"; **Forward-thinking:** "I was in math class one day long ago when we were learning percentages, and I realized I could use what I was learning to figure out exactly how much money stores were talking about when they say 20 percent off this thing or 40 percent off that thing.").

Show students two graphic organizers: Figure 4.1, "Backward-Reaching Transfer," and Figure 4.2, "Forward-Thinking Transfer." Explain that you will give students a copy of each; they need to complete one, though could do both if they have time. Tell students it would be best if they could identify how they had used or would use something they learned or were learning in a situation outside of school. However, if they are having a difficult time thinking of one, they could, instead, identify something they learned in one class that they used or could use in another class. (Note: Until students become much more comfortable and experienced with the concept of learning transfer, it may be much harder for them to think of ways they can apply some new learning to contexts outside of school. Identifying ways to use it in other classes or in other tasks in the same course is a useful way for students to begin to build confidence in their ability to make those kinds of connections—see "Possible Extensions/Modifications" for further information.)

Tell students they will have five minutes to complete at least one sheet and point out that they don't have to write a lot—just one or two sentences in each of the two sections on the sheet.

9. Students work on their sheets while you circulate around the room helping students and identifying examples that you would like to highlight to the entire class. (Note: Depending on how the class goes, it is possible that there will only be time to explain the assignment and distribute the graphic organizers. If that is the case, they can be assigned as homework for students to complete that night. Step ten could then be completed during the first eight minutes of the next day's class.)

10. Ask students to get into groups of three to share verbally what they wrote. After four minutes, highlight particular examples to the entire class. You can

also say that this is not the last time the class will be discussing the idea of learning transfer. Then collect the completed graphic organizers and, if desired, the responses to the two questions to which students wrote responses.

Assessment

1. Collect the completed graphic organizers to assess for understanding of transfer of learning.

2. If you feel a more involved assessment is necessary, you can develop a simple rubric appropriate for your classroom situation. Free online resources to both find pre-made rubrics and to create new ones can be found at http://larryferlazzo.edublogs.org/2010/09/18/the-best-rubric-sites-and-a-beginning-discussion-about-their-use/

Possible Extensions/Modifications

- At the beginning of some regular lessons in the future, copies of Figure 4.1, "Backward-Reaching Transfer," could be distributed and used, along with reminding students of what transfer is and why it's important.

- At the end of some regular lessons in the future, copies of Figure 4.2, "Forward-Thinking Transfer" could be distributed and used, along with reminding students of what transfer is and why it's important. When using this graphic organizer, point out that it is best if they could think of times they could use it outside of school but, if they cannot, sharing how they could use what they just learned in another class is okay.

- After students become familiar with the concept, different graphic organizers can be used at the end of some regular lessons. Figure 4.3, "Hugging for Near Transfer," and Figure 4.4, "Bridging for Far Transfer," could be used, along with quick explanations of the differences. See the beginning of this chapter for explanations of "hugging" and "bridging." These graphic organizers can help students begin to further differentiate between applying transfer to in-school and non-school contexts.

- Figure 4.5, "Transfer Homework Assignment," is another kind of graphic organizer that can be modified in multiple ways. It's just one more example of how students can be encouraged to use transfer.

Ed Tech

Students can use any number of online tools to create simple videos, comics, animations, etc. to illustrate—seriously or with humor—how they could transfer (or have transferred) their academic learning to non-school environments. See "The 'All-Time' Best Web 2.0 Applications for Education" (http://larryferlazzo.edublogs.org/2014/02/24/the-all-time-best-web-2–0-applications-for-education/) and "The 'All-Time' Best Ways to Create Online Content Easily and Quickly" (http://larryferlazzo.edublogs.org/2014/02/23/the-all-time-ways-to-create-online-content-easily-quickly/) for various options of free and easy creation tools.

Figure 4.1   Backward-Reaching Transfer

   Backward Reaching Transfer

Think back – reach back to previous experience to find information or skills that will allow you to solve a current problem.

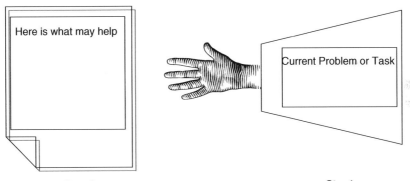

| Step 2 | Step1 |
| What have you learned that you can use to solve your current problem | What problem or task are you currently facing? |

Created by Dr. Fran O'Malley, Delaware Social Studies Education Project, University of Delaware, and reprinted with permission.
Retrieved from: http://www.udel.edu/dssep/transfer/Hugging%20for%20Near%20Transfer.pdf

Figure 4.2   Forward-Thinking Transfer

Forward Thinking Transfer

Think forward – think about what you learned and how you might apply it to a future problem or task.

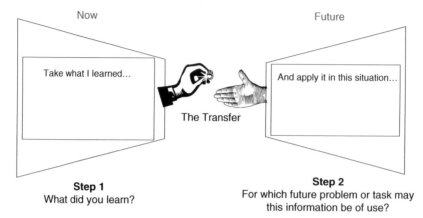

Now

Future

Take what I learned…

And apply it in this situation…

The Transfer

Step 1
What did you learn?

Step 2
For which future problem or task may
this information be of use?

*Created by Dr. Fran O'Malley, Delaware Social Studies Education Project, University of
Delaware, and reprinted with permission.*
Retrieved from: http://www.udel.edu/dssep/transfer/Hugging%20for%20Near%20
Transfer.pdf

Figure 4.3   Hugging for Near Transfer

Hugging for Near Transfer

Transfer what you just learned to a similar but not identical task.

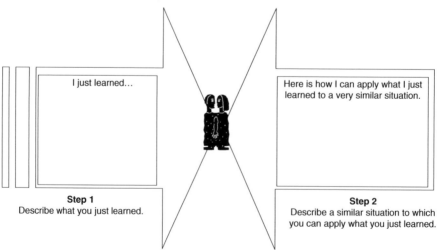

I just learned…

Here is how I can apply what I just
learned to a very similar situation.

Step 1
Describe what you just learned.

Step 2
Describe a similar situation to which
you can apply what you just learned.

*Created by Dr. Fran O'Malley, Delaware Social Studies Education Project, University of
Delaware, and reprinted with permission.*
Retrieved from: http://www.udel.edu/dssep/transfer/Hugging%20for%20Near%20
Transfer.pdf

Figure 4.4 Bridging for Far Transfer

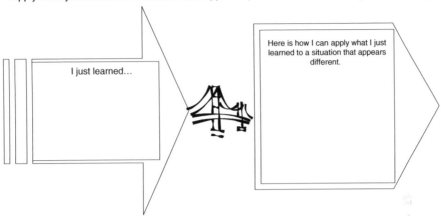

Bridging for Far Transfer

Apply what you learned to a situation that appears quite different from what you learned originally.

I just learned…

Here is how I can apply what I just learned to a situation that appears different.

Step 1
Describe what you just learned.

Step 2
Describe a different situation in which you can use what you just learned.

Created by Dr. Fran O'Malley, Delaware Social Studies Education Project, University of Delaware, and reprinted with permission.

Retrieved from: http://www.udel.edu/dssep/transfer/Bridging%20for%20Far%20Transfer.pdf

Figure 4.5 Transfer Assignment Example

Name: _____

Date: _____

Homework Slip
English 9

Your "homework" is to use the reading strategy of **connecting** in one of your other classes today.

Directions

Pick a piece of text you read in another class and connect it to something else. How does it relate to another piece of text? Television? The world? Your life? Something else?

Class: _____

What is this text about?

This connects to:

Explain how the two things connect:

Developed by Lara Hoekstra, and reprinted with her permission.

(Originally published in *Helping Students Motivate Themselves*, Ferlazzo, 2011, p. 118)

Building a Community of Self-Motivated Learners

References

Backward reaching transfer. (2006). Delaware Social Studies Education Project. Retrieved from: http://www.udel.edu/dssep/transfer/Backward%20Reaching%20Transfer.pdf

Bransford, J. D., Brown, A. L., & Cocking, R. R. (2000). *How people learn: Brain, mind, experience, and school* (expanded ed.). Washington, DC: The National Academies Press. Retrieved from: http://www.nap.edu/openbook.php?record_id=9853&

Bridging for far transfer (2006). Delaware Social Studies Education Project. Retrieved from: http://www.udel.edu/dssep/transfer/Bridging%20for%20Far%20Transfer.pdf

Dadgar, S. (n.d.). *Transfer of learning.* Retrieved from: http://www.etc.edu.cn/eet/articles/transferLearn/start.htm

Darling-Hammond, L., & Austin, K. (n.d.). *Session 11: Lessons for life: Learning and transfer.* Retrieved from: http://www.learner.org/courses/learningclassroom/support/11_learning_transfer.pdf

Dewitz, P., & Graves, M. F. (2014, July 3). Teaching for transfer in the Common Core era. *Wiley Online Library.* Retrieved from: http://onlinelibrary.wiley.com/doi/10.1002/trtr.1290/abstract?deniedAccessCustomisedMessage=&userIsAuthenticated=false

Diving into deeper learning: Mark Chun at TEDxDenverTeachers. (2013, March 24). *YouTube.* Retrieved from: https://www.youtube.com/watch?v=k6BmbdzPcrY

Dolmann, D.H.J.M., De Grave, W., Wolfhagen, I.H.A.P., & van der Vleuten, C.P.M. (2005). Problem-based learning: Future challenges for educational practice and research. *Medical Education, 39,* 732–741. Retrieved from: http://www.google.com/url?sa=t&rct=j&q=&esrc=s&source=web&cd=18&cad=rja&uact=8&ved=0CGUQFjAHOAo&url=http%3A%2F%2Fwww.researchgate.net%2Fpublication%2F7782105_Problem-based_learning_future_challenges_for_educational_practice_and_research%2Ffile%2F504635226d01710b6e.pdf&ei=LZ_QU5qLEIbv8AGq8oGIDA&usg=AFQjCNHlizQcU1HEKTNlnF1l6o9CkgPDGA&sig2=5pgkMmh2IQoJFP_BoRJNCg&bvm=bv.71667212,d.b2U

Ferlazzo, L. (2010, April 2). The best sites for cooperative learning ideas. *Larry Ferlazzo's websites of the day.* Retrieved from: http://larryferlazzo.edublogs.org/2010/04/02/the-best-sites-for-cooperative-learning-ideas/

Ferlazzo, L. (2010, September 18). The best rubric sites (and a beginning discussion about their use). *Larry Ferlazzo's websites of the day.* Retrieved from: http://larryferlazzo.edublogs.org/2010/09/18/the-best-rubric-sites-and-a-beginning-discussion-about-their-use/

Ferlazzo, L. (2011). *Helping students motivate themselves.* Larchmont, NY: Eye on Education.

Ferlazzo, L. (2012, April 15). Videos of Allegory of the Cave. *Theory of knowledge: Resources for Mr. Ferlazzo's TOK class.* Retrieved from: http://theoryofknowledge.edublogs.org/2012/04/15/videos-of-allegory-of-the-cave

Ferlazzo, L. (2013). *Self-driven learning: Teaching strategies for student motivation.* New York: Routledge.

Ferlazzo, L. (2014, February 23). The "All-time" best ways to create online content easily and quickly. *Larry Ferlazzo's websites of the day.* Retrieved from: http://larryferlazzo.edublogs.org/2014/02/23/the-all-time-ways-to-create-online-content-easily-quickly/

Ferlazzo, L. (2014, February 24). The "All-time" best Web 2.0 applications for education. *Larry Ferlazzo's websites of the day.* Retrieved from: http://larryferlazzo.edublogs.org/2014/02/24/the-all-time-best-web-2-0-applications-for-education/

Ferlazzo, L. (2014, July 21). The best movie scenes, stories, and quotations about "transfer of learning"—Help me find more. *Larry Ferlazzo's websites of the day.* Retrieved from: http://larryferlazzo.edublogs.org/2014/07/21/the-best-movie-scenes-stories-quotations-about-transfer-of-learning-help-me-find-more/comment-page-1/

Ferlazzo, L. (2014, July 23). The best online learning simulation games and interactives—Help me find more. *Larry Ferlazzo's websites of the day.* Retrieved from: http://larryferlazzo.edublogs.org/2014/07/23/the-best-online-learning-simulation-games-interactives-help-me-find-more/

Feynman, R. The pleasure of finding things out (2008, March 23). *YouTube.* Retrieved from: https://www.youtube.com/watch?v=MoCVUtfYMmDs

Forward thinking transfer (2006). Delaware Social Studies Education Project. Retrieved from: http://www.udel.edu/dssep/transfer/Forward%20Reaching%20Transfer.pdf

Hart Research Associates (2013, April 10). *It takes more than a major: Employer priorities for college learning and student success.* Retrieved from: https://www.aacu.org/leap/documents/2013_EmployerSurvey.pdf

Hugging for near transfer (2006). Delaware Social Studies Education Project. Retrieved from: http://www.udel.edu/dssep/transfer/Hugging%20for%20Near%20Transfer.pdf

Pellegrino, J. W., & Hilton, M. L. (Eds.) (2012). *Education for life and work: Developing transferable knowledge and skills in the 21st century.* Washington, DC: The National Academies Press. Retrieved from: http://www.nap.edu/openbook.php?record_id=13398&

Perkins, D. N., & Salomon, G. (1992). Transfer of learning. *International encyclopedia of education* (2nd ed.). Oxford, UK: Pergamon Press. Retrieved from: https://learnweb.harvard.edu/alps/thinking/docs/traencyn.htm

Perkins, D. N., & Salomon, G. (n.d.). *The science and art of transfer.* Retrieved from: http://learnweb.harvard.edu/alps/thinking/docs/trancost.pdf

Pugh, K. J., & Bergin, D. A. (2006). Motivational influences on transfer. *Educational Psychologist, 41*(3), 147–160. Retrieved from: http://www.tandfonline.com/doi/abs/10.1207/s15326985ep4103_2#.U9AI5mOwUXE

Rey, G. D. (2010). Instructional advice, time advice and learning questions in computer simulations. *Australasian Journal of Educational Technology, 26*(5), 675–689. Retrieved from: http://www.ascilite.org.au/ajet/ajet26/rey.pdf

Shank, P. (2004, September 7). Can they do it in the real world? Designing for transfer of learning. *Learning Solutions Magazine.* Retrieved from: http://www.

learningsolutionsmag.com/articles/288/can-they-do-it-in-the-real-world-designing-for-transfer-of-learning

Sousa, D. A. (2006). *How the brain learns*. Thousand Oaks, CA: Corwin.

Sparks, S. D. (2013, June 4). Students can learn by explaining, studies say. *Education Week*. Retrieved from: http://www.edweek.org/ew/articles/2013/05/31/33aps.h32.html?tkn=TXCCxteRocKIVU%2BwOUgIxF1P1qe2JQgiE2uR&cmp=clp-sb-ascd

Welcome to my favorite collection proverbs (n.d.). Retrieved from: http://www.khmerkromrecipes.com/pages/quotes.html

Wiggins, G. (2012, January). *The research on transfer and some practical implications (Transfer, part 2)*. Retrieved from: http://grantwiggins.wordpress.com/2012/01/16/the-research-on-transfer-and-some-practical-implications-transfer-part-2

Williams, J. J., & Lombrozo, T. (2010). The role of explanation in discovery and generalization: Evidence from category learning. *Cognitive Science, 34*, 776–806.

Willis, J. (2006). *Research-based strategies to ignite student learning*. Alexandria, VA: ASCD.

Chapter 5

How Can You Help Students Want To Live A Physically Healthy Lifestyle?

So many of my students don't get enough sleep, don't eat enough healthy food, and don't get much exercise. I know that affects how much energy they bring to class and their ability to learn. Any suggestions on what I can do to help students want to better take care of themselves physically?

An increasing amount of research is finding that the elements of a physically healthy lifestyle, particularly around issues of nutrition, exercise, and sleep, are important for student motivation and their readiness to learn in school (*Ready to Learn?*, 2013). For many of our students, these challenges, like so many discussed in this book and in the previous titles in this series, have many causes well beyond the teacher's control, particularly around issues of race and class (Ferlazzo, 2010, December 28). Teachers can organize through community organizations and teachers unions to support public policy solutions to the problems of racism, poverty, and wealth inequality—and their many symptoms, including stress and financial insecurity, which create more difficult conditions for a healthy lifestyle to flourish—and we can help our students learn to become capable participants in public life. At the same time, we can provide information, strategies, and support to help them effectively cope with what they are facing today. The strategies and lessons in this chapter and in this series of books are one small attempt at doing just that.

This chapter includes suggestions for what teachers can do on a day-to-day basis to encourage students to lead a healthy lifestyle, as well as mini-lessons on the importance of eating breakfast, and two full lesson plans—one on junk food and exercise, and the other on sleep. Evidence for their role in enhancing student motivation and the ability to learn is included in both the introduction and the lessons themselves. As in all the chapters, the goal of these lessons is to create the conditions where students will *want* to maintain a healthy lifestyle because *they* see it in their self-interests, not because we do.

These lessons, in addition to corresponding to Common Core Standards, also meet 14 of the 15 "Characteristics of an Effective Health Education Curriculum" developed by the Centers for Disease Control after consulting with experts in the health education field (n.d.). The one they do not meet is because that particular "characteristic" is up to each individual teacher and school:

> **Provides adequate time for instruction and learning.** An effective curriculum provides enough time to promote understanding of key health concepts and practice skills. Behavior change requires an intensive and sustained effort. A short-term or "one shot" curriculum, delivered for a few hours at one grade level, is generally insufficient to support the adoption and maintenance of healthy behaviors. (Characteristics, n.d.)

The healthy lifestyle lessons in this chapter and in previous titles (Ferlazzo, 2011, p. 23) all include suggestions on how to continue bringing up these issues throughout the school year in several ways, including by implementing various "immediate actions," mini-lessons, incorporating them into regular goal-setting exercises, and doing things as simple as drawing attention to student-created posters taped on classroom walls. Despite the fact that these extensions correspond with Common Core Standards and their desire to promote literacy skills, most teachers are also under pressure to "cover" a set curriculum. It will be up to individual teachers and administrators to decide if they believe the increased student motivation and cognitive skills that can result from making these lessons a priority trump full curriculum "coverage."

The Importance of Sleep

Lack of sleep can be one reason for a lack of motivation in some students, and *Helping Students Motivate Themselves* (Ferlazzo, 2011) contains a lesson plan that helps students see that this lack of sleep can lead to weight gain, lower grades, and increased levels of depression. That lesson also includes a goal-setting activity where students reflect on what they have learned and if they want to make any changes (Ferlazzo, 2011, p. 12). The sleep lesson in this chapter is completely different, and can be done at any time before or after that lesson, and can also stand on its own without having to do both.

Research since that lesson was published only reinforces the studies upon which it is based. Columbia University researchers found that after people did not get an adequate amount of sleep, the parts of their brain connected to craving and reward were particularly stimulated by "junk food" and theorized that brain and body needed to seek more energy to get through the day (Sleepy brains, 2012).

In addition, several new studies describe how during sleep the brain needs time to "reactivate and reorganize" learned material (Simon, 2012).

Immediate Actions to Support Student Sleep

Exposing Students to Natural Sunlight

Studies show that exposure to natural light through windows, especially in the morning (Wooten, n.d.), can have a positive effect on reinforcing natural body rhythms that facilitate sleep at night (Bergland, 2013; Windows in the Workplace, 2013).

Keeping classroom curtains open as much as possible, therefore, would be one small action teachers can take to encourage student sleep. In many classrooms, however, light shining through windows can sometimes make it difficult for students to see images shown with a computer projector or document camera. This challenge is just one more of the many balancing acts that teachers must perform during their day, and it could be made easier by explaining to students, perhaps during one of the sleep lessons, why sunlight exposure—inside or outside of the classroom—is important (perhaps important enough to have less-than-clear-cut images on the screen occasionally?)

Helping Students Reduce Their Stress

Experiencing stress can have a negative effect on a person's ability to have a good night's sleep (Barnes, 2013). As discussed in *Self-Driven Learning* (Ferlazzo, 2013, p. 81), research shows that the more powerless you feel in a situation, the more stress you experience (Lehrer, 2012). Supporting student autonomy with many of the suggestions made in Chapter 1, especially around the concept of choice, could have an impact on stress reduction. Teaching the lesson on stress in that same book (Ferlazzo, 2013, p. 82) will provide students with many tools they can use to reduce their own stress levels.

Teaching Students About Sleep

Though it may seem self-apparent, multiple studies show that helping students learn about the importance of sleep have, indeed, had an impact on their sleep habits (Paul, 2014). Teaching this chapter's lesson and the one in *Self-Driven Learning* (Ferlazzo, 2013), along with looking for reminder opportunities, such as encouraging students to include sleep issues in their goal-setting activities, can lead to positive results.

Ed Tech

Supplemental "Read Alouds" and reading material for the "sleep lesson" in *Helping Students Motivate Themselves* (Ferlazzo, 2011) can be found at http://larryferlazzo.edublogs. org/2010/08/05/the-best-resources-for-helping-teens-learn-about-the-importance-of-sleep/. Links there also lead to images comparing brains that have had adequate sleep with those that are sleep-deprived.

Setting the Stage: Students and Sleep Lesson Plan

This one-day lesson, which could be expanded to two or even three based on teacher discretion, has a "text data set" as its centerpiece. This use of inductive learning, where students are provided examples and use them to understand key concepts, was discussed in Chapter 4. It contrasts with deductive learning, where the concepts are given first and then students are provided examples to support them. "Assisted discovery learning" strategies like the inductive model have been found by numerous studies to be a far more effective instructional strategy than direct instruction (Marzano, 2011).

Importance of Sleep Inductive Lesson Plan

Instructional Objectives for Students

- Further develop their ability to practice reading strategies to help comprehend a text.

- Develop experience in working with an inductive data set.

- Learn about the importance of getting a good night's sleep and be able to articulate reasons why it's important.

Duration

One 55-minute class period and 20 minutes the following day, with multiple possible extensions to add one or two more days.

Materials

- Access to the Internet and "The Best Resources for Helping Students Learn About the Importance of Sleep" (http://larryferlazzo.edublogs.org/2010/08/05/the-best-resources-for-helping-teens-learn-about-the-importance-of-sleep/).

- Document camera or overhead projector.

- Student copies of Figures 5.1 and 5.2.

- Construction paper, color markers, and highlighters (all optional).

Common Core English Language Arts Standards

Reading:

- Determine central ideas or themes of a text and analyze their development; summarize the key supporting details and ideas.

- Read and comprehend complex literary and informational texts independently and proficiently.

Writing:

- Write arguments to support claims in an analysis of substantive topics or texts, using valid reasoning and relevant and sufficient evidence (depending upon which, if any, extension the teacher chooses to do).

Speaking and Listening:

- Prepare for and participate effectively in a range of conversations and collaborations with diverse partners, building on others' ideas and expressing their own clearly and persuasively.

Language:

- Demonstrate command of the conventions of standard English grammar and usage when writing or speaking.
- Demonstrate command of the conventions of standard English capitalization, punctuation, and spelling when writing.

Procedure

First Day

1. Explain that the class is going to learn about the importance of sleep today. Show the sleep quotes, Figure 5.1, on the overhead and pass copies to students. Tell the students you are going to read them aloud and that they are going to pick the one they like the most (or dislike the least). They will put a star next to it and at the bottom of the sheet write what they think the quote means and why they like it. Students will have three minutes to complete the task.

2. While students are working, circulate to provide assistance and also identify students who you want to make a point of asking to share with the entire class.

3. Three minutes later, tell students to verbally share what they wrote with a partner (you might want to "mix up" the pairing process a bit by telling students to pick someone with different color hair or different color pants). Then have some students share with the entire class.

4. Next, explain that students are going to use something called an inductive data set. Show the first page of Figure 5.2 on the document camera and only pass out the first page of the data set to students. Tell them to ignore the list of categories at the top for now and read the first passage and explain that you want students to highlight (or underline) three to five words that show the main point of the passage. Do so as a model on the document camera. Then say that good readers ask questions, and you want students to write a question they have about each passage next to it—what would they want to know more about? Then write a model question. Explain that students will work in pairs and that each student will read one passage to another and highlight and write a question—they can do the same on each of their papers if they want. Say that you want students to read with prosody

and explain that means with intonation and feeling. Read the first passage two more times—one in a monotone and one with prosody as a model. Tell students they will have ten minutes to complete this page, and that they will have one minute to find a partner and begin reading.

5. Circulate among the class during those ten minutes, checking on prosody, for understanding, and to identify student work you want to highlight to the entire class.

6. At the end of ten minutes, tell students to stop (if some students finish early, ask them to do tasks like put a star next to the passage they found most interesting and say why they chose it, highlight words that are new to them, etc.). Ask a few students to quickly share the words they highlighted in some passages and questions they wrote.

7. Next, show the second page of the data set on the document camera and repeat the modeling sequence and distribute the second sheet to students. On this page, though, you want students to make a connection to an experience they've had or something else they have read or seen ("This makes me remember . . ."). You can either have students work with the same partners or have, for example, all students on the right move up one seat so they are with a new partner.

8. Circulate during those ten minutes, checking on prosody, for understanding, and to identify student work you want to highlight to the entire class.

9. At the end of ten minutes, tell students to stop (if some students finish early, you can ask them to do tasks like put a star next to the passage they found most interesting and say why they chose it, highlight words that are new to them, etc.). Ask a few students to quickly share the words they highlighted in some passages and some connections they wrote.

10. Next, show the third page of the data set which, depending on how it is copied, will only have one to three passages on it. Explain that you want students to do the same highlighting of important words but, instead of writing a question or making a connection, you want students to visualize—draw a picture of what the passage is making their brain see in their mind. Model visualizing, but do so with one of the passages on the first or second sheet. Explain that they will have five minutes to complete this task.

11. Circulate during those five minutes, checking on prosody, for understanding, and to identify student work you want to highlight to the entire class.

12. At the end of five minutes, the class can have some fun by you inviting certain students to bring up their visualizations to the document camera and explain to the class what they drew.

13. Now brings students' attention to the list of four categories at the top of the first page of the data set. Explain that you want students to categorize each

Building a Community of Self-Motivated Learners

passage—in other words, write down next to each passage the name of the category to which they think it belongs (they can shorten it to "Learning," "Weight," etc. instead of writing out the entire name). They also have to circle the key words—the evidence—that would support their decision to place it in that category. Model it with the first two passages. (Another option is to not provide students with the categories and have them develop their own. However, that possibility should only be considered if students are already familiar with inductive data sets.)

14. There will probably be very little time left in the period at this point. You can decide if you want to assign the categorization task as homework or plan on giving ten minutes of class time the next day to complete it. In my experience, doing the latter usually works better since some students might not complete it as homework.

Second Day

1. Give students ten minutes to do the categorization with a partner. This is the "answer sheet." However, be very open to letting students make a good case to put a passage in a different category:

    Sleep, School, and Learning—6, 7, 12, 13, 16
    Sleep and Weight—4, 8, 14, 15
    Sleep and Mental and Physical Health—2, 3, 10, 11
    Obstacles to Getting Enough Sleep—1, 5, 9

2. Review each item on the data set with the entire class, calling on individual students to share their categories and evidence.

3. Tell students you want them to pick which category they think is most important, and turn it into a short paragraph with a topic sentence and supporting evidence from the data set. Give students a few minutes to complete it and immediately collect it, or first have students verbally share their paragraphs with a partner. You may want to model a topic sentence with supporting evidence, though choosing a different topic (perhaps explaining why you are the greatest teacher in the world—levity can be helpful).

4. Tell students that you hope they will keep this information in mind as they think about goals for themselves.

Assessment

1. The annotated data set and paragraph from each student can easily be evaluated.

2. If you feel a more involved assessment is necessary, you can develop a simple rubric appropriate for your classroom situation. Free online resources to

both find pre-made rubrics and to create new ones can be found at http://larryferlazzo.edublogs.org/2010/09/18/the-best-rubric-sites-and-a-beginning-discussion-about-their-use/

Possible Extensions/Modifications

There are many possible extensions to using any kind of inductive text data set. They could include the following:

- Have students cut and glue the data set passages and group them together under category names instead of just annotating them. This method of organization is particularly useful if you are then going to have students do further research and identify several new additional pieces of information for each category—students can then just write them under each category. Students could search the Internet and/or begin at "The Best Resources for Helping Students Learn About the Importance of Sleep" (http://larryferlazzo.edublogs.org/2010/08/05/the-best-resources-for-helping-teens-learn-about-the-importance-of-sleep/).

- Show students any of the videos on "The Best" list and have them take notes related to each of the categories, again adding new information under each one.

- Have students make a poster divided into four sections—one for each category—and write a summary sentence and draw an illustration for each one.

- Have students write a topic sentence and provide supporting evidence for it for each one of the categories, and then combine them all into one essay with an introduction and conclusion.

- Use any of the online tools suggested in previous chapters to create online representations of what they have learned in this lesson.

Ed Tech

Students could create an infographic using the information they have learned about sleep. They can look at sleep infographics on "The Best Resources for Helping Students Learn About the Importance of Sleep" (http://larryferlazzo.edublogs.org/2010/08/05/the-best-resources-for-helping-teens-learn-about-the-importance-of-sleep/) as models. Resources and lesson plans on creating infographics can be found at "The Best Resources for Creating Infographics" (http://larryferlazzo.edublogs.org/2011/01/11/the-best-resources-for-creating-infographics/).

Building a Community of Self-Motivated Learners

Figure 5.1 Sleep Quotes

1. "As a well-spent day brings happy sleep"
   (Leonardo da Vinci; http://en.wikiquote.org/wiki/Leonardo_da_Vinci)

2. "The woods are lovely, dark and deep. But I have promises to keep, and miles to go before I sleep."
   (Robert Frist)

3. "Then the gods send us their refreshful sleep, Which good and evil from our mind doth sweep."
   (Homer in *The Odyssey*)

4. "I change during the course of a day. I wake and I'm one person, and when I go to sleep I know for certain I'm somebody else."
   (Bob Dylan, "I'm Not There," http://en.wikiquote.org/wiki/I%27m_Not_There)

5. "A good laugh and a long sleep are the best cures in the doctor's book."
   (A supposed Irish proverb)

6. "It is a common experience that a problem difficult at night is resolved in the morning after the committee of sleep has worked on it."
   (John Steinbeck, *Sweet Thursday*; http://en.wikiquote.org/wiki/John_Steinbeck)

Figure 5.2   Sleep Data Set

Categories for Sleep Data Set:
Sleep, School, and Learning
Sleep and Weight
Sleep and Mental and Physical Health
Obstacles to Getting Enough Sleep

1. "Smartphones and tablets can make for sleep-disrupting bedfellows. One cause is believed to be the bright light-emitting diodes that allow the use of mobile devices in dimly lit rooms; the light exposure can interfere with melatonin, a hormone that helps control the natural sleep-wake cycle. But there may be a way to check your mobile device in bed and still get a good night's sleep. A Mayo Clinic study suggests dimming the smartphone or tablet brightness settings and holding the device at least 14 inches from your face while using it will reduce its potential to interfere with melatonin and impede sleep." (Mayo Clinic, 2013, http://www.sciencedaily.com/releases/2013/06/130 603163610.htm?utm_source=feedburner&utm_medium=feed&utm_cam paign=Feed%3A+sciencedaily%2Fmind_brain+%28ScienceDaily%3A+ Mind+%26+Brain+News%29&utm_content=Google+Reader)

2. One study reports that "inadequate sleep worsens a teen's insulin resistance—and therefore probably increases the teen's risk of eventually getting diabetes . . . The American Academy of Sleep Medicine says most adolescents need a little more than nine hours of sleep every night, but the new study says that up to 87 percent of teens don't get enough sleep on school nights." (Akst, 2012, http://blogs.wsj.com/ideas-market/2012/10/03/for-gods-sake-let-the-kids-sleep/?mod=WSJBlog)

3. "When adolescents don't get adequate sleep, they experience health problems, according to the National Sleep Foundation, including impaired alertness and attention, which is important in academics but also important for those teenagers who drive to and from school. Sleep deprivation can also inhibit the ability to solve problems, cope with stress, and retain information, and is often associated with emotional and behavioral problems such as depression and substance abuse." (Cairney, 2013, http://www.edweek.org/ew/articles/2013/03/15/26sleep. h32.html?tkn=NZOFcHYMHycjmHZgFP7ph8fb93il2ZRJOzWB&cmp= clp-edweek)

4. Research shows that the less you sleep, the more your brain craves high-calorie junk foods. And if you're sleeping less, research also shows that the parts of the brain that govern self-control don't work as well. In other

(continued)

Figure 5.2 Sleep Data Set (*continued*)

words, "A sleepy brain appears to not only respond more strongly to junk food, but also has less ability to rein that impulse in."
(O'Connor, 2013, http://well.blogs.nytimes.com/2013/08/06/how-sleep-loss-adds-to-weight-gain/?smid=tw-nytimeswell&seid=auto).

5. One study "showed that two hours of iPad use at maximum brightness was enough to suppress people's normal nighttime release of melatonin, a key hormone in the body's clock, or circadian system. Melatonin tells your body that it is night, helping to make you sleepy. If you delay that signal . . . you could delay sleep."
(Sutherland, 2012, http://www.scientificamerican.com/article/bright-screens-could-delay-bedtime/)

6. "Sleep after learning encourages brain cells to make connections with other brain cells, research shows for the first time. The connections, called dendritic spines, enable the flow of information across the synapses."
(How Sleep After Learning Enhances Memory, 2014, http://www.spring.org.uk/2014/06/how-sleep-after-learning-enhances-memory.php)

7. "Sleep . . . refines the memories formed during the previous day and makes preparations for the learning that will begin the next morning. Irrelevant memories are discarded and important memories are preserved, moved to the brain's long-term storage to make room for new memories."
(Paul, 2014, http://anniemurphypaul.com/2014/07/educating-kids-about-sleep/)

8. In experiments, people gained, on average, 2.2 pounds after five nights of limited sleep.
(Alexander, 2013, http://www.today.com/health/later-you-stay-more-you-eat-study-shows-6C10488450)

9. Researchers have found that "television [is] stimulating for the brain, keeping watchers alert rather than allowing them to start shutting down for the day, the lights from the screen may also act as a biologically-based wake-up call. There is a suggestion that TV affects sleep hormones because screens emit blue light and that could delay sleep onset," says [researcher Louise] Foley.
(Rochman, 2013, http://healthland.time.com/2013/01/16/sleep-stealers-whats-keeping-children-from-getting-enough-shut-eye/)

10. "During sleep, the body produces cytokines, cellular hormones that help fight infections. Thus, short sleepers may be more susceptible to everyday infections like colds and flu."
(Brody, 2013, http://well.blogs.nytimes.com/2013/06/17/cheating-ourselves-of-sleep/?smid=tw-nytimes)

(continued)

Figure 5.2 Sleep Data Set (*continued*)

11. "A . . . study shows that teens who don't get enough sleep are more likely to suffer from depression and have suicidal thoughts—in some cases—much more likely."
    (Sleep-Deprived Teens' Disturbing Thoughts, 2010, http://www.cbsnews. com/news/sleep-deprived-teens-disturbing-thoughts/)

12. Students who sleep one-half more (moving from nine to nine-and-a-half hours) "showed improvement in alertness, behavior and emotions" researchers found in one experiment.
    (Paul, 2012, http://anniemurphypaul.com/2012/10/just-a-little-more-sleep-makes-kids-ready-to-learn/)

13. "Starting school just 30 minutes later [from 8:00 am to 8:30 am] was linked with significant improvements in adolescents' reported sleep times, mood and health," according to one study.
    (Dooren, 2012, http://online.wsj.com/news/articles/SB1000142405274 8704535004575349182901006438?mg=reno64-wsj&url=http%3A%2F %2Fonline.wsj.com%2Farticle%2FSB10001424052748704535004 575349182901006438.html)

14. In one study, "sleep-deprived eaters ended up eating more calories during after-dinner snacking than in any other meal during the day. Over all, people consumed 6 percent more calories when they got too little sleep. Once they started sleeping more, they began eating more healthfully, consuming fewer carbohydrates and fats."
    (Parker-Pope, 2013, http://well.blogs.nytimes.com/2013/03/18/lost-sleep-can-lead-to-weight-gain/?partner=rss&emc=rss&smid=tw-nytimes)

15. "Metabolism slows when one's circadian rhythm and sleep are disrupted; if not counteracted by increased exercise or reduced caloric intake, this slow-down could add up to 10 extra pounds in a year."
    (Brody, 2013, http://well.blogs.nytimes.com/2013/06/17/cheating-oursel ves-of-sleep/?smid=tw-nytimes)

16. "We are actually learning during sleep," says [sleep expert Helene] Emsel-lem. In some sleep stages, our brains are taking the information we've gath-ered during the day "and laying it down into the memories that are going to allow us to retrieve the information" at a later time, she explains.
    (Aubrey, 2013, http://www.npr.org/blogs/health/2013/03/01/173150 812/sacrificing-sleep-makes-for-run-down-teens-and-parents)

Good Nutrition

Similar to sleep problems, nutrition-related issues can also have an impact on student motivation—a diet rich in "junk food" can cause fatigue, make it more difficult for the brain to learn and remember (Walton, 2012), and increase the chances of suffering from depression ("The Link Between Fast Food," 2012).

Immediate Actions to Support Student Nutrition

Teachers Modeling Healthy Eating

Researchers have found (Osowski et al., 2013, p. 425) that teachers modeling eating a healthy diet can have a positive effect on student nutrition. This practice is also recommend by the Centers for Disease Control (Promoting Lifelong Healthy Eating, n.d.). Of course, teachers need to also have their lunch breaks honored, so teachers eating regularly in the school cafeteria is not a reasonable or fair expectation. However, teachers letting students eat their lunches in classrooms is not an uncommon experience in many schools, and provides an opportunity for this kind of teacher modeling.

Healthy Nutrition Posters in the Classroom

Studies have also found that classroom posters publicizing healthy nutrition habits can also positively affect student nutrition habits (Osowski et al., 2013, p. 425). One extension activity for the "Nutrition and Exercise" lesson plan is to have students create posters documenting what they learned, and to hang them up on the classroom walls and/or other places around the school.

Making Sure That Any Teacher-Provided Food is Healthy

In *Helping Students Motivate Themselves* (Ferlazzo, 2011), I discussed research—and my own experience—that found that a loss of self-control can sometimes be connected to a loss of glucose, and that teachers providing particularly challenging students on occasion with graham crackers, peanut butter, or trail mix (of course, being conscious of students with allergies) could be an option worth considering (p. 51). In addition, despite the availability of free meals at lunch, it's not unusual to find many of our students often hungry. I'm sure I'm not alone in having food available for when that situation arises, and teachers can be conscious about the type we offer to students.

Helping Students Motivate Themselves (Ferlazzo, 2011) has a chapter on using learning games (particularly ones played in small groups) in the classroom (p. 173). In my experience, students get so involved in the fun and friendly competition that the majority of time there is no need for any other kind of reward. At times, though, despite all of my commentary against the use of rewards, a small one can be a nice bonus to offer "winners" of a classroom game. Some nutrition advocates oppose the idea of offering any kind of food as a reward (Alternatives to Food Rewards, 2011), but most of the negative feelings revolve around the common use of candy for that purpose. Since I do not use it often in my classroom, I find that graham crackers, healthy granola bars, and 100 percent fruit rolls are relatively inexpensive alternatives.

Setting the Stage: Nutrition and Exercise Lesson

Research also shows that classroom lessons on nutrition can have a positive impact on student health (Brownstein & MyHealthNewsDaily, 2011). The danger, of course, in tackling any issue like this is that "preaching" to students is unlikely to be effective. This lesson, as with other lessons in this chapter and in this book, tries to take what researchers recommend about giving advice (Ferlazzo, 2013, p. 14)—providing information people do not know is better than telling them what you think they should do—to heart. This perspective promotes autonomy, though doesn't preclude us from asking questions that might help others clarify their own thinking (Bluestein, 2013).

The lesson also incorporates another important finding made by researchers—that teenagers learning about how much exercise would be required to "work off" the food they eat is much more effective at making them conscious of nutrition than calorie counts on food labels (Shea, 2012).

Ed Tech

The Nutrition Lesson Plan is designed to last three class periods. However, numerous possible extension activities are also listed, including expanding it to include a more complete review of advertising techniques, using infographics, and exploring online interactive exercises and games. Resources to support these extension activities can be found at http://larryferlazzo.edublogs.org/2010/01/19/the-best-sites-for-learning-about-nutrition-food-safety/; at http://larryferlazzo.edublogs.org/2009/07/19/the-best-sites-to-learn-about-advertising/; and "The Best Resources for Creating Infographics" (http://larryferlazzo.edublogs.org/2011/01/11/the-best-resources-for-creating-infographics/).

Breakfast Mini-Lesson

An increasing amount of research is reinforcing the legitimacy of calling breakfast "the most important meal of the day." Eating breakfast, particularly a healthy one, is linked to improved cognition and mental and physical health for students (Basch, 2010, p. 50). Specifically, it improves "alertness, attention, memory, processing of complex visual display, problem solving" (Health and Academic Achievement, 2014, p. 2)

The "Breakfast" mini-lesson, which should last approximately 30 to 35 minutes, can be taught at some point prior to, or following, the "Junk Food" lesson. Teaching it is another opportunity to respect the Centers for Disease Control's urging that health and nutrition information not be done as a single lesson during the school year and, instead, be reinforced regularly.

Nutrition and Exercise Lesson Plan

Instructional Objectives for Students

- Students will read several complex texts on nutrition, advertising and neuroscience and apply reading strategies to assist in comprehension.

- Students will synthesize what they learn and present it to their classmates.

- Students will make it relevant to their lives by applying what they learned towards making specific nutrition-related goals.

Duration

Three 60-minute periods, though it might take three-and-a-half periods.

Materials

- Document camera or overhead projector with screen.

- Access to a computer lab on the third day, or laptops for each student.

- Highlighters for each student.

- Copies for each student of the article "The Connection Between Good Nutrition and Cognition" (Walton, 2012) (http://www.theatlantic.com/health/archive/2012/01/the-connection-between-good-nutrition-and-good-cognition/251227/).

- Student copies of "Junk Food and Your Brain" Read Aloud (Figure 5.3); "What Foods Seem to Help the Brain?" (Figure 5.4) and "Nutrition Planning Sheet" (Figure 5.5).

- Student copies of: Bittman (2011); Taylor (n.d.); Harris, Schwartz, & Brownell (2010) (p. ix starting at "Results" and p. x—only).

Common Core English Language Arts Standards

Reading:

- Determine central ideas or themes of a text and analyze their development; summarize the key supporting details and ideas.

Speaking and Listening:

- Prepare for and participate effectively in a range of conversations and collaborations with diverse partners, building on others' ideas and expressing their own clearly and persuasively.

- Adapt speech to a variety of contexts and communicative tasks, demonstrating command of formal English when indicated or appropriate.

Language

- Demonstrate command of the conventions of standard English grammar and usage when writing or speaking.

Procedure

First Day

1. Write on the board, or show on an overhead, this question as students enter the classroom: "What shrinks your brain, can turn you into an addict, and costs a fair amount of money?" Ask students to think about this question for 30 seconds without saying what they believe to be the answer. Then asks students to share their response with a neighbor. You might want to go quickly through the room and ask students to shout out what they answered and keep a "running tally" on the board.

2. You might say that students correctly identified a few answers that were correct, and today the class is going to focus on one—junk food. Ask students to write down on a piece of paper what they think "junk food" is and include examples. After one minute, begin calling on students to share what they wrote and write them on the overhead. Ask students to raise their hand if they have eaten junk food in the past 24 hours.

3. Say that everyone knows that eating a lot of junk food can make you put on weight, and that it isn't healthy. But today, the class is primarily going to learn about other impacts of junk food. Explain that the class is first going to start by reading a short article in pairs but, first, you want to review two words. Write "cognitive" and "trans fats" on the board, ask students to take 20 seconds to think about the two words, then share with a neighbor what they think it means. Call on a student or two to share, then clarify what the two words mean.

4. Explain that you are going to give an article to each student, and they will work in pairs (sometimes it can be a nice change of pace to pair up students creatively—"work with someone who has the same color socks . . . different color shirt . . . same color shoelaces"). Distribute highlighters, and explain that each student will take a turn reading a paragraph to the other student. As they read, they are to highlight three to six words in each paragraph that are important to the main idea of the passage and they are to pick one paragraph where they write a question and another where they make a connection to a personal experience, another text they've read, or a movie they've seen. Model doing this in the first paragraph after reading it out loud. Also read it aloud with prosody (with feeling) and asks students to do the same when they are reading to their partners. Contrast that by reading one sentence in a monotone. After they are done, students should

write a one-sentence summary of the entire article. Explain that they will need to save all their nutrition materials and will hand them in as packets at the end of the unit. They will have ten minutes. Then distribute the article, "The Connection Between Good Nutrition and Cognition" (Walton, 2012) to each student.

5. When the assignment is completed, ask a few students to share their summary sentence with the entire class.

6. Say you want to let students know about a few other things junk food does to the brain, and put the Read Aloud titled "Junk Food and Your Brain" (Figure 5.3) on the overhead. Ask students to read along silently as you read it to the class. Afterwards, distribute copies to the class, and asks students to put a check mark next to a piece of information they think is most surprising or interesting to them. Also ask them to write a sentence at the bottom of the sheet saying why they found it surprising or interesting.

7. Ask students to share with a new partner—someone they haven't already worked with today—which point on the Read Aloud they chose and why they chose it. Circulate and identify two or three students to share with the entire class afterwards.

8. Explain that tomorrow students will learn a few more things about junk food, including what advertisers do to persuade you to buy and eat it. Then, on the third and last day of this unit, students will be going to the computer lab and will list what junk food they eat and visit a website that will tell them how much they have to exercise in order to "work it off."

Second Day

1. Write on the board or overhead, "What is the most important thing you learned yesterday?" before students enter the classroom. As they sit down, point to the question and ask students to take out a piece of paper and write their response, and say you would like them to try to be specific.

2. After a minute, ask students to pair-share what they wrote—telling them and not just giving them the piece of paper. Call on a few students to share with the entire class.

3. Explain that today the class is going to do something called a "jigsaw." You are going to give everyone a number—either 1, 2, or 3 (it might be easier to organize if you just divide the room into thirds and everyone on the left third is a number 1, if they are in the middle they are a 2, and on the right they're a 3). Each number will get a different article. They will pair up with another student with the same number, taking turns reading each paragraph, and then writing one sentence summarizing each page. In addition,

they are to use the reading strategy of visualizing by drawing a picture of what the text is making them see in their mind on one page, and on another page they are to write about a connection they can make to the text from their personal experience or another text they have read. Then, each pair will complete a graphic organizer or complete the assignments that you write on the overhead. This organizer/assignment could vary, but it might include listing three important points in the article, one or two quotations, a drawing, and questions they might have. Each pair should prepare a presentation—involving both in speaking roles—that should last no longer than four minutes. Begin the process by distributing copies of the three articles: Bittman "http://www.nytimes.com/2011/09/25/opinion/sunday/is-junk-food-really-cheaper.html?pagewanted=all&_r=0" Is Junk Food Really Cheaper? (http://www.nytimes.com/2011/09/25/opinion/sunday/is-junk-food-really-cheaper.html?pagewanted=all&_r=0) (2011); Taylor "http://fit.webmd.com/teen/food/article/fast-food-advertising" Are Fast-Food Advertisers Playing You? (http://fit.webmd.com/teen/food/article/fast-food-advertising) (n.d.); Harris et al. "http://www.fastfoodmarketing.org/media/FastFoodFACTS_Report.pdf" Fast Food FACTS (http://www.fastfoodmarketing.org/media/FastFoodFACTS_Report.pdf) (2010) (page ix starting at "Results" and p. x—only)—giving each student only the article that he/she will be presenting to the class. Give students 20 minutes to complete this activity. (Note: Research shows that students are more highly motivated to learn, and retain more information, when they know they are going to teach material to someone else (Expecting to teach, 2014).)

4. Create groups of six students each—one pair who are each numbers 1, 2, and 3. Students get into their groups and make their presentations. Give students 20 minutes to complete this activity. Afterwards, give students copies of all three articles.

5. Bring everybody back together and ask them to think for a few seconds and be prepared to share the most interesting thing they learned today. Ask students to quickly share with a partner and then asks a few students to share with the entire class.

Third Day

1. Explain that we've been learning a lot about the problems caused by eating junk food. One way to deal with it is by eating less, and we can also eat foods that help our brain. The same research that shows junk food can damage our brain says that eating food high in Omega 3 fatty acids can help reduce the damage the junk food causes.

2. Put "What Foods Seem to Help the Brain?" (Figure 5.4) on the overhead and read it. Then give each student a copy of it, and tell them to put it with all the rest of their nutrition materials.

3. Next, ask students to make a list of anything they would consider junk food that they have eaten in the past week (you can refer back to the class list they made on the first day). Say that students can be honest, and that no one will see this list but them. Explain that the class is going to go to the computer lab (or use laptops in class) and go to a site called Calorie King (http://www.calorieking.com). (A site called "Lose It" [http://loseit.com/] provides similar information but it is more complicated to use and requires registration [if neither site is available, an alternative is to have students go to one of the many sites on the Web that list calories for every food and then go to one of the other numerous sites, like My Fitness Pal [http://www.myfitnesspal.com/exercise/lookup], that tell you how many calories you burn doing what kind of exercise for what amount of time.) You can write the URL on the overhead and ask students to copy it down. Tell students that after they type in each kind of junk food they ate, Calorie King will show how many minutes they have to jog, walk, ride a bicycle, or swim in order to "work off" the calories they ate. Ask them to list the number of minutes students have to jog for each piece of food (studies have shown that the number of jogging minutes makes the most impression on teens because it is one of the least enjoyable exercises for many of them [Shea, 2012]; however, you might want to be flexible if there are a few students who want to choose one of the other forms of exercise listed. The most important point is that they use the *same* exercise for all their foods). Then, after they go through all their listed foods, they should add up the total number of minutes and write it down.

4. Bring the students to the computer lab (or distribute laptops), where they should be able to complete the activity in 20 minutes.

5. If you feel comfortable sharing, it might be useful to share your list and say something like, "This is pretty scary to me—I certainly don't get enough exercise to work off the junk food I eat." However, you probably do not want to ask students to share because some student responses might create an opportunity for ridicule—if not in class, then perhaps later. The point of the activity is for students to see for themselves how much junk food they eat and its potential consequences.

6. Show the "Nutrition Planning Sheet" (Figure 5.5) on the overhead. Explain that students are now going to reflect on what they have learned over the past three days and decide if they want to apply any of it to their lives. Model completing the sheet and explain that research shows that framing goals as

a question and then answering it generates a stronger feeling of commitment (Ferlazzo, 2011, p. 11), and that's why the sheet is set up the way it is.

Also explain that you understand students are not necessarily in complete control of the food choices they have (though they do have some choices—for example, if they eat a school-provided lunch they can choose which one they eat). Because of that, if they decide they want to eat more of a particular food, they might have to talk with their parent or guardian. If they choose to have that conversation, they might want to keep in mind what research says about how to give advice effectively—instead of just telling people what to do, giving them new information to consider works better. You can say that this is the way this whole lesson has been designed—you are not telling people they have to make diet changes, you are just providing information that they can consider. Students could use the same strategy when talking to their families.

Model taking out the "What Foods Seem to Help the Brain?" hand-out and choosing one, and then write out a strategy you'll use to implement it ("Talk to my partner about the importance of Omega 3 fatty acids in helping the brain.")

Then model looking at the list of junk foods you made and choosing one you want to eat less. Then explain that research shows that a good strategy to combat temptation is to plan ahead for a way to distract yourself (ideally, the class has already learned this through the "Self-Control" lesson plan in *Helping Students Motivate Themselves* (Ferlazzo, 2011, p. 57) using the famous marshmallow experiment). Write down something you will use (for example, "I will visualize my brain being eaten away by the junk food").

Also explain that students will be able to choose a "buddy" with whom they'll meet every week for a few minutes to see how each one of them is doing in achieving their goals and to offer advice to the other on challenges they might be facing. They can also decide if they want to add new goals in the future.

Explain that it is fine if any students decide they don't want to make any changes in the food they eat, too. If that is the case, they should just write a couple of sentences explaining why they do not.

7. If there is time in the class period, pass out the Planning Sheets for students to complete. If not, you can either assign it as homework or wait to pass out the sheets the next day and give students seven minutes to complete them. Afterwards, students can pick their "buddies" (you could also consider allowing groups of three). Collect the Planning Sheets, make copies that day, and return the originals to the students. Any student who has decided not to make a food change can read a book quietly during this time. Complete the lesson by asking a few students to share their goals with the class. In addition, ask students to staple all the other materials they have used and annotated during the lesson together in the correct order (you can write them on the overhead), put their name on it, and then turn them in.

8. If there is not enough time to complete the Planning Sheet and discussion, the class can complete it during the first portion of the fourth day. It is important not to shortchange this part of the lesson.

9. During the next few weeks, "buddies" could meet for a few minutes during class every Friday.

Assessment

1. The annotated student packets and planning sheets should provide a good enough representation of student work for assessment.

2. If desired, you could develop your own rubrics for use with this activity. See Ferlazzo (2010, September 18) for multiple free online tools for use in easily creating a rubric.

3. You could also ask students to write an "ABC" paragraph (see previous lesson plan) responding to the question, "What do you think is the worst thing about junk food?"

Possible Extensions/Modifications

Most of the following extensions can be done immediately following the lesson or at any other point. In fact, spreading them out as "mini-lessons" throughout the year would serve as a useful reminder to students about what they have learned related to nutrition and their own health.

- Student can spend half a class period using online nutrition interactives and games. See the Ed Tech: Nutrition and Advertising Resources box for the sites where students can access them.

- You could spend another period or two doing an expanded lesson on the types of persuasive techniques that advertisers use. The resources listed in the Ed Tech box lead to multiple useful lesson plans and online interactives.

- Students can review the nutrition infographics available in the Ed Tech box and create their own infographic displaying important information they have learned. Those tools are also accessible through links in the Ed Tech box.

- You can show excerpts of the movie *Super Size Me*—available free online in a number of places (search online). Multiple engaging movie-related lesson plans are also available by searching the Web.

- This nutrition lesson plan can be connected to the lesson plans on sleep in *Helping Students Motivate Themselves* (Ferlazzo, 2011) and in this chapter, and the research mentioned earlier in this chapter about how lack of sleep generates junk food cravings.

- Students can research the nutritional guidelines used by the school district for school-provided lunches and see if they want to meet with staff to suggest improvements.

- Students can turn the goals and strategies they wrote about in their Planning Sheets into posters with drawings and text that can be hung on the classroom's walls as a reminder to the class.

- Students can create posters for the classroom and other areas of the school where they share information they have learned about nutrition.

Figure 5.3   Junk Food and Your Brain Read Aloud

- A University of California-Los Angeles study in 2012 showed that a diet high in sugar and corn syrup makes it more difficult for your brain to learn and remember. Those are key ingredients in items like soda and other processed food (Schmidt, 2012).

- People who eat a lot of fast food are 51 percent more likely to suffer from depression than those who don't eat any or very little ("The Link Between Fast Food and Depression," 2012).

- "Research suggests that processed foods and sugary drinks . . . aren't simply unhealthy. They can hijack the brain in ways that resemble addictions to cocaine, nicotine and other drugs. The data is so overwhelming the field has to accept it," said Nora Volkow, director of the National Institute on Drug Abuse. "We are finding tremendous overlap between drugs in the brain and food in the brain." (Langreth & Stanford, 2011).

- Eating food high in trans-fats has been found to make people more irritable and aggressive (Chan, 2012).

Figure 5.4 What Foods Seem to Help the Brain?

Eating foods rich in Omega-3 fatty acids seems to help the brain counteract some of the damage caused by junk food. These foods include:

salmon	spinach
walnuts	sardines
Brussel sprouts	tuna
salad greens	mackerel
green beans	
shrimp	
strawberries	
kale	
kiwi fruit	
canola oil	
soybean oil	
flaxseeds	

Sources: Schmidt (2012)
Wolpert (2008)
"Your Omega-3 Shopping List" (n.d.)
"Ask the Expert: Omega-3 Fatty Acids" (n.d.)

Building a Community of Self-Motivated Learners

Figure 5.5 Nutrition Planning Sheet

Student Name _____

One food I will eat more of . . .

Can I eat more _____?

Yes, I can eat more _____.

I will help make this happen by _____

_____.

One food I will eat less of . . .

Can I eat fewer _____?

Yes, I can eat fewer _____.

If I am tempted to eat _____,
I will distract myself by _____.

My support buddy is _____.

Breakfast Mini-Lesson Plan

Procedure

1. Begin by asking students to think for a minute about the last three days and ask them to write first if they ate breakfast on each of those days and, if so, what they ate on each of them. After a minute, ask students to share what they wrote with a partner.

2. Ask for a show of hands of students who have eaten breakfast on each of those days. Then, if you have already taught the longer "junk food" lesson, you can say we're going to do a very short follow-up lesson to the one on junk food we did a month ago (or whenever it was done). If that lesson hasn't been taught, you can just say we're going to spend a few minutes talking about breakfast and its importance.

3. Show one of the videos at "The Best Resources on Why Breakfast is Important for Teenagers" (http://larryferlazzo.edublogs.org/2014/07/27/the-best-resources-on-why-breakfast-is-important-for-teenagers/) which show news reporters giving a short report on why researchers say breakfast is the most important meal of the day. Prior to showing the video, ask students to plan on writing down two things they find interesting—they can write them down on the same piece of paper. Each video is only two to four minutes long (the direct links to two of them are "Breakfast Exercise Boost Brain Activity" (http://www.clickondetroit.com/news/Good-Health-Breakfast-exercise-boost-brain-activity/20108460) and "Importance of Eating Breakfast" (https://www.youtube.com/watch?v=jV_OdWTM9QQ)—more can be found on the previously mentioned "Best" list.

4. Then give half of the class the article "A Better Breakfast Can Boost a Child's Brainpower" (Aubrey, 2013, http://www.npr.org/templates/story/story.php?storyId=5738848) and the other half the article "Breakfast Keeps Teenagers Lean" (http://news.bbc.co.uk/2/hi/7275554.stm). Tell them that they can read the article together with another student who has the same article (taking turns reading each paragraph aloud) and highlight or underline a few key words in each paragraph—no more than three to six words in each. They each then have to make their own very simple poster, using a piece of paper and markers, that lists the three most important points made in the article, features a drawing illustrating the main idea of the article, and lists one thing they believe they might remember about the article in the future and why they think it might stick with them. In 15 minutes they will be paired with a student reading the other article, and then they each have to verbally present their poster to each other. Circulate throughout the class

during this time, telling students to whom they will be presenting, and asking them to write down the name of that person so they don't forget. Also note which students you might want to make a point of asking later to share with the entire class.

5. At the end of 15 minutes, tell students to go to their new partner and give them five minutes to present to each other.

6. After five minutes call on a few students to share with the entire class what they listed as the point they will remember after today. Then ask students to take a minute to think about if they want to do anything differently in their mornings based on what they learned today. If they do, ask them to write it down on the sheet of paper where they wrote what they had for breakfast the previous days, and to also write a few words about why they want to make that change—one sentence would be fine. It's okay to feel like they don't want to make any changes, either—they just need to write down why on that same sheet. Circulate for that minute or two to see what students are writing to identify people you might want to call on to share with the entire class.

7. End the lesson by calling on certain students to share things they might want to do differently, making sure most are positive comments. Then say students can remember these as potential items for their goal sheets (see Chapter 1). Say you will collect the sheets and posters and put some up on the classroom walls as reminders.

8. You can end it there or, if there is time and if desired, end it by showing the *Sesame Street* video "The Most Important Meal Song" (https://www.you tube.com/watch?v=LPqvODHZt_c) for fun. My teenage students still love *Sesame Street*, but teachers should use their own judgment.

References

Akst, D. (2012, October 3). For God's sake, let the kids sleep! *The Wall Street Journal*. Retrieved from: http://blogs.wsj.com/ideas-market/2012/10/03/for-gods-sake-let-the-kids-sleep/?mod=WSJBlog

Alexander, B. (2013, June 30). The later you stay up, the more you eat, study shows. *Today Health*. Retrieved from: http://www.today.com/health/later-you-stay-more-you-eat-study-shows-6C10488450

Alternatives to food rewards (2011, November). Connecticut State Department of Education. Retrieved from: http://healthymeals.nal.usda.gov/hsmrs/Connecticut/Food_As_Reward.pdf

Ask the expert: Omega-3 fatty acids (n.d.). Harvard School of Public Health. Retrieved from: http://www.hsph.harvard.edu/nutritionsource/questions/omega-3/index.html

Aubrey, A. (2006, September 4). A better breakfast can boost a child's brain-power. *NPR*. Retrieved from: http://www.npr.org/templates/story/story.php?storyId=5738848

Aubrey, A. (2013, March 1). Sacrificing sleep makes for run-down teens—and parents. *NPR*. Retrieved from: http://www.npr.org/blogs/health/2013/03/01/173150812/sacrificing-sleep-makes-for-run-down-teens-and-parents

Barnes, C.M. (2013, June 11). Lack of sleep and stress—a vicious cycle you can escape. *Huffington Post*. Retrieved from: http://www.huffingtonpost.com/christopher-m-barnes/sleep-and-stress_b_3415480.html

Basch, C.E. (2010, March). Healthier students are better learners: A missing link in school reforms to close the achievement gap. *Equity Matters* (Research Review No. 6). Retrieved from: http://www.equitycampaign.org/i/a/document/12557_EquityMattersVol6_Web03082010.pdf

Bergland, C. (2013, June 5). Exposure to natural light improves workplace performance. *Psychology Today*. Retrieved from: http://www.psychologytoday.com/blog/the-athletes-way/201306/exposure-natural-light-improves-workplace-performance

Bittman, M. (2011, September 24). Is junk food really cheaper? *The New York Times Sunday Review*. Retrieved from: http://www.nytimes.com/2011/09/25/opinion/sunday/is-junk-food-really-cheaper.html?pagewanted=all

Bluestein, J. (2013, May 8). *An alternative to advice giving*. Retrieved from: http://janebluestein.com/2013/an-alternative-to-advice-giving

Breakfast "keeps teenagers lean" (2008, March 3). *BBC News*. Retrieved from: http://news.bbc.co.uk/2/hi/7275554.stm

Brody, J.E. (2013, June 17). Cheating ourselves of sleep. *The New York Times*. Retrieved from: http://well.blogs.nytimes.com/2013/06/17/cheating-ourselves-of-sleep/?smid=tw-nytimes

Brownstein, J., & MyHealthNewsDaily (2011, December 7). Childhood obesity best battled in schools, research finds. *Scientific American*. Retrieved from: http://www.scientificamerican.com/article.cfm?id=childhood-obesity-best

Cairney, G. (2013, March 15). Experts make a case for later school start times. *Education Week*. Retrieved from: http://www.edweek.org/ew/articles/2013/03/15/26sleep.h32.html?tkn=NZOFcHYMHycjmHZgFP7ph8fb93iI2ZRJ0zWB&cmp=clp-edweek

Chan, A.L. (2012, March 13). Trans fats linked with aggression, study finds. *Huffpost Healthy Living*. Retrieved from: http://www.huffingtonpost.com/2012/03/13/trans-fats-aggression-irritability-crabby_n_1342856.html

Characteristics of an effective health education curriculum (n.d.). Centers for Disease Control. Retrieved from: http://www.cdc.gov/healthyyouth/sher/characteristics

Dooren, J.C. (2010, July 6). Later start to school boosts teens' health. *The Wall Street Journal*. Retrieved from: http://online.wsj.com/news/articles/SB10001424052748704535004575349182901006438?mg=reno64-wsj&url=http%3A%2F%2Fonline.wsj.com%2Farticle%2FSB10001424052748704535004575349182901006438.html

Expecting to teach enhances recall, learning. (2014, August 8). Retrieved from: http://www.eurekalert.org/pub_releases/2014–08/wuis-ett080814.php

Ferlazzo, L. (2009, July 19). The best sites to learn about advertising. *Larry Ferlazzo's websites of the day.* Retrieved from: http://larryferlazzo.edublogs.org/2009/07/19/the-best-sites-to-learn-about-advertising/

Ferlazzo, L. (2010, January 19). The best sites for learning about nutrition & food safety. *Larry Ferlazzo's websites of the day.* Retrieved from http://larryferlazzo.edublogs.org/2010/01/19/the-best-sites-for-learning-about-nutrition-food-safety/

Ferlazzo, L. (2010, August 5). The best resources for helping teens learn about the importance of sleep. *Larry Ferlazzo's websites of the day.* Retrieved from: http://larryferlazzo.edublogs.org/2010/08/05/the-best-resources-for-help ing-teens-learn-about-the-importance-of-sleep/

Ferlazzo, L. (2010, September 18). The best rubric sites (and a beginning discussion about their use). *Larry Ferlazzo's websites of the day.* Retrieved from: http://larryferlazzo.edublogs.org/2010/09/18/the-best-rubric-sites-and-a-begin ning-discussion-about-their-use/

Ferlazzo, L. (2010, December 28). The best places to learn what impact a teacher and outside factors have on student achievement. *Larry Ferlazzo's websites of the day.* Retrieved from: http://larryferlazzo.edublogs.org/2010/12/28/the-best-places-to-learn-what-impact-a-teacher-outside-factors-have-on-stud ent-achievement

Ferlazzo, L. (2011). *Helping students motivate themselves.* Larchmont, NY: Eye on Education.

Ferlazzo, L. (2011, January 11). The best resources for creating infographics. *Larry Ferlazzo's websites of the day.* Retrieved from: http://larryferlazzo.edublogs.org/2011/01/11/the-best-resources-for-creating-infographics/

Ferlazzo, L. (2013). *Self-driven learning: Teaching strategies for student motivation.* New York: Routledge.

Ferlazzo, L. (2014, July 27). The best resources on why breakfast is important for teenagers. *Larry Ferlazzo's websites of the day.* Retrieved from: http://larry-ferlazzo.edublogs.org/2014/07/27/the-best-resources-on-why-breakfast-is-important-for-teenagers

Good health: Breakfast, exercise boost brain activity (2013, May 11). *Clickon Detroit.* Retrieved from: http://www.clickondetroit.com/news/Good-Health-Breakfast-exercise-boost-brain-activity/20108460

Harris, J. L., Schwartz, M. B., & Brownell, K. D. (2010, November). *Fast Food FACTS: Evaluating fast food nutrition and marketing to youth.* New Haven, CT: Yale Rudd Center for Food Policy and Obesity. Retrieved from: http://www.fastfood marketing.org/media/FastFoodFACTS_Report.pdf

Health and academic achievement. (2014, May). Centers for Disease Control. Retrieved from: http://www.cdc.gov/healthyyouth/health_and_academics/pdf/health-academic-achievement.pdf

How sleep after learning enhances memory (2014, June 10). *PsyBlog.* Retrieved from: http://www.spring.org.uk/2014/06/how-sleep-after-learning-enhan ces-memory.php

I'm not there (n.d.). *Wikiquote*. Retrieved from: http://en.wikiquote.org/wiki/I%27m_Not_There

Importance of eating breakfast (2010, November 15). Gunderson Health System. *YouTube*. Retrieved from: https://www.youtube.com/watch?v=jV_OdWTM9QQ

John Steinbeck (n.d.). *Wikiquote*. Retrieved from: http://en.wikiquote.org/wiki/John_Steinbeck

Langreth, R., & Stanford, D.D. (2011, November 11). Fatty foods addictive as cocaine in growing body of science. *Bloomberg BusinessWeek*. Retrieved from: http://www.businessweek.com/news/2011–11–11/fatty-foods-addictive-as-cocaine-in-growing-body-of-science.html#p1

Lehrer, J. (2012, June 8). It's good to be the top banana. *The Wall Street Journal*. Retrieved from: http://online.wsj.com/news/articles/SB10001424052702303830204577446831263993506

Leonardo da Vinci (n.d.). *Wikiquote*. Retrieved from: http://en.wikiquote.org/wiki/Leonardo_da_Vinci

The link between fast food and depression has been confirmed (2012, March 30). AlphaGalileo Foundation. Retrieved from: http://www.alphagalileo.org/ViewItem.aspx?ItemId=118970&CultureCode=en

Marzano, R.J. (2011). The perils and promises of discovery learning. *Educational Leadership*, *69*(1), 86–87. Retrieved from: http://www.ascd.org/publications/educational-leadership/sept11/vol69/num01/The-Perils-and-Promises-of-Discovery-Learning.aspx

Mayo Clinic (2013, June 3). Are smartphones disrupting your sleep? *Science Daily*. Retrieved from: http://www.sciencedaily.com/releases/2013/06/130603163610.htm?utm_source=feedburner&utm_medium=feed&utm_campaign=Feed%3A+sciencedaily%2Fmind_brain+%28ScienceDaily%3A+Mind+%26+Brain+News%29&utm_content=Google+Reader

O'Connor, A. (2013, August 6). How sleep loss adds to weight gain. *The New York Times*. Retrieved from: http://well.blogs.nytimes.com/2013/08/06/how-sleep-loss-adds-to-weight-gain/?smid=tw-nytimeswell&seid=auto

Osowski, C.P., Goranzon, H., & Fjellstrom, C.H. (2013). Teachers' interaction with children in the school meal situation: The example of pedagogic meals in Sweden. *Journal of Nutrition Education and Behavior*, *46*(5), 420–427. Retrieved from: http://www.sciencedirect.com/science/article/pii/S1499404613001036

Parker-Pope, T. (2013, March 18). Lost sleep can lead to weight gain. *The New York Times*. Retrieved from: http://well.blogs.nytimes.com/2013/03/18/lost-sleep-can-lead-to-weight-gain/?partner=rss&emc=rss&smid=tw-nytimes

Paul, A.M. (2012, October 17). *Just a little more sleep makes kids ready to learn*. Retrieved from: http://anniemurphypaul.com/2012/10/just-a-little-more-sleep-makes-kids-ready-to-learn

Paul, A.M. (2014, July 10). *Educating kids about sleep*. Retrieved from: http://anniemurphypaul.com/2014/07/educating-kids-about-sleep

Promoting lifelong healthy eating among young people (n.d.). Centers for Disease Control. Retrieved from: http://www.cdc.gov/HealthyYouth/nutrition/pdf/help.pdf

Ready to learn? The science behind the experiment—video (2013, March 29). *The Guardian*. Retrieved from: http://www.theguardian.com/science/video/2013/mar/29/ready-to-learn-science-behind-experiment-video

Rochman, B. (2013, January 16). Sleep stealers: What's keeping children from getting enough shut-eye? *Time*. Retrieved from: http://healthland.time.com/2013/01/16/sleep-stealers-whats-keeping-children-from-getting-enough-shut-eye/

Schmidt, E. (2012, May 15). This is your brain on sugar: UCLA study shows high-fructose diet sabotages learning, memory. *UCLA Newsroom*. Retrieved from: http://newsroom.ucla.edu/portal/ucla/this-is-your-brain-on-sugar-ucla-233992.aspx

Sesame Street: The most important meal song. (2010, December 6). *YouTube*. Retrieved from: https://www.youtube.com/watch?v=LPqvODHZt_c

Shea, C. (2012, January 26). Improving calorie counts. *The Wall Street Journal*. Retrieved from: http://blogs.wsj.com/ideas-market/2012/01/26/improving-calorie-counts/?mod=WSJBlog/

Simon, H. B. (2012, February 15). Sleep helps learning, memory. *Harvard Health Publications*. Retrieved from: http://www.health.harvard.edu/blog/sleep-helps-learning-memory-201202154265

Sleep-deprived teens' disturbing thoughts. (2010, January 14). *CBS News*. Retrieved from: http://www.cbsnews.com/news/sleep-deprived-teens-disturbing-thoughts

Sleepy brains drawn to junk food (2012, June 10). *CNN Health*. Retrieved from: http://thechart.blogs.cnn.com/2012/06/10/sleepy-brains-drawn-to-junk-food/?hpt=hp_c2

Sutherland, S. (2012, December 19). Bright screens could delay bedtime. *Scientific American*. Retrieved from: http://www.scientificamerican.com/article/bright-screens-could-delay-bedtime/

Taylor, J. (n.d.). Are fast-food advertisers playing you? *Fit WebMD*. Retrieved from: http://fit.webmd.com/teen/food/article/fast-food-advertising

Walton, A. G. (2012, January 13). The connection between good nutrition and good cognition. *The Atlantic*. Retrieved from: http://www.theatlantic.com/health/archive/2012/01/the-connection-between-good-nutrition-and-good-cognition/251227/

Windows in the workplace linked with better sleep (2013, June 12). *Huffington Post*. Retrieved from: http://www.huffingtonpost.com/2013/06/12/windows-workplace-sleep-sunlight-exposure_n_3415797.html

Wolpert, S. (2008, July 9). Scientists learn how and what you eat affects your brain—and those of your kids. *UCLA Newsroom*. Retrieved from: http://newsroom.ucla.edu/portal/ucla/scientists-learn-how-food-affects-52668.aspx

Wooten, V. D. (n.d.). *How to fall asleep*. Retrieved from: http://health.howstuffworks.com/mental-health/sleep/basics/how-to-fall-asleep2.htm

Your Omega-3 shopping list (n.d.). *WebMD*. Retrieved from: http://www.webmd.com/diet/your-omega-3-family-shopping-list

Chapter 6

How Can You Help Students Get Into a State of "Flow"?

I've heard about something called "flow." I think it means being so focused on what you're doing that you lose track of time. Do you have any suggestions for how I can create conditions in my classroom that would encourage it, and help my students want to seek it out?

"Flow," a term originally coined by professor and researcher Mihaly Csikszentmihalyi, is the highest level of intrinsic motivation—the "optimal experience" (Csikszentmihalyi, 2009, p. 3)—which makes it a fitting topic for the final chapter in this book. Flow is what people feel when they are enjoying doing an activity so much that they are "being carried away in a current" (Csikszentmihalyi, 1990, p. 127) and lose track of time. There are few comments from a student that will warm my heart more than "This class goes so fast!"

People have been found to learn faster when they are in a state of flow (Adee, 2012) because they are more focused and because their enjoyment of the activity creates a higher motivation to repeat it (Engeser & Rheinberg, 2008, p. 9)—often at an increased level of challenge (Csikszentmihalyi, 1997). Research on student engagement has found a direct connection between frequency of flow experiences and longer-term academic interest and motivation (Shernoff, 2002). In addition, Csikszentmihalyi suggests that the happiest people are those who have the most flow experiences (2009, p. 267).

So, what exactly is flow?

Csikszentmihalyi found that there are several elements of flow—what people experienced when they were in that state and what conditions were necessary to achieve it (note that at different times and in different situations it appears he may have made some minor adjustments to the list—this is an amalgam based on his writing and his speaking and all, if not otherwise indicated, comes from Csikszentmihalyi, 2009, and Mihaly Csikszentmihaly, 2008).

Flow

What People Feel While in a State of Flow

1. Concentrating completely on the activity.
2. Losing track of time.
3. Feeling a great sense of intrinsic motivation—doing the activity is its own reward.
4. Having a sense of clarity about what needs to be done.
5. Forgetting their worries and concerns.
6. Feeling like "you're not doing your everyday routine" (Csikszentmihalyi, 2008).
7. Feeling a sense of control over the actions needed to successfully complete the task, similar to feelings of autonomy and competence that have been discussed earlier in this book as prerequisites for intrinsic motivation.

Necessary Conditions to Achieve a State of Flow

1. You receive clear and regular feedback enabling you to make adjustments to what you are doing.
2. You must have a clear goal.
3. The activity is challenging to your skill level. Csikszentmihalyi recommends doing something 10 percent outside one's comfort level to attain a state of flow. His research found that being completely over-matched led to anxiety; doing something too easy led to boredom; and a feeling of apathy is experienced when the challenge and the skill of the person are both low. It's essential to find just the right balance (Shernoff, 2002; Shernoff & Csikszentmihalyi, n.d., p. 132).

Of course, some of the things people feel while in flow could also be listed under the "necessary conditions." For example, people are more likely to be able to concentrate in situations where they get fewer interruptions. In addition, people need to feel that they are in control and have the capability of dealing with the task at hand, and part of that means being in a place where they have the autonomy to do so. Finally, if people are going to feel like they are not in their "everyday routine"—especially in the case of a classroom—we need to remember that, though some "routine" is important to provide to our students (especially to those who have very little of it outside of school), too much of a good thing can be bad. We should keep in mind that the root word of "routine" means "road, way, path" (Route, n.d.) and such a road can take many forms.

Though he hasn't included it in his well-known list of ten "criteria" for flow, Csikszentmihalyi has differentiated between what he calls "junk flow" and flow that "makes you grow" (Mihaly Csikszentmihalyi on Flow, 2014). He defines "junk flow" as something that might have been flow in the beginning, but gradually turns into an "addiction." He specifically refers to playing video games as one example of how, if done to excess, something can turn into "junk flow":

> You can do it faster and faster and play higher and higher levels, but after a while either you can't go anymore because you are not fast enough, or you wake up one morning and say, "Why the heck am I doing this kind of thing? It just doesn't give me any hope for the future." (Mihaly Csikszentmihalyi on Flow, 2014)

Csikszentmihalyi goes on to say:

> The meaning is important. The Greek philosopher Plato wrote a thousand years ago that the greatest challenge for teachers and parents is to teach young people to find pleasure in the right things. He called it pleasure, but actually what he meant was enjoyment. The problem is that it's much easier to find pleasure or enjoyment in things that are not growth-producing but are attractive and seductive. After a while you get trapped by a cycle of short term bursts of excitement, and then it becomes a habit; and now you feel bad if you can't play, but you don't feel good when you can play. That's a problem that goes beyond flow. It goes to the philosophy of life. (Mihaly Csikszentmihalyi on Flow, 2014)

How often are people in a state of flow? In Csikszentmihalyi's international research, he found a fairly common breakdown in different countries—20 to 23 percent say flow happens to them often; 40 percent say sometimes; rarely, 25 percent, and 10 to 12 percent say never (Csikszentmihalyi, 1997, p. 2). Unfortunately, research has also found that, apart from when they are doing paid work like flipping burgers or washing dishes, students feel a sense of flow less in class than at any other time (Bronson, 2010).

The "Immediate Actions" section of this chapter and the lesson plan that follows it will share ideas on what teachers can do to help create conditions conducive to flow and what students can do to maximize their odds of reaching it—and why they would want to!

Immediate Actions

Demonstrate Enthusiasm and Humor

Studies have found that when educators are experiencing flow in their teaching, their state of flow can "cross over" to students (Shernoff & Csikszentmihalyi, n.d., p. 143). In addition, teachers demonstrating humor have also been found to increase student engagement leading to flow (Suttie, 2012, April 17). Of course, this fact is probably not surprising to veteran teachers who know their mood can have a huge impact on what will happen in the classroom on any given day.

Turn Learning Tasks into Puzzles

Many people derive enjoyment from solving puzzles, and Csikszentmihalyi and others have found that looking at learning tasks and challenges as "puzzles" is a common occurrence among those in a state of flow (Shernoff, 2013). Teachers can frame any number of learning activities as a sort of puzzle—for example, sequencing activities where students have to put cut-up pieces of text into the correct order (Ferlazzo, 2011, p. 95), or clozes, (also known as "gap-fills" or "fill-in-the-gaps") where readers have to identify correct words that belong in the "blanks" (Csikszentmihalyi also suggests that an even better flow activity would be having students create their own "puzzles" that others can then solve [Csikszentmihalyi, 2009, p. 129]).

Student readers can even be encouraged to become "lost" in a book by considering its puzzle elements, including "anticipating turns of the plot" (Csikszentmihalyi, 1990, p. 132) and imagining alternate endings.

Reduce Interruptions

It is not unusual for teachers to assign a task to students and then proceed to interrupt them regularly while they are working on the activity. Sometimes those interruptions are worthwhile—for example, showing an example of student work on the document camera that others can use as a model. However, often it is because we have forgotten to tell them something or because we misjudge the importance of the information we want to share. Separate studies have found that students' learning appears to be reduced by 20 percent with multiple interruptions—both in information retained and in writing quality (Robb, 2014; Sullivan & Thompson, 2013). Before teachers disrupt the potential of student flow, we should ask ourselves, "Is the cost of the interruption I am going to make worth what I think is the benefit of students hearing it?"

Create Opportunities for Regular Feedback

In order to enter a flow state, students need to receive regular feedback so they can make any adjustments needed to complete their goal. This flow criteria needs to be balanced with their same need to not have many interruptions to their concentration. Some ways to handle feedback effectively without interrupting flow are:

◆ Teaching students to self-monitor through the use of metacognition. There is a metacognition lesson plan in *Self-Driven Learning* (Ferlazzo, 2013, p. 99).

◆ Providing a rubric that, ideally, has also been developed with some input from students.

◆ If students are working in small groups, encouraging them to provide candid feedback to each other.

◆ Teachers providing selective feedback occasionally and not constantly.

Promote Higher-Leveling Thinking and Use Appropriately Challenging Activities

Flow is most likely to occur when students are at an interconnection between high skills and high challenge, and differentiation strategies (see Chapter 1) will be critical to increase the chances of each student reaching that nexus. In addition to formulating the appropriately challenging specific lesson tasks for students, there are many other "layers" of deeper level thinking that can be applied to any lesson, including challenging students to:

◆ Identify ways they can transfer their learning in that lesson to another environment (see Chapter 4).

◆ Seriously practice the art of listening and conversation, including asking thoughtful questions of each other during classroom sharing opportunities. These kinds of serious conversations can promote flow (Csikszentmihalyi, 2009, p. 129) and provide opportunities to reinforce lessons on asking questions (Ferlazzo, 2013, p. 109) and good listening (Ferlazzo, 2013, p. 62). When students are sharing with each other and are directed to ask each other questions, framing the instruction as part of a strategy towards developing flow could result in at least some students taking the assignment more seriously.

♦ Accept personal responsibility for taking actions that could create flow. We can help students understand that flow is not something that happens *to* them. Rather, flow is something that we *make* happen to ourselves. Similar to the message sent in the lesson on boredom in Chapter 2, Csikszentmihalyi writes:

Take control of your boredom—Roman Emperor Marcus Aurelius wrote: "If you are pained by external things, it is not they that disturb you, but your own judgment of them. And it is in your power to wipe out that judgment now." (Csikszentmihalyi, 2009, p. 5)

♦ These student actions can include providing feedback to teachers about what actions they take that seems to facilitate or work against student flow. Csikszentmihalyi suggests that using a few minutes to periodically reflect in a journal about what activities were the high points during a day or during a class can help inform us about what we should be doing more or less of in our classrooms (http://www. psychologytoday.com/articles/199707/finding-flow).

♦ Help their classmates. Research has found that many people get what is called a "helper's high"—a physical and psychological sensation—from helping another person (http://www.webmd.com/ balance/features/science-good-deeds and http://www.psychology today.com/blog/raising-happiness/201002/what-we-get-when- we-give). Facilitating this kind of altruism in the classroom can function as a "gateway" to student flow (Kotler, 2014). Teachers could "prep" certain students prior to a lesson so they can function as "teaching assistants," ask students who complete an assignment early to help others or, if teaching the same lesson that's taught in the morning to a later class, make arrangements for some of those earlier students to come in and help during the afternoon.

Encourage Use of Mental Imagery

Csikszentmihalyi suggests that using mental imagery—practicing tasks in your mind—promotes flow because it "increases complexity of consciousness" (Csikszentmihalyi, 2009, p. 120). More information, including a full lesson plan, can be found in *Self-Driven Learning* (Ferlazzo, 2013, p. 39) on helping students effectively visualize for success.

Use Cooperative Learning and Other Interactive Strategies

Research has shown that students are more likely to experience flow while participating in cooperative learning activities and, in fact, studies—both in high school and in college—found that those group activities encouraged "high concentration and high enjoyment," both essential for flow (Sawyer, 2007; Shernoff & Csikszentmihalyi, n.d., p. 134). Here are a few guidelines for small-group learning that have been found to be particularly effective for encouraging flow—most are similar to typical guidelines issued by teachers, but—if framed as more "flow-producing" after teaching the lesson later in this chapter—might "carry a little more weight" (*Helping Students Motivate Themselves*, Ferlazzo, 2011, has an entire chapter on cooperative learning):

◆ Making sure the group's goal is clear.

◆ Encouraging students to listen to each other and having everyone participate.

◆ Being positive and supportive to group members.

◆ Concentrating more by not talking and being distracted by people in other groups.

In addition, teachers will want to build in as much autonomy (choice) as possible into how students accomplish the task. Lastly, sometimes offering the option of students choosing their own teammates can facilitate flow. Familiarity with teammates and their work and "communication" styles can encourage the likelihood of more effective immediate feedback (Sawyer, 2012).

That doesn't mean, however, that flow is not possible while learning in other ways. Csikszentmihalyi writes:

> If you look at academic classes, they [students] would report flow especially when they work on team projects. That's the most enjoyable part of school. Next comes working on your own on a project and you can go down and the lowest one [in promoting flow] is listening to a lecture and audio/visual. Anything that involves them, that has goals where they can try to achieve, solve a problem,

or do something it's going to be much more likely to produce flow. (Mihaly Csikszentmihalyi, 2002)

Build Positive Teacher–Student Relationships and Ensure Lesson Relevance

It's no surprise that it's been found that a positive teacher-student relationship (see Chapter 1) also helps create the conditions for student flow (Suttie, 2012, April 17), as does ensuring that students feel lessons are relevant to their lives (Suttie, 2012, April 16). Student-created goals—and teachers being aware of them in their lesson-planning and implementation—can be a helpful tool to ensuring the latter condition is present. The four key components behind intrinsic motivation described in Chapter 1—autonomy, competence, relatedness, and relevance—are all directly connected to elements required for flow.

 Ed Tech

Encouraging students to not be afraid of making mistakes and, instead, to learn from them and move on is another lesson that can help students enter a state of flow (http://www.health.harvard.edu/blog/go-with-the-flow-engagement-and-concentration-are-key-201307266516). There are many texts that can be used as short "Read Alouds" and videos that can be shown to reinforce that message at "The Best Posts, Articles and Videos About Learning From Mistakes and Failures" (http://larryferlazzo.edublogs.org/2011/07/28/the-best-posts-articles-videos-about-learning-from-mistakes-failures/).

Setting the Stage

Flow Lesson

The "Flow" lesson plan introduces the concept of "flow" (and its benefits) to students through videos, examining their own prior experiences, and by reading an excerpt from one of Csikszentmihalyi's books. Then, students create a series of specific actions that they and their teacher can do to facilitate a flow state in the classroom.

The lesson provides a basis to support many of the "immediate actions" listed earlier in the chapter, and also offers—in the lesson itself and through suggested extension activities—a number of ways it can be reinforced throughout the school year.

Flow Lesson Plan

Instructional Objectives for Students

- Further develop their ability to practice reading strategies to help comprehend a text.

- Understand the importance of flow and design an effective action plan to help achieve it.

Duration

Two 55-minute class periods and various short follow-up activities during the rest of the year.

Materials

- Access to the Internet and a computer projector to show videos from "The Best Resources for Learning About Flow" (http://larryferlazzo.edublogs.org/2012/04/26/the-best-resources-for-learning-about-flow/).

- Student copies of "Finding Flow" (http://www.psychologytoday.com/articles/199707/finding-flow); Figure 6.1, "What Is Flow?", and Figure 6.2, "Teacher and Student Actions to Help 'Flow.'"

- Document camera, overhead projector or whiteboard.

- Paper and color markers.

Common Core English Language Arts Standards

Reading:

- Determine central ideas or themes of a text and analyze their development; summarize the key supporting details and ideas.

- Read and comprehend complex literary and informational texts independently and proficiently.

Writing:

- Write arguments to support claims in an analysis of substantive topics or texts, using valid reasoning and relevant and sufficient evidence.

Speaking and Listening:

- Prepare for and participate effectively in a range of conversations and collaborations with diverse partners, building on others' ideas and expressing their own clearly and persuasively.

Language:

- Demonstrate command of the conventions of standard English grammar and usage when writing or speaking.

- Demonstrate command of the conventions of standard English capitalization, punctuation, and spelling when writing.

Procedure

First Day

1. Explain that you are going to show students three videos and you want students to write down on a sheet of paper what you think the videos have in common. Then show students your choice of the short film, basketball, or commercial video clips from "The Best Resources for Learning About Flow" list.

2. After the videos are done, give students one minute to identify what they have in common and then ask them to share what they wrote with a partner. Call on a student or students to share with the entire class. The students should say something like "They are all in 'the zone.'"

3. Agree, and ask students to take five minutes and write about as many times as they can remember when they have been in "the zone." You can give an example when you had that experience. As students are writing, walk around identifying students you would like to have share with the entire class.

4. After five minutes, ask students to verbally share what they wrote with a different partner (you can have some fun with the pairing—choose someone with the same or different color socks, etc.). After they have shared, call on certain students to briefly share with the entire class. Ask students to raise their hands if they liked how they felt when they were "in the zone." Most, if not all, the students are likely to raise their hand.

5. Then explain that the class is going to learn about "being in the zone" today. Ask students to raise their hands if they had any classroom experience on their list when they were feeling "in the zone." It is likely that few, if any, will have included one (though some might have an after-school or art class experience). Say that you are not surprised—that research shows that, apart from working at an after-school job, young people say the classroom is where they feel "in the zone" the least. The point of the lesson today is to see if both you and they can do anything to change that.

6. Explain that some researchers call being "in the zone" "flow." Put the "What Is Flow?" Read Aloud (Figure 6.1) on the document camera and distribute copies to all students. Ask students to read along silently as you read, and think about whether the activities they listed as times when they felt they had been "in the zone" had those same qualities. Read it to the class. Afterwards, you can give another example of when you were in a flow state and explain that, at least for you, the Read Aloud describes how you felt. Tell the class you will give them a minute to think about whether that describes how they felt during their "zone" experiences or at least during some of them. After a minute, ask students to share with another partner about an experience they had that might sound like being in a flow state.

7. Explain that students are now going to do a "jigsaw" activity. Pass out an excerpt from one of Csikszentmihalyi's articles about flow (Finding Flow, 1997), and explain that each of them only has to read two small sections of it. Then they will have to teach others about what they learned. Distribute the excerpt and have students "count off" to six and write their number on the front page. Explain that there are actually seven sections of the excerpt and give these instructions (showing them on a document camera or whiteboard would be helpful):
   - Everyone will read the short introduction.
   - The "ones" will read the section titled "Where to Find Flow."
   - The "twos" will read the section titled "Flow at Work." When they are reading that section, though, students should see if and when they can substitute the word "school" for "work" or "job."
   - The "threes" will read the section titled "Flow at Play."
   - The "fours" will read the section titled "Social Flow."
   - The "fives" will read the section titled "Overcoming Obstacles."
   - The "sixes" will read "Finding A Goal."
   - Each student will "pair up" with another student who has the same number. They will take turns reading paragraphs from the introduction and their assigned section, and they should read with prosody—with some feeling. Model reading with prosody and then reading in a monotone. As students read, they should highlight key points—no more than six words in each paragraph.
   - Then, each student needs to create their own poster that they will teach to another group. The posters students are making as they are working in pairs can be very similar. The poster should include:
     - a one-sentence summary of the introduction and a picture illustrating its main idea
     - a few key words describing the three most important points of the section they read, along with a picture illustrating its main idea

Building a Community of Self-Motivated Learners

- a list of the specific suggestions in the excerpt about what people can do to help them get into flow (if it makes any)
- one piece of information they found particularly interesting and why they thought it was interesting.

Students should prepare a short oral presentation to go along with their poster that is more than just reading it to other students. Students need to remember that a poster is not an essay. Instead, it highlights key points that the speaker will elaborate on when he/she speaks. Give students 15 minutes to read the text and prepare their poster.

8. Circulate around the room during those 15 minutes to ensure students are on task and also assigns each student to a letter group to which they will be teaching. For example, go to a student who is a "one" and tell him he will teach in "A" group and have him write "A" on his paper. Then go to a "two" and tell her she will teach in "A" group; then go to a "three" and tell him she will teach in "A" group, etc., until there are six students in "A" group. Then repeat the process to create a "B" group and so on.

9. At the end of 15 minutes, you can assign different sections of the room to letter groups and, depending on the class time that is remaining, they can go there and begin teaching (using their prepared presentation and poster) in the order of their number. Explain that they will finish the next day. If there is not enough time to begin, you can explain they will begin the next day.

Second Day

1. Remind students that the class is studying "flow" and asks students to immediately move to their letter groups and begin teaching in the order of their number. Tell students they will have ten minutes to complete their teaching. If they are done early, say that you would like students to ask each other questions about the sections they read or to highlight/underline their favorite passages in the text. Circulate during this period to monitor that students are indeed developing an accurate understanding of flow.

2. Explain that, as the excerpt pointed out, there are several elements that help people get into a flow state, including getting feedback so you can make adjustments on what you are doing; what you are doing has to be connected to a goal that you're interested in achieving; the activity has to be challenging to your skill level; you need to be able to concentrate; have some control over what you are doing and how you are doing it; and it needs to be a little out of your everyday routine. You can write these elements on a document camera or on a whiteboard.

3. Show and review Figure 6.2 on the document camera. Explain that you now want students to come up with ideas on what you can do under each

category to help create better classroom conditions for flow to occur for students, and then you want students to come up with ideas on what they think they can do to help increase the chances of their experiencing flow here in the classroom. Each student will write on their own sheet, but they will work together in their group of six and all six sheets can say the same thing. They can get ideas from the excerpt they just read and think up ideas of their own. Point out the two ideas listed in the first category as examples. (Note: Do not show students Figure 6.3, which is an "answer sheet" including many ideas. You should have it available, but you should first elicit ideas from students and then only in the latter portion of the class share the items on the list that students don't mention.) Announce that students will have six minutes to come up with a list.

4. Walk around to the groups and give hints if you feel that some are stuck, or give more examples from the front if you feel they're necessary to move things along. It's not important if students come up with ideas in the same categories as in Figure 6.3 (for example, they might think of an idea that is listed there under "Challenge" and put it under "Everyday Routine" instead)—it's the ideas for actions that are important. And they may very well think of additional good ideas, or the same ideas but worded in different ways from the "answer sheet." While you are walking around, you should also quietly give each student in each group a number from one to six and have them write it down on their paper.

5. After six minutes, announce that students from each group are going to share the ideas they wrote down with students from the other groups. Announce the location where all the "ones" will meet; all the "twos" will meet, etc., up to the "sixes." Tell students they will have five minutes to share, starting with the "ones," what they wrote on their papers. They should write down ideas that they don't have already, and they don't have to repeat ones that have already been said. In other words, at the end of five minutes, all students should have the same ideas listed on each of their papers.

6. At the end of five minutes, borrow a student sheet that is relatively legible and put it on the document camera. Praise students for good thinking and hard work while giving specific examples you saw of both. Then, without making it obvious that you have an "answer sheet" (a "guessing what is in my head" activity can often be very irritating to students), announce that you'd like to share a few additional ideas. Then add some of the ideas from the answer sheet (though you don't have to add them all) and any additional ones you have thought of on your own. Ask students to copy them down on their lists.

7. Ask students to circle two ideas under each of the six categories (one for the teacher and one for the students) that they think would work the best.

8. Say that you will make a poster for the classroom wall including these ideas so the class can see them each day and, after you collect and return each student's sheet, you want them to keep their own copy, too. To finish-up the lesson, ask students to write a simple ABC paragraph—Answer the question, Back it up with evidence (like a quotation from the excerpt), make a Connection with a previous experience or a previous reading and make a Comment. The question is: "What is flow and what is one thing I can do to help get it in class?"

9. Depending on how much class time is left, students can be given five to ten minutes to write it, share it verbally with a partner, and then turn it in, along with the jigsaw poster and "Actions to Help Flow" sheet.

Assessment

1. You can collect and review the "jigsaw" poster, the "plan of action" sheets, and the ABC paragraph to evaluate student work.

2. If you feel a more involved assessment is necessary, you can develop a simple rubric appropriate for your classroom situation. Free online resources to both find pre-made rubrics and to create new ones can be found at http://larryferlazzo.edublogs.org/2010/09/18/the-best-rubric-sites-and-a-beginning-discussion-about-their-use/

Possible Extensions/Modifications

- Students could be periodically shown videos from a link on "The Best Resources for Learning About Flow" list that have people talking about when they experience flow. Students could use them as models to create their own similar videos and/or presentations.

- Students could be asked to keep a weekly or even daily journal listing when they felt they were in flow or closest to flow that day.

- Students could create posters highlighting all the different actions required for flow, with examples.

- You could post versions of either Figures 6.4 and 6.5 on the classroom wall that illustrate the different levels of challenge and skill and what kind of feelings they each tend to generate (see the explanation earlier in the chapter). The figures are versions of a chart created by Csikszentmihalyi

(2009, p. 74) that has been widely distributed in different versions. One teacher made an interpretation (http://www.learningspy.co.uk/featured/2-minute-lesson-plan/) of the Flow Chart that I further modified in Figure 6.5. Teachers could post either Figure 6.4 or 6.5 on the wall and, at the end of some classes, have students write down anonymously on a small piece paper which section best described how they felt about that day's class and turn it in. It could function as a useful formative assessment opportunity.

Figure 6.1   What is Flow?

"Flow" is a term originally coined by professor and researcher Mihaly Csikszentmihalyi. Flow is like "being in the zone"—it's what people feel when they are enjoying doing an activity so much that they are "being carried away in a current." When people are having a flow experience, they tend to lose track of time, feel challenged, and are concentrating completely on an activity.

People have been found to learn faster when they are in a state of flow because they are more focused and because their enjoyment of the activity creates a higher motivation to repeat it—often at an increased level of challenge. In addition, Csikszentmihalyi suggests that the happiest people are those who have the most flow experiences.

Flow is something that people *make* happen for themselves, not something that others do *to* or *for* them.

Figure 6.2 Teacher and Student Actions to Help "Flow"

Challenge

What can the teacher do to make sure the learning activity is appropriately challenging to each student?

Get to know each student's strengths and challenges and plan lessons with those in mind.

What can students do to help make sure their classroom activities are challenging to them?

Think about ways they can use what they are learning in class in other classes or outside of school (transfer of learning).

Feedback

What can the teacher do to provide effective feedback to students?

What can students do to obtain effective feedback?

Goals

What can the teacher do to encourage students to identify clear goals that they care about and to make sure that each lesson's goal is clear?

What can students do to identify clear goals that they care about and to make sure that each lesson's goal is clear?

Concentration

What can the teacher do to help students focus on the learning activity?

(continued)

Figure 6.2   Teacher and Student Actions to Help "Flow" (*continued*)

What can students do to help themselves focus on the learning activity?

Control

What can the teacher do to help students have more control over what students are learning and how they are learning it?

What can students do to have more control over what they are learning and how they are learning it?

Everyday Routine

What can the teacher do to help make sure learning activities in the classroom are interesting and not the same every day?

What can students do to help make sure learning activities in the classroom are interesting and not the same every day?

Figure 6.3   Teacher and Student Actions to
Help "Flow" ("Answer Sheet")

Challenge
What can the teacher do to make sure the learning activity is appropriately challenging to each student?
Get to know each student's strengths and challenges and plan lessons with those in mind.

What can students do to help make sure their classroom activities are challenging to them?
Think about ways they can use what they are learning in class in other classes or outside of school.

Think about what was learned in the mini-lesson on how to deal with boredom (see Chapter 2).

Take responsibility for figuring out ways to make the lesson more interesting to themselves.

Write down in a journal each week or day what activities are particularly challenging and communicate it to the teacher.

Think of ways the lesson can be made better and communicate those ideas to the teacher in a respectful way.

If a student understands something and a classmate is having difficulties, think about how they can help teach that student so he/she understands it better ("helper's high").

Ask thoughtful questions of other students and the teacher.

Feedback
What can the teacher do to provide effective feedback to students?
Highlight both what a student is doing well and what a student can do to improve.

If there is going to be a rubric, make sure it's clear.

Be nice.

What can students do to obtain effective feedback?
Be willing to listen to helpful comments—both ones that are positive and ones that suggest improvement—from the teacher and from classmates.

Be willing to give helpful comments—both ones that are positive and ones that suggest improvement—to classmates and to the teacher.

(continued)

Figure 6.3   Teacher and Student Actions to Help "Flow" (*continued*)

Goals

What can the teacher do to encourage students to identify clear goals that they care about and to make sure that each lesson's goal is clear?

Give students time to regularly think about, write, and discuss their goals.

Make sure that the purpose and goal of every assignment is clear.

What can students do to identify clear goals that they care about and to make sure that each lesson's goal is clear?

Take goal-setting and their regular review of them seriously.

Take time to think about how different assignments will help them achieve their goals and, if they are not clear about how they connect, ask the teacher and classmates for their ideas on how they do.

If students are not clear about the purpose and goal of an assignment, ask their classmates and/or the teacher.

Concentration

What can the teacher do to help students focus on the learning activity?

After assigning a task, try to interrupt students as few times as possible.

What can students do to help themselves focus on the learning activity?

Not sit next to people who they think might be distracting.

"Don't eat the marshmallow"—remember what we learned about self-control and the Marshmallow Experiment.

Control

What can the teacher do to help students have more control over what they are learning and how they are learning it?

Give students as much of a choice as possible—within reason—about how much time students are given to complete an assignment, what the exact assignment is, who they can work with, and how they do it.

What can students do to have more control over what they are learning and how they are learning it?

Act responsibly and hold classmates accountable for doing the same.

(continued)

Figure 6.3   Teacher and Student Actions to Help "Flow" (*continued*)

Everyday Routine
What can the teacher do to help make sure learning activities in the classroom are interesting and not the same every day?

Not do the same thing every day in class—mix things up.

Have pair and larger group work as much as possible.

What can students do to help make sure learning activities in the classroom are interesting and not the same every day?

Act responsibly when the teacher does try different activities.

Tell the teacher in a respectful manner what activities they like to do and help them learn best.

Offer suggestions—in a respectful manner—about what they think the teacher can do differently.

Figure 6.4 Flow Chart I

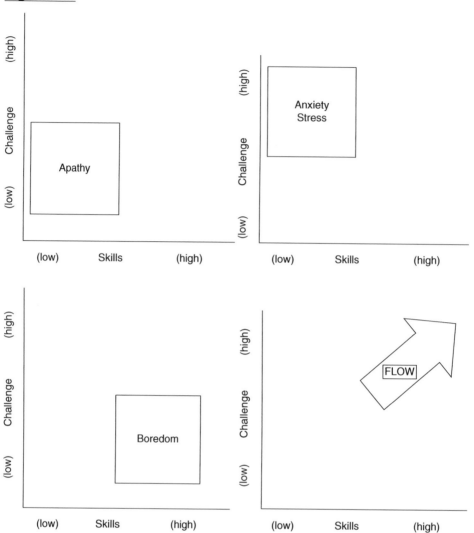

Adapted from "Flow: The Psychology of Optimal Experience" by Mihaly Csikszentmihalyi (p. 74)

Building a Community of Self-Motivated Learners

Figure 6.5 Flow Chart II

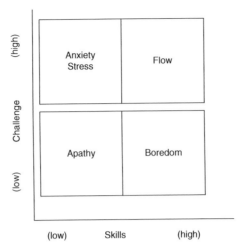

Modified from http://www.learningspy.co.uk/featured/2-minute-lesson-plan/

References

Adee, S. (2012, February 6). Zap your brain into the zone: Fast track to pure focus. *NewScientist*. Retrieved from: http://www.newscientist.com/article/mg2132 8501.600-zap-your-brain-into-the-zone-fast-track-to-pure-focus.html

Bronson, P. (2010, May 18). Motivation and flow: The teenager edition. *Newsweek*. Retrieved from: http://www.newsweek.com/motivation-and-flow-teenager-edition-223476

Csikszentmihalyi, M. (1990). Literacy and intrinsic motivation. *Daedalus, 119*(2), 115–140. Retrieved from: https://www.msu.edu/~dwong/CEP991/CEP991 Resources/Csikszentmihalyi-Lit&Mot.pdf

Csikszentmihalyi, M. (1997, July 1). Finding flow. *Psychology Today*. Retrieved from: http://www.psychologytoday.com/articles/199707/finding-flow

Csikszentmihalyi, M. (2008). Flow, the secret to happiness. *TED*. Retrieved from: https://www.ted.com/talks/mihaly_csikszentmihalyi_on_flow/transcript

Csikszentmihalyi, M. (2009). *Flow: The Psychology of Optimal Experience*. Harper-Collins e-books. Retrieved from: http://www.amazon.com/Flow-P-S-Mihaly-Csikszentmihalyi-ebook/dp/B000W94FE6/ref=tmm_kin_swatch_0?_encoding=UTF8&sr=&qid=page%20three

Didau, D. (2012, November 17). Go with the flow: The 2 minute lesson plan. *David Dadau: The learning spy*. Retrieved from: http://www.learningspy.co.uk/featured/2-minute-lesson-plan

Engeser, S., & Rheinberg, F. (2008). Flow, performance and moderators of challenge-skill balance. *Motivation and Emotion*. doi 10.1007/s11031-008-9102-4. Retrieved from: http://www.psycho.wi.tum.de/Publ/34857.pdf

Ferlazzo, L. (2010, September 18). The best rubric sites (and a beginning discussion about their use). *Larry Ferlazzo's websites of the day*. Retrieved from: http://

larryferlazzo.edublogs.org/2010/09/18/the-best-rubric-sites-and-a-begin
ning-discussion-about-their-use/

Ferlazzo, L. (2011). *Helping students motivate themselves: Practical answers to class-room challenges*. New York: Routledge.

Ferlazzo, L. (2011, July 28). The best posts, articles and videos about learning from mistakes and failures. *Larry Ferlazzo's websites of the day*. Retrieved from: http://larryferlazzo.edublogs.org/2011/07/28/the-best-posts-articles-videos-about-learning-from-mistakes-failures

Ferlazzo, L. (2012, April 26) The best resources for learning about 'flow'. *Larry Ferlazzo's websites of the day*. Retrieved from: http://larryferlazzo.edublogs.org/2012/04/26/the-best-resources-for-learning-about-flow/

Ferlazzo, L. (2013). *Self-driven learning: Teaching strategies for student motivation*. New York: Routledge.

Kotler, S. (2014, February 9). Flow states: Answers to the three most common questions about optimal performance. *Forbes*. Retrieved from: http://www.forbes.com/sites/stevenkotler/2014/02/09/flow-states-answers-to-the-three-most-common-questions-about-optimal-performance

Mihaly Csikszentmihalyi: Motivating people to learn (2002, April 11). *Edutopia*. Retrieved from: http://www.edutopia.org/mihaly-csikszentmihalyi-motivating-people-learn

Mihaly Csikszentmihalyi: Flow, the secret to happiness (2008). *YouTube*. Retrieved from: https://www.youtube.com/watch?v=fXIeFJCqsPs

Mihaly Csikszentmihalyi on flow, intrinsic motivation, and happiness (2014, April 20). *Real Leaders Project*. Retrieved from: http://realleaders.tv/portfolio/mihaly/#sthash.8sB0slHj.dpuf

Phillips, E. (2013, July 26). Go with the flow: Engagement and concentration are key. *Harvard Health Publications*. Retrieved from: http://www.health.harvard.edu/blog/go-with-the-flow-engagement-and-concentration-are-key-201307266516

Robb, A. (2014, July 16). Interruptions are even worse than we thought. *New Republic*. Retrieved from: http://www.newrepublic.com/article/118714/interruptions-work-make-you-way-less-productive

Route. (n.d.). *Online etymology dictionary*. Retrieved from: http://www.etymonline.com/index.php?term=route&allowed_in_frame=0

Sawyer, K. (2007). *Group genius: The creative power of collaboration*. Basic Books. Retrieved from: http://books.google.com/books?id=YIoGFZz4yQMC&pg=PA43&lpg=PA43&dq=people+who+participated+in+group+flow+were+the+highest+performers&source=bl&ots=_-W6h33BeQ&sig=lAFJbI1Ab XmHTXIjpHbB__gCXc0&hl=en&sa=X&ei=grndU8bVMoeT8gGGhYCw BA&ved=0CB8Q6AEwAA#v=onepage&q=people%20who%20partici pated%20in%20group%20flow%20were%20the%20highest%20perfor mers&f=false

Sawyer, K. (2012). What Mel Brooks can teach us about "group flow." *Greater good*. Retrieved from: http://greatergood.berkeley.edu/article/item/what_mel_brooks_can_teach_us_about_group_flow

Shernoff, D. (2002, February 27). *Flow states and student engagement in the classroom.* Retrieved from: http://www.amersports.org/library/reports/8.html

Shernoff, D.J. (2013). *Optimal learning environments to promote student engagement.* Springer eBooks. Retrieved from: http://books.google.com/books?id= wnnu9IOA6vQC&pg=PA67&lpg=PA67&dq=Csikszentmihalyi+puzzles& source=bl&ots=NilohIjZ8r&sig=MURETxbT3MuWq3jh0h5LIQHP0ac&hl= en&sa=X&ei=Y93jU6W7FsnE8AG2r4GACQ&ved=0CFwQ6AEwCA#v= onepage&q=Csikszentmihalyi%20puzzles&f=false

Shernoff, D.J., & Csikszentmihalyi, M. (n.d.). *Flow in schools: Cultivating engaged learners and optimal learning environments.* Retrieved from: http://www.cedu. niu.edu/~shernoff/shernofffsc.pdf

Sullivan, B., & Thompson, H. (2013, May 3). Brain, interrupted. *The New York Times.* Retrieved from: http://www.nytimes.com/2013/05/05/opinion/sun day/a-focus-on-distraction.html?_r=0

Suttie, J. (2012, April 16). Can schools help students find flow? *Greater good.* Retrieved from: http://greatergood.berkeley.edu/article/item/can_schools_ help_students_find_flow

Suttie, J. (2012, April 17). Eight tips for fostering flow in the classroom. *Greater good.* Retrieved from: http://greatergood.berkeley.edu/article/item/eight_tips_ for_fostering_flow_in_the_classroom

Don't miss
Larry Ferlazzo's
other acclaimed books on student motivation!

These lively, research-based books provide strategies and Common-Core-aligned lessons that you can use immediately to increase achievement by helping students motivate themselves.

Self-Driven Learning
Teaching Strategies for Student Motivation

This volume is filled with practical ideas for helping students build intrinsic motivation about their learning. You'll find out how to get students to feel positive about their classes, to enjoy reading and writing, to want to think critically, to not be burned out by tests, and more!

© 2013 : 224 pages : 978-1-59667-239-0

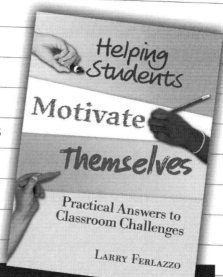

Helping Students Motivate Themselves
Practical Answers to Classroom Challenges

This volume offers helpful ideas for managing and structuring your class in a way that will teach students self-motivation. You'll discover how to get the year off to a good start, use leftover class time, incorporate games and technology, keep kids focused at the end of the year, and more!

© 2011 : 208 pages : 978-1-59667-181-2

Routledge
Taylor & Francis Group

Routledge... think about it
www.routledge.com